The Light of Wisdom

THE LIGHT
OF WISDOM

THE ROOT TEXT
Lamrim Yeshe Nyingpo
BY PADMASAMBHAVA

as recorded by Yeshe Tsogyal *and revealed*
and decoded by Jamyang Khyentse Wangpo
and Chokgyur Lingpa

THE COMMENTARY
The Light of Wisdom
BY JAMGÖN KONGTRÜL THE GREAT

THE NOTES
Entering the Path of Wisdom
BY JAMYANG DRAKPA

as recorded by Jokyab Rinpoche
Supplemented with clarifying remarks by
H. H. Dilgo Khyentse Rinpoche *and*
H. E. Tulku Urgyen Rinpoche

Translated from the Tibetan according to the teachings of
His Eminence Tulku Urgyen Rinpoche
by Erik Pema Kunsang

SHAMBHALA · *Boston & London* · 1995

Shambhala Publications, Inc.
Horticultural Hall
300 Massachusetts Avenue
Boston, Massachusetts 02115

9 8 7 6 5 4 3 2 1

First Edition

Printed in the United States of America on acid-free paper ∞
Distributed in the United States by Random House, Inc.,
and in Canada by Random House of Canada Ltd

Library of Congress Cataloging-in-Publication Data
Koṅ-sprul Blo-gros-mtha'-yas, 1813–1899.
[Lam rim ye śes sñiṅ po'i 'grel pa ye śes snaṅ ba rab tu rgyas pa. English]
The light of wisdom / the root text, Lamrim yeshe nyingpo by Padmasambhava as
recorded by Yeshe Tsogyal and revealed and decoded by Jamyang Khyentse
Wangpo and Chokgyur Lingpa: the commentary, the light of wisdom by Jamgön
Kongtrül the Great; the notes, entering the path of wisdom by Jamyang Drakpa, as
recorded by Jokyab Rinpoche; supplemented with clarifying remarks by H.H.
Dilgo Khyentse Rinpoche and H.E. Tulku Urgyen Rinpoche; translated from the
Tibetan according to the teachings of His Eminence Tulku Urgyen Rinpoche by
Erik Pema Kunsang.—1st ed.
p. cm.
ISBN 0-87773-566-2
1. Mchog-gyur-gliṅ-pa, Gter ston, 1829–1870. Lam rim ye śes sñiṅ po. 2. Tantric
Buddhism—Doctrines. I. Mchog-gyur-gliṅ-pa, Gter ston, 1829–1870. Lam rim
ye śes sñiṅ po.
BQ8918.3.M353K6613 1995 94-44059
294.3'925—dc20 CIP

Teachers consulted for transmission and clarifications:

HIS HOLINESS DILGO KHYENTSE RINPOCHE

HIS EMINENCE TULKU URGYEN RINPOCHE

CHÖKYI NYIMA RINPOCHE

TULKU PEMA WANGYAL RINPOCHE

CHAGDUD TULKU RINPOCHE

ORGYEN TOBGYAL RINPOCHE

KHENPO PEMA SHERAB

LAMA PUTSI PEMA TASHI

Prepared by Rangjung Yeshe Translations,
P.O. Box 1200, Kathmandu, Nepal

Translator: Erik Pema Kunsang
Associate translator: Marcia Binder Schmidt
Editors: Judy Amtzis *and* John Frederick
Assistants: Graham Sunstein *and* Ben Rosenzweig

Contents

THE ROOT TEXT

THE COMMENTARY

Section One
Prologue and Teachings on the Title, the Sign Script, and the Homage

Section Two
The Explanation of the Actual Body of the Text

Contents

Section Three
Path

APPENDICES AND NOTES

Foreword

The root text of *Lamrim Yeshe Nyingpo,* a terma revealed by the great treasure-finder Chokgyur Lingpa, and its commentary by Kongtrül Rinpoche, the great translator Vairochana in person, form together a complete scripture that embodies all the tantras, statements, and instructions of the Nyingma School of the Early Translations, which is most rare to find in the past, present, or future.

At this time when the sunlight of the precious teachings of the Buddha spread throughout foreign countries, the bright Dane Erik Pema Kunsang, with the thought to help others, has translated into English the sections on the preliminaries and the attitude of awakened mind. I find it important that all Dharma practitioners study and reflect upon this book.

This was written by old Dilgo Khyentse on the tenth day of the first month in the Year of the Iron Sheep [February 24, 1991] in order to inspire further goodness.

Translator's Introduction

Lord of all mandalas, Lake-Born Vajra Holder,
Manifest in the form of a supreme vidyadhara,
Great lord and treasure revealer, only refuge for the people of
    Tibet,
Chokgyur Lingpa, I supplicate at your feet.

—*written by* JAMYANG KHYENTSE WANGPO

Knower of all things as they are and how they exist,
Through nonconceptual compassion, you consider all beings
    your children.
King of Dharma, who overturns the depths of samsara,
Khyentse Wangpo, I supplicate at your feet.

—*written by* JAMGÖN KONGTRÜL

Perceiver of all to be known, treasure of an ocean of virtues,
Lodrö Thaye, foretold by the Victorious One,
Lord who encompasses all families, Padma Gargyi Wangpo,
Great Charioteer of the Jambu Continent, I supplicate you.

—*written by* JAMYANG KHYENTSE WANGPO

Having begun with three verses chosen by His Eminence Tulku
Urgyen Rinpoche as worthy of summarizing the life and examples
of the three great masters whose enlightened qualities form the basis

for this book, in this introduction I would like to explain where the teachings contained in *The Light of Wisdom* came from, the masters who revealed, propagated, and preserved its tradition, as well as the style of the book itself and how to approach it.

The Light of Wisdom presents the first part of *Lamrim Yeshe Nyingpo* accompanied by a commentary composed by the illustrious nineteenth-century Buddhist master Jamgön Kongtrül the Great.

THE NATURE OF LAMRIM YESHE NYINGPO

The *Lamrim Yeshe Nyingpo,* the title of which is translated as the *Gradual Path of the Wisdom Essence,* is a sacred scripture that records oral teachings of the Second Buddha, Padmasambhava, given while he blessed Tibet with a fifty-five-year visit during the ninth century. This most precious, concise, profound teaching of Padmasambhava is a condensation of the entire path to enlightenment and, in its full version, it contains the pith instructions of the Three Inner Tantras: Maha, Anu, and Ati Yoga. Padmasambhava himself describes *Lamrim Yeshe Nyingpo* in the following words:

> This essence of the causal and resultant vehicles,
> Especially the core of the realization of the three sections of the
>   inner tantras,
> Linking together the ground with the path,
> Makes you abandon the temporary defilements along with their
>   tendencies,
> Realize fruition, and quickly accomplish the welfare of self and
>   others.
> In this way it is in conformity with each yet exalted above them
>   all.

> This path of the wisdom essence, the epitome of all,
> Is a magical means for realizing fruition.

Merely seeing it causes the great splendor of blessings to shower
    down.
By hearing it one understands the meaning, and experience and
    realization burst forth spontaneously.
By practicing it for six months, giving up distractions,
The wisdom of the three vajras will naturally manifest.

Since Samantabhadra, Vajrasattva, and Padmakara
Are ultimately indivisible and spontaneously complete as one,
I am the emanation-basis for all the infinite tantras,
The essential meaning and the oral instructions.

Yet, in appearance I manifest in all kinds of ways as magical
    displays of deeds in different modes of appearing,
Such as emerging miraculously in Dhanakosha
Or being born from a womb and so forth,
For the sake of guiding the disciples on the Jambu Continent.

Lord Amitayus at Maratika
And Maha Shri Heruka at Yanglesho
Bestowed upon me with the natural sound of dharmata
This sole quintessence of all the oral instructions.

If Garab Dorje, Shri Singha, the eight vidyadharas,
And all the supreme siddhas from whom I received the stages of
    the path
Were to hold a great Dharma discussion with one another,
There would be no other summary-manual than this compiling
    their realization.

Throughout the countries of Uddiyana, India, Tibet, and
    elsewhere,
This is the unmistaken condensed meaning

Of all the infinite, profound, and extensive wheels of the
   Dharma,
Such as guru sadhana, the Great Perfection, the Great
   Compassionate One, and the Eight Sadhana Teachings.[1]

In short, there does not exist an ultimate instruction other than
   this.
Expressed in few words yet including all that should be
   expressed,
Easy to comprehend and convenient to practice,
Without depending on anything else, it perfects the paths for
   those of lower, medium, and higher faculties.

This is the self-resounding tantra of dharmata, the indestructible
   essence,
From the space of luminosity in the five-colored sphere within
   the heart of me, Padmasambhava.
It is the path traversed by all the buddhas of the three times.

Praised by Jamyang Khyentse Wangpo as being more valuable than
thirty yak loads of scriptures, the *Lamrim Yeshe Nyingpo*, together
with the commentary by Jamgön Kongtrül, comprises the important
last volume in both the collections of termas and teachings renowned
as *Rinchen Terdzö* and *Chokling Tersar*.

Several biographies of Padmasambhava, the Lotus-Born Master,
have been published in English, including *The Lotus-Born* (Shambhala, 1993) and Jamgön Kongtrül's essay in *Dakini Teachings* (Shambhala, 1990). It is, therefore, better for the reader to refer to them
than for me to try to add anything here other than historical data.

Padmasambhava or Guru Rinpoche was renowned for establishing
the tantric teachings in Tibet in the ninth century. He ordered the
concealment of his oral instructions in the form of hidden treasures,

termas, to be revealed by the destined disciple at the appropriate time. *Lamrim Yeshe Nyingpo* is one such treasure.

YESHE TSOGYAL

The dakini Yeshe Tsogyal wrote down and hid many of Padmasambhava's teachings, including the *Lamrim Yeshe Nyingpo.* In his *Ocean of Blessings,*[2] Jamgön Kongtrül says:

Yeshe Tsogyal appeared as an emanation of Dhatvishvari Vajra Yogini and was in essence not different from the consorts of the five buddhas. In the dharmakaya aspect she is known as Samantabhadri or Prajnaparamita; in the sambhogakaya level she manifests in the form of the great consort Dhatvishvari; and from there she displays an inconceivable number of nirmanakayas, appearing in whichever way is necessary to influence whoever is in need. In the pure lands she appears in the form of Sarasvati, the noble Goddess of Eloquence, and shows the skillful means for generating the light of wisdom in all aspects of knowledge, both the outer and inner levels of philosophy. In the presence of Buddha Shakyamuni she emanated in the form of Ganga Devi and acted as the custodian of the treasury of the Mahayana teachings. In this snowy land [of Tibet] she took rebirth as a qualified dakini into the family line of the Kharchen clan and became a consort accepted by Guru Rinpoche. By the power of her immense training, she accomplished perfect recall. Traversing the secret path of Vajrayana, right to the letter, she achieved the supreme vajra abode of the twelfth bhumi. Perfecting the great power of realization of the natural Great Perfection, she arrived at the stage that is at the end of the four visions. Acting as the compiler of all Guru Rinpoche's words, she visited everywhere in the central and surrounding lands of Tibet and concealed innumerable major and minor termas. At present she resides in the indestructible form of the rainbow body in the Palace of Lotus Light on [the continent of] Chamara where she is indivisible from the never-ending adornment wheels of Guru Rinpoche's body, speech, mind, qualities, and activities, pervading as far as the reaches of space to benefit beings for as long as samsara exists.

ENTRUSTMENT

The main recipients of the *Lamrim Yeshe Nyingpo* were the king, the princes, the incarnated translator Vairochana, and Yeshe Tsogyal, the spiritual consort of Padmasambhava. The great master entrusted these teachings to a small gathering of his personal disciples during which he concluded with these words:

> I will entrust it to the assembly of suitable vessels, the destined
>   and qualified ones,
> The king and his sons, who are worthy recipients for the
>   instructions,
> Vairochana, whose realization is equal to mine,
> And my spiritual consort, who has rendered perfect service.
>
> Do not let it dissipate; retain it in the core of your hearts.
> Rely on it, engage in it, expound and practice it.
> By means of it may all the infinite number of disciples
> Accomplish the wisdom essence within the very same lifetime.

PRINCE MURUB TSEYPO

One of the principal recipients of the *Lamrim Yeshe Nyingpo* was the second prince, known variously under the names Yeshe Rölpa Tsal, Murub Tseypo, or Mutri Tseypo. An untitled and unpublished manuscript written by His Holiness Dilgo Khyentse Rinpoche explaining the *Sheldam Nyingjang,* herein called *Commentary on the Essence Manual of Instructions,* contains some background information on this prince:

The single father, King Trisong Deutsen, had three sons of which the middle one was called Murub Tseypo, a lord of the tenth bhumi who in actuality and visibly had achieved the noble qualities of abandonment and realization. Also known as the Prince Translator, he reached perfection in learning. At the end, his bodily form vanished into the body of light, and he attained the supreme accomplishment of perceiving the primordial wakefulness. It is his magical reincarnation who appeared during this age of degeneration, renowned worldwide under the title Orgyen Chokgyur Dechen Shikpo Lingpa, the universal ruler over an ocean of accomplished revealers of Dharma treasures.[3]

THE THREE MASTERS

In addition to the second prince, who was reborn as Chokgyur Lingpa, another important person present during Padmasambhava's transmission of *Lamrim Yeshe Nyingpo* was King Trisong Deutsen, who later incarnated as Jamyang Khyentse Wangpo. Jamgön Kongtrül Lodrö Thaye is regarded as the emanation of the translator Vairochana. These three great masters met together again in the middle part of the nineteenth century in accordance with numerous predictions of Guru Rinpoche. During a short period of time they revealed to the world an immense treasury of precious teachings. To expand upon these masters, I requested Tulku Urgyen Rinpoche to provide a short essay on their lives and qualities, and his beautifully expounded anecdotes are included right after this Introduction. More details of the lives of these most wonderful masters can be found in *The Nyingma School of Tibetan Buddhism* by His Holiness Dudjom Rinpoche, pages 839–868.

CHOKGYUR LINGPA

His Holiness Dilgo Khyentse Rinpoche describes Chokgyur Lingpa in his *Commentary on the Essence Manual of Instructions:*

Quoting the omniscient Yönten Gyatso [Jamgön Kongtrül], "Your excellent aspiration is to consider the beings of the dark age; your excellent activity is to manifest in accordance with those to be tamed; your excellent life example is to uphold an unprecedented treasury of secrets; I supplicate you who are endowed with this threefold excellence." In accordance with these words, the embodied forms of the activity of the king [Trisong Deutsen] and his sons, who will never forsake the beings of this world, are to an increasing degree unimpeded, even in this period of the dark age. And thus, there arose a new auspicious coincidence, the wonderful nature of which resembles the appearance of the Buddha in the world.

The most important among the profound termas of this great revealer of Dharma treasures was the *Four Cycles of Guru Sadhana,* belonging to the Sadhana Section, and the *Seven Profound Cycles,* belonging to the Tantra Section, the latter of which were expressed in a terminology that is in harmony with the Oral Transmission [of Kama]. Each of these were endowed with the complete aspects of empowerment, sadhana, tantra, development stage, and completion stage, each of which again were adorned with wonderful and profound details. In this way his Dharma treasures were totally unmatched.

Together with these Dharma treasures he [Chokgyur Lingpa] also revealed sacred substances and innumerable, most amazing representations of enlightened body, speech, and mind. He was an unprecedented lord of a treasury of secrets, as if Dharmevajra [compiler of the tantras] had appeared in person.

Moreover, the activity of his enlightened deeds was beyond partiality in exposition, practice, and action, to such an extent that an untold number of learned and accomplished masters of Sakya, Geluk, Kagyü, and Nyingma—headed by the two lords of the Land of Snow, who are like the sun and moon in presiding over the chariot of the Dharma in this world, as well as their disciples and lineage holders—all directly or indirectly accepted the nectar of his deep teachings. And thus the sunlight of these profound and extensive termas has shone far and wide for the Buddhadharma and all beings.[4]

Chokgyur Lingpa was assigned to become a master over one hundred sacred places and treasure troves and would have done so had the auspicious circumstances all been perfected. Nevertheless, there are thirty-seven profound termas well-known within the general domain of experience. The most complete and concise is the root of blessings, the *Heart Practice of the Vidyadhara Guru,* endowed with an outer, inner, secret, and innermost section.

The *Lamrim Yeshe Nyingpo* belongs to this fourth, the *Innermost Cycle Dorje Drakpo Tsal.*

JAMYANG KHYENTSE WANGPO

Jamyang Khyentse Wangpo (1820–1892) was one of the greatest masters of the last century. Regarded as the last of the five tertön kings,[5] he became the master and teacher of all the Buddhist schools of Tibet and one of the founders of the nonsectarian Rimey movement. Described as a holder of the seven transmissions, he was together with his close friend Jamgön Kongtrül one of the codifiers of the Eight Chariots of the Practice Lineage. There are ten volumes of his works in addition to his termas. In his *Wish-Fulfilling Source of Splendor,*[6] Jamgön Kongtrül describes his close friend, guru, and lineage holder in these words, "Jamyang Khyentse Wangpo, Dorje Ziji Tsal, the king of all learned and accomplished masters, was the combined incarnation of the great pandita Vimalamitra and Tsangpa Lhayi Metok, King Trisong Deutsen appearing as a nirmanakaya for the sake of beings."[7] Among his other names are Künga Tenpey Gyaltsen, Ösel Trülpey Dorje, and his tertön name Padma Ösel Dongak Lingpa.

JAMGÖN KONGTRÜL

Jamgön Kongtrül (1813–1899) is also known as Lodrö Thaye, Yönten Gyatso, Padma Garwang, and by his tertön name, Padma Tennyi Yungdrung Lingpa. He was one of the most prominent Buddhist masters in nineteenth-century Tibet and placed special focus upon a nonsectarian attitude. Renowned as an accomplished master, scholar, and writer, he authored more than one hundred volumes of scriptures. The best-known are his Five Treasuries, among which are the sixty-three volumes of the *Rinchen Terdzö,* the terma literature of the one hundred great tertöns. It is impossible to adequately describe the full scope of the impact this master has had on Tibetan Buddhism.

THE COMMENTARY

In the author's colophon at the end of the commentary on *Lamrim Yeshe Nyingpo,* Jamgön Kongtrül explains why he made the effort to write this text:

> This brief commentary on the *Oral Instructions in the Gradual Path of the Wisdom Essence,* the background teachings for the *Four Cycles of Guru Sadhana,* [was written based on] receiving the command of both vidyadhara gurus, the two great treasure revealers and all-encompassing masters and lords of the circle; the spiritual sons of the fourteenth Omniscient King of the Victorious Ones, the two supreme incarnations in his family at Tsurphu who illuminate the teachings of the Kamtsang; and also the wise dakini Dechen Chödrön, had for a long time encouraged me [to write] with a gift of a golden flower.[8]
>
> Later on, in the company of the son of the tertön, the vidyadhara Tsewang Drakpa,[9] she again asked me. Headed by the bodhisattva spiritual teacher Tsa-nyag Lama Sherab, other devoted people also made insistent requests. For these reasons, taking as the chief material the outline bestowed by the omniscient Jamgön Lama Rinpoche[10] and the nectar of his words, which I received directly, I have used whatever was present within the realm of my mind. Taking also several appropriate parts from the eloquent expositions of other learned masters, this was written down in a legible and concise manner by an ignorant meditator, the mere image of a renunciant, by

the name of Padma Garwang Lodrö Thaye, also known as Chimey Tennyi Yungdrung Lingpa Tsal, at the upper retreat of Palpung Shri Devi Koti known as the practice center of Tsandra Rinchen Drak. May it be a cause for the unwaning light of benefit and welfare for the teachings and beings to spread and flourish!

REVELATION OF THE TERMA

The *Lamrim Yeshe Nyingpo* is a terma revealed in unison by Chokgyur Lingpa and Jamyang Khyentse Wangpo and belongs to the fourth cycle from an amazing set of terma teachings renowned as the *Four Cycles of Guru Sadhana*. In his *Key That Opens One Hundred Doors to Accomplishment,* Jamgön Kongtrül describes the lineages for these four cycles:[11] "In general, the outer, inner, secret, and innermost *Four Cycles of Guru Sadhana* were first received by Padma Ösel Do-ngak Lingpa. Later Chokgyur Lingpa revealed, as his personal destiny, the *Barchey Künsel* and so forth, establishing these terma teachings as perfectly trustworthy by combining mother and child, like joining two rivers into one." The *Lamrim Yeshe Nyingpo* belongs to the fourth of the four cycles, the innermost cycle of the wrathful form of Padmasambhava, Dorje Drakpo Tsal, meaning "Powerful Vajra Wrath."

Lamrim Yeshe Nyingpo was revealed according to Orgyen Tobgyal Rinpoche in *The Life and Teaching of Chokgyur Lingpa*[12] in the following way:

Chokgyur Lingpa traveled again to Derge in Eastern Tibet, now as a great lama. Everyone considered him Guru Rinpoche in person and he brought great benefit to others. At this time he was invited to Dzongsar Monastery in Derge, from where he went to Rongmey. At Rongmey, Khyentse Rinpoche and Chokgyur Lingpa called for Jamgön Kongtrül. Chokgyur Lingpa told Khyentse, "A precious terma treasure is to be discovered, but you must call the king of Derge." Khyentse Rinpoche wrote a letter and the Derge king came with many chiefs, filling the whole area with horses and men. Everyone went to Karmo Taktsang. At the end of the town was a big cave where Guru Rinpoche had appeared in his wrathful form of Dorje Drolö. There Chokgyur Lingpa sang many songs, saying, "Now I will take out some termas. If everything is auspicious, and works out well, I have things to do for Tibet." Even Khyentse Rinpoche was amazed and sang a lot of songs. Chokgyur Lingpa told everyone to recite the Vajra Guru mantra and the Dusum Sangye prayer. He said, "If the three of us work together, we can really do something." Proceeding to where the terma treasure was located, Chokgyur Lingpa Rinpoche put a note on a pine tree telling the guardian of the terma to give it to him. Then they went to a rock. Chokgyur Lingpa opened the rock and extracted a vajra, leaving it half out and half in just for show. He removed a terma box and let everyone come and touch it with his head. That was the *Lamrim Yeshe Nyingpo*.

PROPAGATION

As soon as the root text was revealed, Jamyang Khyentse Wangpo taught it in detail after having established the outline, which flowed forth from his vast realization. Jamgön Kongtrül Lodrö Thaye used this outline as the framework for his commentary. In the *Key That Opens One Hundred Doors to Accomplishment,* Jamgön Kongtrül says:

> The most secret cycle for accomplishing the guru in the form of Powerful Vajra Wrath was revealed by [Jamyang Khyentse Wangpo and Chokgyur Lingpa] together at Rongmey Karmo Taktsang.[13] From this cycle the Omniscient Guru [Jamyang Khyentse Wangpo] decoded only the *Lamrim Yeshe Nyingpo,* while the other teaching cycles were at that point not accessible.

In *Clarifying the Aspects of the Auspicious Melody,*[14] Könchok Gyurmey Tenpey Gyaltsen, the second incarnation of Chokgyur Lingpa explains:

The thirty-first terma, the cycle of the secret sadhana Dorje Drakpo Tsal, was revealed from the left side of the Secret Cave at Karmo Taktsang after having broken through thirteen consecutive seals. But, due to circumstances, it could not be written down in its entirety. Nevertheless, Chokgyur Dechen Lingpa succeeded in revealing the *Lamrim Yeshe Nyingpo,* which is superior to one hundred loads of terma teachings. As the extracted essence of the tantras, statements, and instructions, it is the background teaching for all terma treasures in general and for the *Four Cycles of Guru Sadhana* in particular. Padma Ösel Do-ngak Lingpa [Jamyang Khyentse Wangpo] decoded it from the yellow parchment and Chimey Tennyi Yungdrung Lingpa [Jamgön Kongtrül Lodrö Thaye] wrote a commentary upon it. Thus they established the tradition for expounding and studying this profound teaching, which will shatter samsaric existence by merely hearing its name, which causes unconditioned wakefulness to grow forth when one studies it and reflects upon it, and which bestows the fruition of buddhahood when applying it in practical experience. The commentary itself was also a terma teaching that arose from the expanse of sublime wisdom, and a normal person, no matter how learned, will not be able to write such a book.

In the *Garland of Jewels,* Tekchok Tenphel, the third tulku of Neten Chokling, summarizes:[15]

The cycle of the secret sadhana Dorje Draktsal was revealed as Chokgyur Lingpa's thirty-first terma from the left side of the Secret Cave at Chimey Taktsang, but due to a lack of auspicious circumstances all its parts were not written down in full. Nevertheless, Chokgyur Lingpa took out the terma of *Lamrim Yeshe Nyingpo,* and Jamyang Khyentse Wangpo decoded it from the yellow parchment. Immediately upon being decoded, this profound teaching, which was clarified by Jamgön Rinpoche [Lodrö Thaye], was twice explained in great detail by the omniscient Dorje Ziji [Jamyang Khyentse Wangpo]. [Jamgön Kongtrül later] gave the transmission for the commentary *Spreading the Light of Wisdom* and also the reading transmission mixed with explanations for the root text and commentary combined.

In the words of Tulku Urgyen Rinpoche:

> Prior to this, Jamyang Khyentse Wangpo had been presented with a scroll containing the list of the termas through which he had gained certainty as to the preciousness of the *Lamrim Yeshe Nyingpo*. At a certain point in time after that, he and Chokgyur Lingpa met together during a perfect coincidence of time and place. This was predicted by Guru Rinpoche as the reunion of father and son in the sense that Jamyang Khyentse was the reincarnation of King Trisong Deutsen, while Chokgyur Lingpa was the rebirth of the prince, the king's second son. It was at Karmo Taktsang that they then revealed the cycle of termas within which the *Lamrim Yeshe Nyingpo* is included.

TRANSMISSION TO THE PRESENT

After Chokgyur Lingpa and Jamyang Khyentse Wangpo had established the root text, this precious scripture was propagated by their chief disciples, headed by Jamgön Kongtrül, and it has been transmitted in an unbroken lineage to this very day. Every lama who possesses the lineage for the *Rinchen Terdzö* or *Chokling Tersar* will evidently also be a holder of the reading transmission for *Lamrim Yeshe Nyingpo*. What follows are just a few of the many lineages for these two major sets of Vajrayana precepts.

His Holiness the sixteenth Karmapa, Rangjung Rigpey Dorje, mentions in his *Tob-yig,* a record of teachings received, for the *Chokling Tersar,* that his transmission for the *Lamrim Yeshe Nyingpo* came through Dorje Ziji Tsal [Jamyang Khyentse Wangpo], Padma Garwang [Jamgön Kongtrül], Khewang Loten Chögyal, Tsewang Norbu, Lama Chimey, [Surmang] Tenga Rinpoche, and then to himself.

H. H. Dilgo Khyentse Rinpoche similarly states that his lineage comes from Chokgyur Lingpa to the two great masters, Jamyang Khyentse Wangpo and Jamgön Kongtrül, and from all three of them to Tsewang Norbu, the son of Chokgyur Lingpa. Tsewang Norbu transmitted this to both Pema Gyurmey Tekchog Tenphel, the incarnation of Chokling at Neten Gompa, and to Könchok Gyurmey Tenpey Gyaltsen, the other incarnation of Chokgyur Lingpa who took up residence at Tsikey Monastery. Dilgo Khyentse Rinpoche's root guru, the illustrious master Jamyang Khyentse Chökyi Lodrö Rinpoche received the lineage from both incarnations of Chokgyur Lingpa. His Holiness also mentions an alternate line of transmission as having passed from Tsewang Norbu through Katok Situ Pandita Orgyen Chökyi Gyatso and Yabje Rigdzin (Serpa Tersey) Gyurmey Tsewang Gyatso to Khyentse Chökyi Lodrö, as well as from Tsewang Norbu to Samten Gyatso Rinpoche to Khakhyab Dorje, the fifteenth Karmapa, who wrote many of the arrangements.

Tekchok Tenphel, the third incarnation of Chokgyur Lingpa at Neten, who is the father of Dzigar Kongtrül Rinpoche and Orgyen Tobgyal Rinpoche, explains that his lineage for the *Lamrim Yeshe Nyingpo* originated with Chokgyur Lingpa, who took out the yellow parchment and gave it to Jamyang Khyentse Wangpo, who then decoded the symbolic dakini script. Having received detailed teachings twice from Jamyang Khyentse Wangpo, Jamgön Kongtrül wrote the commentary. From them the lineage went to the great Khenpo Rinchen Namgyal, then to the second Chokling, and from him to Khyentse Chökyi Lodrö, his root guru. Another lineage is from Tsewang Norbu to Chökyi Lodrö, and a third line goes through Jamgön Kongtrül to Lama Tendzin Chögyal, to Tsewang Norbu, to Situ Gyurmey Tsewang Gyatso, to Khyentse Chökyi Lodrö, and then to himself. This is the lineage held by Lama Putsi Pema Tashi.

The lineage of Tulku Urgyen Rinpoche, Tsewang Chokdrub Palbar, is traced through Chokgyur Lingpa, Jamyang Khyentse Wangpo, Jamgön Kongtrül, Tsewang Norbu, and Samten Gyatso, as well as through Samten Gyatso to Gyalwang Karmapa Khakhyab

Dorje, and then to Jamgön Palden Khyentse Öser, from whom Tulku Urgyen Rinpoche received the *Rinchen Terdzö*. In addition, Tulku Urgyen received detailed instruction from Jokyab Rinpoche. Jamgön Palden Khyentse Öser, the son of the fifteenth Karmapa, was the reincarnation of Jamgön Kongtrül, as well as the root guru of Kalu Rinpoche.

In recent years, the transmission for *Lamrim Yeshe Nyingpo* and its commentary has also been passed on to most of the incarnate lamas of the Karma Kagyü lineage by Kalu Rinpoche and Tulku Urgyen Rinpoche. Among the living masters of our time who either have or are about to transmit the *Rinchen Terdzö* or *Chokling Tersar* we also find His Holiness Penor Rinpoche, Dodrub Chen Rinpoche, Kela Chokling Rinpoche, and Khenchen Thrangu Rinpoche.

The reason I mention this is that now, while you are holding this book in your hands, I encourage you to make the wish to request the transmission for *Lamrim Yeshe Nyingpo* from one of these many authentic masters of the living tradition.

It has been a tradition to give a lengthy exposition of *Lamrim Yeshe Nyingpo* as the "background teaching" when conferring the empowerments for the *Chokling Tersar*. For instance, His Holiness Dilgo Khyentse in 1978 passed on the transmission for the entire termas of Chokgyur Lingpa at Ka-Nying Shedrup Ling Monastery in Boudhanath, Nepal, to a large group of incarnate masters and ordained and lay practitioners, including reincarnations of Chokgyur Lingpa, Jamyang Khyentse Wangpo, and Jamgön Kongtrül, headed by Trülshik Rinpoche, Shechen Rabjam Rinpoche, Dzongsar Jamyang Khyentse, Chokling Mingyur Dewey Dorje, Chökyi Nyima Rinpoche, Orgyen Tobgyal Rinpoche, Tulku Pema Wangyal, Tulku Jigme Khyentse, Dzigar Kongtrül Rinpoche, Chagdud Tulku Rinpoche and his son Jigme Norbu Rinpoche, and many, many others. During this time, His Holiness continued every day explaining Jamgön Kongtrül's commentary *The Light of Wisdom,* showing its great importance. Being both deaf and dumb regarding the Tibetan language, it was during this time I formed the strong wish to understand and translate *Lamrim Yeshe Nyingpo.*

Many years later, when requesting clarification on *The Light of Wisdom,* His Holiness Dilgo Khyentse gave me his blessings and permission to translate the entire commentary, and he also strongly suggested that I read the *Notes,* a collection of annotations by Jokyab Rinpoche, entitled *Entering the Path of Wisdom.* When mentioning this to Tulku Urgyen Rinpoche, he revealed that he had personally carried this manuscript out of Tibet and, possessing the only extant copy, later lent it to His Holiness for publication. This original manuscript was often consulted for verification.

STRUCTURE OF THE SCRIPTURES

The English translation of *The Light of Wisdom,* vol. 1, is a combination of three texts:

- *Lamrim Yeshe Nyingpo* (The Gradual Path of the Wisdom Essence), the terma root text recorded by Yeshe Tsogyal
- *The Light of Wisdom*
- *Entering the Path of Wisdom,* the notes collected by Jokyab Rinpoche

THE *LAMRIM YESHE NYINGPO* ROOT TEXT

The Gradual Path of the Wisdom Essence is the root text *Lamrim Yeshe Nyingpo.* It contains Guru Rinpoche's oral instructions on the gradual path to enlightenment according to the Three Inner Tantras—Maha, Anu, and Ati Yoga—as recorded by the dakini Yeshe Tsogyal and is a terma revealed by Chokgyur Lingpa and Jamyang Khyentse Wangpo. The translated portion of the root text presented here includes the historical narration and the instructions that are common for all levels of practitioners.[16]

THE LIGHT OF WISDOM

The Light of Wisdom is a commentary on *Lamrim Yeshe Nyingpo* by Jamgön Kongtrül the First. Because of its depth and encompassing scope, this exposition of Guru Rinpoche's teachings is considered by many masters to be a mind treasure in itself. I shall now briefly sketch the contents of Jamgön Kongtrül's commentary as it is structured here in *The Light of Wisdom,* vol. 1. Jamgön Kongtrül follows the traditional writing style of a pandita with numerous levels and sublevels. These divisions and their names are retained within the text, but as a kindness to the general reader, I have also used the structure of sections and chapters: three sections with a total of fifteen chapters.

The first section contains three chapters covering the traditional front matter, in which the author pays his respects to the masters of the lineage, here Padmasambhava, Jamyang Khyentse Wangpo, and Chokgyur Lingpa. This homage, followed by the author's pledge to complete his writing, his synopsis of the topic, and his method of explanation, are all included in Chapter 1.

Chapter 2 contains his clarification on the various levels of meaning expressed in the title, with special emphasis on the words *Yeshe Nyingpo,* "Wisdom Essence."

Chapter 3 covers the significance of the dakini script, a secret code that is legible only to masters possessing the transmission of Padmasambhava. These characters are included on page 1 at the beginning of the root text.

The second section is called "The Explanation of the Actual Body of the Text" and contains five chapters. The first two, Chapter 4, "The Setting," and Chapter 5, "The Circumstances," are titles often used in the tantras, the sacred literature of Vajrayana. These two chapters cover the historical background, "The Setting" explaining where and when, and "The Circumstances" detailing why and who requested the great master Padmasambhava to give this most precious teaching.

Chapter 6 is a detailed clarification of "The Four Vajra Sylla-bles"—OM AH HUNG HOH—explaining how these four tantric sylla-bles demonstrate the nature of all aspects of spirituality, here known as ground, path, and fruition.

In Chapter 7 Jamgön Kongtrül clarifies the meaning of the five perfections—teacher, place, retinue, teaching, and time. Together these five aspects show the Buddhist cosmology for propagating the Dharma on the three levels of dharmakaya, sambhogakaya, and nir-manakaya. This chapter concludes with Padmasambhava's injunction to his present and future followers, explaining the value of retaining and practicing the teachings.

Chapter 8 covers the meaning of the buddha nature, here called the ground. The clarification of the ground, our basic enlightened essence, details both the basis for confusion as well as enlightenment, according to the general system of Mahayana as well as from the extraordinary perspective of the Great Perfection.

The third section is called "Path." By "path" is meant the period from the very outset of awakening faith and interest in liberation from samsaric existence and the attainment of complete enlighten-ment. Among the seven chapters in this section, Chapter 9 covers the details of how to carefully and genuinely connect with a spiritual teacher.

Chapter 10 explains how to develop true renunciation by means of reflection on "The Four Mind Changings"—the preciousness of our human life, the sad fact that everything is impermanent, the inev-itable consequences of our actions, and the painful nature of exis-tence while under the power of ignorance and delusion.

In Chapter 11 Jamgön Kongtrül describes in detail the reason and method for taking refuge under seven points.

Chapter 12 covers the teachings on how to develop the genuine wish to attain enlightenment for the welfare of all sentient beings, here called the "Conventional Bodhichitta of Aspiration."

Chapter 13 details how to implement this wish in action, how to train in the six paramitas and four means of attraction—the conduct of a genuine bodhisattva.

In Chapter 14 is explained "The View of Ultimate Bodhichitta," the nature of the emptiness of all things, both phenomena and the individual self.

Chapter 15 clarifies "The Meditation of Ultimate Bodhichitta," as well as the path and result of Mahayana, leading to the state of unexcelled, true, and complete enlightenment.

THE NOTES

Entering the Path of Wisdom is a collection of annotations to the above commentary, spoken by Jamyang Khyentse Wangpo to one of his learned disciples, Jamyang Drakpa, and written down by Jokyab Rinpoche, a student of Jamyang Drakpa. *Entering the Path of Wisdom* was written down as fragmented pieces of information and additional explanations to be used when teaching *The Light of Wisdom*. They cast invaluable light on some of the more profound parts of Jamgön Kongtrül's words and also fill out places with explanation that he had assumed would be already understood by the person giving the teachings.

To shed further light on how the oral transmission of these teachings took place, I will repeat the words of Tulku Urgyen Rinpoche:

> Jamyang Drakpa was a student of both Jamgöns [Jamyang Khyentse Wangpo and Jamgön Kongtrül] and was present when the root text was revealed. He is one of the sixteen destined disciples who would spread the teaching and is predicted in the root text *Lamrim Yeshe Nyingpo*. Consequently, Jamyang Khyentse Wangpo told him, "Your activity for the welfare of others is to propagate the *Lamrim Yeshe Nyingpo*. So do it!" The explanatory lineage for the *Lamrim Yeshe Nyingpo* at one point rested on him. He had reached an advanced age, above eighty, by the time Jokyab Rinpoche came to receive the transmission for the *Lamrim*. I knew Jokyab Rinpoche personally, since I was fortunate enough to receive the teachings on

the *Lamrim Yeshe Nyingpo* from him. Jokyab Rinpoche also received the entire transmission for the *Chokling Tersar* from my uncle and guru Samten Gyatso Rinpoche, as well as the *Damngak Dzö* from Khyungtrül Karjam Rinpoche.[17]

Samten Gyatso Rinpoche sent a message to Dru Jamyang Drakpa, requesting teachings on the *Lamrim Yeshe Nyingpo* on behalf of Jokyab Rinpoche. Jokyab remained with the great master Jamyang Drakpa for an entire year, but the teachings on the *Lamrim* did not commence during the first six months, due to the master's advanced age and fragile health. The first months were spent on questions on the *Guhyagarbha Tantra* with which Jamyang Drakpa was quite familiar, knew by heart, and therefore did not have to look at pages in order to consult. The second half of the year was spent on the *Lamrim.*

When Jamyang Drakpa finally began the explanations, Jokyab took notes on small pieces of paper, one after the other, so that at the end he had a heap almost the size of a volume of scriptures. Having returned to Tsikey Monastery, he organized and transcribed his notes, and this collection is what is now known as the *Zurgyen,* the "Side Ornament."[18] After this he went to Central Tibet.

His Eminence Tulku Urgyen Rinpoche received transmission for *Lamrim Yeshe Nyingpo* from many great masters, including the reincarnation of Jamgön Kongtrül who was the son of the fifteenth Karmapa, but the detailed explanation he received from Jokyab Rinpoche himself.

In addition to the notes by Jokyab Rinpoche, I have added some clarifications from other masters. In order to identify the various sources explained in the notes, I have used the following codes: "[JOKYAB]" means that it is translated from *Entering the Path of Wisdom.* His Holiness Dilgo Khyentse Rinpoche later corrected this text, and where his opinion differs from the original words, the mark "[DKR]" follows the note. "[TUR]" means that the information was transmitted orally by Tulku Urgyen Rinpoche. Clarifications from Chökyi Nyima Rinpoche are followed by "[CNR]." Annotations followed by

"[EPK]" are my own, but of course based on oral teachings I have received from living teachers.

In addition, two other texts have been used to substantiate the three above. *Illuminating Sunlight* by Khenpo Rinchen Namgyal[19] is a short commentary, a simplified version of Jamgön Kongtrül's *Light of Wisdom*, embellished with his own learning and eloquence. Also used is Mipham Rinpoche's *Outline for Teaching the Light of Wisdom*.[20] This outline was made according to the oral teachings of Jamyang Khyentse Wangpo.

Jamgön Kongtrül's commentary, *The Light of Wisdom*, makes reference to the root text, *The Wisdom Essence*, only in an abbreviated way. For the sake of easy reading, I have inserted the root verses in full at the appropriate places. All quotations from the root text are denoted by indented italic type and are preceded by "The *Lamrim Yeshe Nyingpo* root text says."

HOW TO STUDY THE LAMRIM YESHE NYINGPO

Level one: The root text by itself in connection with the oral instructions of a living master.

Level two: The root text with Jamgön Kongtrül's short commentary immediately following the quotations from the root text. This short commentary is usually the first paragraph following the root text.

Level three: The root text with the extensive commentary by Jamgön Kongtrül, *The Light of Wisdom*.

Level four: *The Light of Wisdom* together with the notes and appendices from *Entering the Path of Wisdom*.

This present book combines all four levels in the following way:

1. The root verses are found separately in the beginning of the book.

2. The simplified commentary is what immediately follows the root verses and contains the words used in these verses.

3. The extra quotations from the scriptures and additional explanations.

4. The appendices and notes at the end of the book.

ACKNOWLEDGMENTS

I would never have been able to undertake and complete such a difficult work without the help of many kind masters of the present time. Due to their great kindness, it has been my fortune to receive teachings and clarify questions chiefly from Tulku Urgyen Rinpoche and Chökyi Nyima Rinpoche, as well as other learned teachers, including H. H. Dilgo Khyentse Rinpoche, Tulku Pema Wangyal, Chagdud Tulku Rinpoche, Orgyen Tobgyal Rinpoche, Khenpo Pema Sherab, Lama Putsi Pema Tashi, Khenpo Tashi Palden, and Acharya Tubten Chöphel. May this work in some way repay their kindness.

Also, my thanks to George MacDonald, Graham Sunstein, and Philippe O'Sullivan who at several stages financially supported the translation work.

Many of my friends have given generously of their time and energy, lending their different skills in editing: Judy Amtzis, John Fredricks, and Ben Rosenzweig. Also, thanks to my friends who read through the manuscript at various stages: Ani Jinpa Palmo, Ani Lodrö Palmo, Larry Mermelstein, Michael Tweed, and Thomas Doctor. Special thanks to Graham Sunstein for helping in locating information. Last, but not least, the completion of this work is due to my wife, Marcia, who helped at all stages of the production.

I dedicate whatever merit may arise from completing this work to the great masters of our day; may their lives be firm. May this effort act as a conduit to the flourishing of Padmasambhava's precious teachings, and may innumerable beings benefit from putting these instructions into practice.

To conclude, I would like to repeat some of Padmasambhava's words from the end of *Lamrim Yeshe Nyingpo.*

There will be eight people with mind transmission,
Twenty-five supreme vidyadharas,
Sixteen who will uphold and spread it,
And two times five authentic dakinis.
If all of them are able to practice it,
They will achieve special supreme and common siddhis.[21]

Moreover, there will be one hundred destined ones,
One thousand and eight who attain siddhi,
And eighteen times a hundred thousand who gain connection.
Thus, there will be an inconceivable number
Of human and nonhuman disciples.

Whoever writes down with precious gold
This *Gradual Path of the Wisdom Essence*
Sprinkles it with the five nectars,
And, together with the samaya substances of means and
    knowledge,
Attaches it around the neck,
Or binds it at the top of the head,
Will be liberated through sight, hearing, remembering, and
    touch,
And the wisdom of realization will effortlessly dawn.

Likewise, whoever reads and memorizes it,
Recites, explains, or studies it,
Will be blessed by me, Padma.
So it's needless to mention about someone who practices it
    correctly.

Erik Pema Kunsang
Ka-Nying Shedrup Ling Monastery
Boudhanath, 1993

Essay on the Three Great Masters

SPOKEN BY

HIS EMINENCE TULKU URGYEN RINPOCHE

Jamyang Khyentse Wangpo, Jamgön Kongtrül, and Chokgyur Lingpa were each other's teachers as well as disciples.

I'll begin with Jamyang Khyentse Wangpo, who was born in the district of Derge in Kham. Derge means "virtue and happiness." This area was traditionally saturated with the practice of Buddhism, a virtuous and perfect place for the Dharma, which was ruled by kings in accordance with spiritual principles. Throughout the centuries these kings had promoted the most favorable conditions for the Buddhadharma and, in recent times, the religious king by the name Tenpa Tsering was a disciple of the great master Situ Chökyi Jungney.

One day while going to the toilet the king thought that maybe it was possible for him to have woodblocks carved with the entire body of the Buddha's teachings, comprised of the *Translated Words,* the *Kangyur,* and the *Translated Treatises,* its commentaries, known as the *Tengyur.* Arriving back in the presence of his root guru, he felt he should relate his new idea, so he said, "Today I had a thought."

"What was that?" the master asked.

"I formed the wish to carve blocks for both the *Kangyur* and *Tengyur.* What do you think? Will it be successful?"

Situ Chökyi Jungney replied, "Don't ever give up this thought!"

"Very well!" the king agreed. "If I arrange for the carving, will you be able to do the proofreading?"

"I will take care of the proofing," Situ Rinpoche promised.

No more conversation than that took place initially. Situ Chökyi Jungney later proofread the woodblocks thirteen times, which is why the Derge edition was regarded as being of such a high standard. Situ was renowned as an equal to Sakya Pandita and was often called Situ Pandita. Thus the entire body of the translated words of the Buddha with their commentaries was carved and verified within the lifetimes of King Tenpa Tsering and Situ Chökyi Jungney, a task which till then had been insurmountable for the government in Central Tibet. It was in such a spiritual environment that Jamyang Khyentse Wangpo took birth.

Jamyang Khyentse Wangpo was the combined reincarnation of Vimalamitra, King Trisong Deutsen, Longchen Rabjam, and the omniscient master Jigmey Lingpa. He is renowned as the lord of seven transmissions, an incredibly learned and accomplished master. Here is a story I heard from one of my own teachers, Khyungtrül Rinpoche.

At this time there were six major monastic centers for the Nyingma tradition in Tibet: Shechen and Dzogchen in Lower Kham, Katok and Palyül in the middle, and Dorje Drag and Mindröl Ling in Upper Tibet. While Tutob Namgyal was the khenpo, the master in charge of higher studies, at Shechen Monastery in Kham, Jamyang Khyentse Wangpo, Jamgön Kongtrül Lodrö Thaye, and Paltrül Rinpoche were classmates. Jamyang Khyentse was nobility from the influential Dilgo clan, housing a line of ministers, one of which held the power equal to one quarter of the Derge kingdom. Jamgön Kongtrül was born into the Khyungpo clan, the same as Milarepa and Khyungpo Naljor, the founder of the Shangpa Kagyü school. The Khyungpo clan included both Buddhists and Bönpos, as shown by Chimey Tennyi Yungdrung Lingpa, the title Jamgön Kongtrül later received, which has a slight Bönpo connotation.

During their studies, these three young prodigies were receiving

teachings in philosophy from the great master Tutob Namgyal. Paltrül Rinpoche, in those days known simply as Palgye, was from the
Golok district, a virtuous country of highland nomads. Jamgön
Kongtrül's family was either poor or far away, and often he had no
food, while Jamyang Khyentse Wangpo was well off due to his rich
father, so Kongtrül often ate the leftover tsampa balls from his friend's
plate. After the meals Paltrül Rinpoche would lie down, covering his
head with his monk's shawl. When Khyentse and Kongtrül told him
he better study, Palgye replied, "Isn't it enough to just repeat what
the teacher said? Why should I worry?" If Paltrül Rinpoche was
called upon to explain the topic of the previous day, he would repeat
it, almost verbatim and nearly better than the khenpo himself.

Later Paltrül Rinpoche departed for the district of Dza Chukha,
while Jamgön Kongtrül, who belonged to the Kagyü School, went
to reside at Palpung Monastery.

Jamyang Khyentse originally was from the Gönchen at Derge, a
monastery belonging to the Sakya tradition. In the early part of his
life, he went to Central Tibet, where he received a vast number of
teachings from numerous masters. Later in his life, on a second visit
to Central Tibet, it seems like he transmitted all these teachings back
to others. It was therefore said, "Before he was a disciple; now he is
the master himself!"

At one point Jamyang Khyentse had a deep spiritual experience
involving a vision of Chetsün Senge Wangchuk after which he established in writing the precious teaching known as *Chetsün Nyingtig*.
At Sakya in Central Tibet he did a retreat on Manjushri and had the
experience of dissolving into the heart of his yidam, so the great
treasure mine of courageous eloquence overflowed from within his
state of realization. Thus he became like a king of all learned and
accomplished masters.

Having begun as a simple monk at the Gönchen Monastery, Jamyang Khyentse Wangpo later moved to Dzongshö, a place situated
above Dzongsar Monastery in Kham, where he made his residence.
This seat was later known as Deshek Düpey Phodrang, the "Palace

of the Assemblage of Sugatas." This is where he lived in the latter part of his life.

Chokgyur Lingpa was from the district of Nangchen and grew up, as a simple monk, in the Nangchen Tsechu Monastery. Once, during the tantric dances performed yearly, he fell out of rhythm and danced on independently of the others. The dance master, of course, got upset and wanted to give Chokgyur Lingpa a beating. Present in assembly was Adhi Rinpoche, the guru of the king of Nangchen as well as the son of the previous king and therefore holder of a very powerful position in the kingdom. Earlier, on a visit to China, Adhi Rinpoche had received the grand religious position of Hutuktu, and during those days there was no higher lama in Nangchen. Adhi Rinpoche, who had clairvoyant abilities, came now to Chokgyur Lingpa's rescue, saying, "Don't beat him! He has his own style. Just leave him to himself."

Soon after, Chokgyur Lingpa asked permission to leave the monastery, and Adhi Rinpoche consented, saying, "Yes, you can go. Travel freely wherever you like and benefit beings!" Before taking leave, Chokgyur Lingpa requested the king of Nangchen to give him a mount and provisions, but the king, being of a hardheaded character, was displeased with his departure and said, "The crazy tertön has given me a figure that is neither clay nor stone.[22] Give him an old horse and a riding mat." Due to this inauspicious circumstance, Chokgyur Lingpa never settled in Nangchen.

Chokgyur Lingpa first went to Derge where he met with Jamgön Kongtrül Lodrö Thaye, who later said, "When you see the terma teachings of this man who doesn't even know spelling or grammar, it is most amazing! It is really strange that such wonderful writing can come through a man who cannot even spell!" Jamgön Kongtrül showed great fondness for Chokgyur Lingpa and for his terma writings. During this time, Jamgön Kongtrül fell very sick and was unable to see. Chokgyur Lingpa gave him the empowerment for Vajrapani from his terma treasure called *Sangdak Dorje Bechön,* the *Vajra Club of the Lord of Secrets,* and told him to do some recitations of the mantra.

"Unless you do this practice, nothing else will help you regain your eyesight!" he said. That was their first connection.

In those days one needed a letter of introduction in order to gain audience with a lama of high standing, so Chokgyur Lingpa requested such a letter, saying, "I want to go and see Jamyang Khyentse Wangpo; please give me a petition letter." Jamyang Khyentse Wangpo was known by the name Shabdrung Rinpoche, Shabdrung being a religious rank two steps below the highest hierarch of the Sakya School, and of the nature of Dorje Lobpön, the vajra master in charge of tantric ceremonies. So Jamgön Kongtrül replied, "Of course I will write a letter introducing you to Shabdrung Rinpoche!" With the letter in hand, Chokgyur Lingpa then went to the residence of Jamyang Khyentse Wangpo.

Prior to this, Jamyang Khyentse Wangpo had written down a gongter, a mind treasure, containing the complete teachings of the famous terma *Tukdrub Barchey Künsel.* Now, when Chokgyur Lingpa arrived, also with a version of the *Tukdrub Barchey Künsel,* which had been revealed and decoded at the sacred place of Khala Rong-go and kept secret for eight years, he explained the story of his revelation, the time and place and the nature of the terma teaching. When comparing the two versions of the terma, they found them to be totally identical, without even one word of difference. This was a major reason for gaining profound trust in each other as being authentic major tertöns. During their first meeting they both had many auspicious dreams and visions, and Jamyang Khyentse Wangpo accepted Chokgyur Lingpa as his disciple, conferring some important empowerments upon him. After this Chokgyur Lingpa again went to see Jamgön Kongtrül at his residence located at the famous Tsandra Rinchen Drak, on the slope above Palpung Monastery in Kham.

At this point, Jamgön Kongtrül had completed the recitation retreat of the tantric deity Sangdak Dorje Bechön and had suddenly recovered completely from his disease. Relating the story of his recovery to Chokgyur Lingpa, Chokgyur Lingpa responded: "Of course you recovered. In your past life as the great translator Vairochana, you put a curse of leprosy on the evil Queen Margyenma and therefore had to undergo the ripening of that karmic deed. Because of the severity of your former action, the karmic ripening corresponded with a type of leprosy on your retinas, a disease influenced by the naga spirits. Padmasambhava designed this particular sadhana of Vajrapani to cure you from that naga disease, which is why I gave you that empowerment." From then on, Jamgön Kongtrül and Chokgyur Lingpa gained even stronger confidence in each other, fortified by several auspicious dreams and visions.

Jamgön Kongtrül often said, "Jamyang Khyentse Wangpo is the only one who can really distinguish between what is Dharma and what is not." After Jamyang Khyentse Wangpo passed away, Jamgön Kongtrül exclaimed, "The omniscient Dorje Ziji has left us! Now we are left behind in pitch-black darkness, not knowing right from wrong!" This was because Jamyang Khyentse Wangpo was the one whom he would ask for advice in all matters of importance, calling him the ultimate pandita. The most important of these three masters was Jamyang Khyentse Wangpo.[23]

Chokgyur Lingpa never went through formal studies, and so he could neither spell nor write with correct grammatical structure, and yet Jamgön Kongtrül later called him a true pandita. You can find the details of his total change in his extensive biography. This change took place while Chokgyur Lingpa remained in a strict retreat, traditionally lasting three years and three fortnights, at his residence above Karma Gön in Kham. During this retreat, phrased in his own words, he "unraveled slightly the intent of the tantras, statements, and instructions" of Maha, Anu, and Ati Yoga. During a vision of Padmasambhava, Chokgyur Lingpa received this advice, which is included in the text of the famous Ngakso which is based on the *Tukdrub Barchey Künsel:* "During this part of the dark age there is almost no Tibetan who hasn't received an empowerment for the Vajra Vehicles of Secret Mantra. The samaya is that which retains the life-force of empowerment. Without observing the samayas, the life-force of the empowerment vanishes, like a feather blown away in the wind, and will not bring you any benefit." For this reason Chokgyur Lingpa requested a method for regularly restoring the samayas, the tantric commitments, which he then received, based on the *Barchey Künsel* teachings. Following that he "unraveled slightly the intent of the tantras, statements, and instructions." This practice is now widely known as the Ngakso.[24]

When I received the transmission for the *Rinchen Terdzö* from Karsey Kongtrül, alias Jamgön Palden Khyentse Öser, the son of Khakhyab Dorje, the fifteenth Karmapa, he once explained that Jamgön Kongtrül had found a prophecy by Padmasambhava that he was to compose five great treasuries. Jamgön Kongtrül himself had access to decode a vast number of Dharma treasures, but, seeing that the older termas had great value, he gave rise to the wish to gather them all into a collection now renowned as *Rinchen Terdzö*, the "Precious Treasury of Termas."[25] So he sent a message to Chokgyur Lingpa, "You often meet Padmasambhava in person. Please ask him permission for me to collect the *Precious Treasury of Termas!*" Later Chokgyur Lingpa sent back this reply, "I asked Padmasambhava. He said, 'Most excellent!' Since that is the case, you must definitely undertake this task!" Karsey Kongtrül, who was in charge of the library at Tsandra Rinchen Drak, still had that letter and told us so in the presence of the sixteenth Karmapa while giving teachings in the main shrine hall.

While Jamgön Kongtrül was in the process of collecting these Dharma treasures, the lineage for many of the termas of former tertöns had disappeared. These were revived as *yangter*, "rediscovered treasures," by Jamyang Khyentse Wangpo. In this way Jamyang Khyentse Wangpo supplied the important termas for the *Rinchen Terdzö*, while Chokgyur Lingpa was the one who asked Padmasambhava for permission. The main work was carried out by Jamgön Kongtrül. Thus the incredible, important collection of the *Precious Treasury of Termas* was a combined effort of all three masters.

Jamgön Kongtrül, Jamyang Khyentse Wangpo, and Chokgyur Lingpa went on several journeys together, during which time they in unison discovered several terma teachings. *Lamrim Yeshe Nyingpo* is one of these Dharma treasures.

This is all I feel like telling here; also, I don't know much more than this. You can find the details of their lives in their respective biographies. I haven't made up any of these stories myself; I have only repeated the words I have heard from my teachers, Khyungtrül Rinpoche, Samten Gyatso Rinpoche, and others.

ཨོཾ༔ ཅཏྲ་མའི་ཕུགས་སྐྱབ་རྗེ་རྗེ་དག་ཚུལ་ལས༔
ཞལ་གདམས་ལམ་རིམ་ཡེ་ཤེས་སྙིང་པོ་བཤུགས་སོ༔
པདྨ་སོ་སྲུ་བའི་སྙིང་ཏིག་གོ།

Lamrim Yeshe Nyingpo

The Wisdom Essence of
Oral Instructions in Stages of the Path

The Heart Essence of Padmasambhava
According to The Guru's Heart Practice of
Dorje Drakpo Tsal, Powerful Vajra Wrath

Spoken by Padmasambhava
Recorded by Khandro Yeshe Tsogyal
Revealed and decoded by Jamyang Khyentse Wangpo
and Chokgyur Lingpa

ༀཨ་མ་གུ་རུ་སརྦ་སིདྡྷི་ཧཱུྃ༔

Homage to Dorje Drakpo Tsal, Powerful Vajra Wrath, embodiment of the Three Roots. ༔

The essence of all the buddhas of the three times, the supreme sovereign of all power-wielding vidyadharas, the all-encompassing lord of the ocean of peaceful and wrathful yidams, the chief of the gatherings of all the dakas and dakinis, the great being who by his splendor outshines all the vajra protectors of the Dharma and the haughty forces of appearance and existence, is the one renowned throughout the infinite realms of the teachers of the three kayas as Mahaguru Padmasambhava. ༔

Invited by Manjushri's incarnation, the Dharma-upholding King Trisong Deutsen, he came to this snowy land of Tibet, the realm of the noble Great Compassionate One. He placed all the vicious elemental forces under the majestic seal of his command, erected the triple-styled Unchanging and Spontaneously Perfected Temple, a palace with shrines, and strewed the flowers of consecration. He established the great tradition of expounding and practicing the entire doctrine of the Buddha and, in particular, he turned an infinite variety of the Dharma Wheels of the tantras, statements, and instructions of Vajrayana. ༔

He visited personally all the sacred places, the snow mountains, caves, and lakes, blessed them, and concealed innumerable named and unnamed treasures. Thus his immeasurable kindness permeates all of Tibet, both the central and surrounding lands, and will remaina right up to the last day of the final future age. SAMAYA. ⁑

At that time and occasion, the moment had come for the ripening of the result of perverted aspirations made through many lifetimes, showing itself as the hostile and evil-minded ministers and Queen Margyenma, engaging in various kinds of perverted thoughts and deeds. In the presence of the king they said:

> This sorcerer from the borderland of Mön has deceived you, the king, with all kinds of deceit, trickery, and optical illusions. At worst, he will deprive you of your life. Second to that, he will rob the kingdom. At the least, he will make the people revolt, spreading slander between the king, ministers, and queens. He should therefore be thrown in the river before the eyes of everyone. ⁑

As they insisted in this way, the king became saddened and related in detail to Guru Rinpoche the story of what had happened. "What will you do about this?" he asked. Tears streamed from the king's eyes and for a short while he fell unconscious from intense devotion. When he regained his senses after a few moments, Guru Rinpoche laughed and with a beaming smile said in the fearless voice of a roaring lion:

> Great king, you need not feel even slightly disheartened about this. Formerly, Mara and the heretics also tried to harm the truly perfected Buddha, but rather than causing even the smallest injury to the Three Jewels, they could only reveal his supreme enlightened virtues. Likewise, since I have attained mastery over the expression of awareness, I can transform the phenomenal world into whatever I desire. Since I have accomplished the indestructible form of the rainbow body, the four elements cannot inflict the least harm on me. Even if all the three realms were to rise up as an enemy toward me, the pandita of Uddiyana and the successor of all the victorious ones and bodhisattvas of the three times will only help in revealing my supreme miraculous powers, and surely not find any opportunity to cause me harm or even shake a tip of my hair. ⁑

When Guru Rinpoche had spoken in this way, the great king felt
deep devotion and rejoiced. He prostrated numerous times and made
this supplication:

> How wonderful, nirmanakaya Guru! ፨
> There is never any deception ፨
> In whatever vajra words you utter, ፨
> Since you are the embodiment of all the masters, ፨
> The great lord encompassing the ocean of yidams, ፨
> And the chief of the assemblies of dakinis. ፨
>
> Please subdue the evil-minded ministers ፨
> By the miraculous power of your compassion ፨
> In order that we, your devoted disciples, ፨
> May rejoice and be inspired, ፨
> And that the precious doctrine ፨
> Of the Buddha, Dharma, and Sangha may flourish. ፨

Since the king supplicated in this way, the guru joyfully promised,
"I will do that!" And in the center of the nine regions of Tibet and
Kham, in the courtyard of Golden Orphan Temple at Glorious
Samye, he entered the samadhi that tames the hordes of Mara. ፨

During this time, in the middle of the great courtyard amidst his
gathered retinue—panditas, translators, monks, mantrikas, the king,
ministers, queens, and common subjects—the guru, while remaining
seated, performed billions of unfathomable and miraculous displays
to tame beings according to their needs, such as letting his body disappear, becoming a blazing fire, making the earth quake, manifesting
peaceful and wrathful deities together with their assemblages, and
filling the sky with the thunderlike sounds of mantras. ፨

At this time, all the classes of maras were subdued and lost their
power to inflict harm. The power of faith was fully established in
both intermediate beings and nonbelievers. The faith of the believers
was increased even further, and they yearned to drink the nectar of

his words. All the people whose minds were ripened achieved the supreme siddhi of liberation, and the liberated ones attained the state of realization of Guru Rinpoche himself, in which the retinue is indivisible from the teacher. ፥

Because of these marvelous and inconceivable deeds, His Majesty the king felt even greater faith and devotion. In particular, at a time when Guru Rinpoche was staying in the Shining Turquoise Temple in the middle story of Samye, thinking of the future disciples in the age of degeneration, the king arranged upon a mandala plate of gold shining heaps of precious turquoise resembling huge and radiant stars. The king and the princes made numerous prostrations and, together with the incarnated translator Vairochana and myself, who was granted to be the spiritual consort, made this supplication:[26] ፥

> You are the fully perfected body, speech, mind, qualities, and
>   activities ፥
> Of all the buddhas and their sons of the ten directions and four
>   times. ፥
> Lotus Vajra body, untainted by a womb, ፥
> Mahaguru, we prostrate at your feet. ፥
>
> Protector, equal to all the buddhas, ፥
> Your kindness toward the beings in the Land of Snow is
>   exceedingly great. ፥
> In particular, there exists for us, the gathering of king and
>   subjects, ፥
> No other crown jewel. ፥
>
> Your special display of great miracles ፥
> Has subdued the impure hordes of Mara. ፥
> Raising the victory banner of the Buddha's teachings throughout
>   the ten directions, ፥
> You have ripened and freed the fortunate ones and established
>   them on the path of enlightenment. ፥

Your benefiting whoever is linked with you is an inconceivable
  wonder. ঃ
So our accumulations must be extremely great. ঃ
However, when in the future the age of degenerations arrives, ঃ
The side of virtue will be feeble and the evil forces raised high. ঃ

With the violation-demons visibly possessing people's hearts, ঃ
Buddhism, the doctrine holders, ঃ
And the happiness of sentient beings will be ravaged and
  destroyed, ঃ
And the evil ages of plagues, famine, warfare, and conflict will
  therefore simultaneously well up. ঃ

Since there will be no other refuge than you, the guru, ঃ
When this ocean of misery overflows Tibet and Kham, ঃ
We beg you to consider us with kindness ঃ
And, for the sake of us and the disciples in the future, ঃ
Bestow the quintessence of all the profound and vast
  instructions ঃ
That temporarily subjugates the outer and inner maras, ঃ
Effortlessly accomplishes the four activities, ঃ
And ultimately is the method for attaining the bhumi of
  Unexcelled Wisdom, ঃ
The light-body of the fivefold essence. ঃ

When we had made this supplication, Guru Rinpoche manifested
himself in an instant in the form of the vidyadhara Dorje Drakpo
Tsal and bestowed all the empowerments and oral instructions. Following this, he displayed, in the manner of totally filling up dharmadhatu, the miracle of emanating and absorbing in a single moment
infinite deities with retinues, the "approach" as the single mudra heruka, the manner with the elaborations of heads and arms of "full
approach," "accomplishment," and "great accomplishment."[27]
Through the great splendor of blessings, he manifested everywhere

throughout the central and surrounding areas of Tibet and Kham magical and miraculous displays of rainbows, lights, rains of flowers, earth tremors, spontaneous sounds and self-resounding music, and the vajra wisdom in actuality descending into the fortunate disciples. ፨

Once again, the Guru appeared majestically in the form of Padmasambhava, of the nature of light, and uttered with his vajra voice of dharmata this, the ultimate vajra speech, the stages of the path condensed to the essence. SAMAYA. ፨

OM AH HUNG HO ፨
The essence of primordially pure space is Samantabhadra, ፨
The spontaneously present awareness is Padmasambhava, ፨
And their indivisible unity, Dorje Drakpo Tsal, ፨
Is the heruka, the supreme sovereign of all mandalas. ፨

In the realm of the great sphere, the all-pervasive
    dharmadhatu, ፨
In the sambhogakaya palace with the fivefold luminosity, ፨
And in all the indefinite places of nirmanakayas who tame
    beings, ፨
They turn throughout the three times ፨
The wheel of Dharma of the inconceivable number of causal and
    resultant vehicles, ፨
For oceanlike assemblies of disciples possessing potential, ፨
In accordance with the various types of suitability and capacity
    of each individual. ፨

I will now teach to my closest disciples ፨
The quintessence of all these condensed into one, ፨
The essence of my heart, the ultimate counsel, ፨
As a direct instruction that is easy to understand and simple to
    apply. ፨
Don't let it dwindle away, but practice one-pointedly. ፨

It has that to be understood, that which causes realization, and
the final result. ჶ
Thus it is demonstrated by these three aspects. ჶ

The ground to be understood is the all-pervasive sugata
essence. ჶ
Uncompounded, luminous, and empty, it is the natural state of
awareness. ჶ
Beyond confusion and liberation, it is completely quiescent, like
space. ჶ
Although it abides without separation in samsara or joining in
nirvana, ჶ
Due to the great demon of coemergent and conceptual
ignorance, ჶ
From the solidified habitual patterns of grasping and fixation, ჶ
And the different perceptions of worlds and inhabitants, ჶ
The six classes of beings appeared as a dream. ჶ

Although this is so, you have never moved and will never
move ჶ
From the original condition of the essence. ჶ
Endeavor therefore in purifying the temporary stains. ჶ

The stages of the path that bring about realization are
innumerable. ჶ
Purify your being, sow the seeds, and cultivate them. ჶ
Remove the hindrances, and likewise bring forth
enhancement. ჶ
Thus enter the correct path through these five aspects. ჶ

First of all is to purify your mind and being. ჶ
The vajra master, the root of the path, ჶ
Is someone who has the pure conduct of samaya and vows. ჶ

He is fully adorned with learning, has discerned it through
    reflection, ⁝
And through meditation he possesses the qualities and signs of
    experience and realization. ⁝
With his compassionate action he accepts disciples. ⁝

Serve a master endowed with these characteristics by means of
    the three pleasing actions, ⁝
And do not commit the displeasing ones for even an instant. ⁝
Take the pledge to accomplish whatever he commands ⁝
By the skill of correctly training in his thoughts and deeds. ⁝

The master should give the teachings suited to the mind of the
    disciple ⁝
Who has faith, renunciation, and compassion, ⁝
And who has sharp faculties, intelligence, and discipline. ⁝
He should not give instructions that are inappropriate for the
    recipient. ⁝

For the way of guiding gradually in accordance with the types of
    mental capacity, ⁝
(1) First, keep far away from places of disturbance ⁝
By going to a place of solitude and giving up worldly activities. ⁝

Sit on a comfortable seat, straighten your body, and expel the
    stale breath. ⁝
Supplicate the Three Jewels and generate devotion to your
    guru. ⁝
Apply mindfulness and reflect in the following way. ⁝

This bodily support adorned with the perfect freedoms and
    riches, ⁝
Like the udumbara flower, is extremely hard to find. ⁝
If you skillfully take advantage of it, ⁝

Then this find has great value, exceeding that of a wish-fulfilling
   gem. ⁝
Therefore follow spiritual guides and virtuous friends ⁝
At all times and on all occasions. ⁝

Giving up concerns for this life, and for the sake of the future, ⁝
Exert yourself quickly to take advantage of it, for if you don't, [it
   will not last]. ⁝

Like the rising and setting of the sun and moon, composite things
   are impermanent. ⁝
The time of death lies uncertain, like a flash of lightning in the
   sky. ⁝
At the time of death nondharmic things are of no help at all, ⁝
So practice the sacred and sublime Dharma correctly. ⁝

The root of practicing the sacred Dharma is the law of karma. ⁝
Through evil deeds and nonvirtues you will go to the three
   lower realms. ⁝
By virtuous actions you achieve the higher realms and
   liberation. ⁝
Therefore confess evil deeds and make the wholehearted vow to
   refrain from them. ⁝

Diligently take up the roots of virtue. ⁝
Prostrations and circumambulations purify the wrongdoings of
   your body. ⁝
Reciting and reading the Buddha's words purify the obscurations
   of your speech, ⁝
And supplicating the Three Jewels pacifies the faults of your
   mind. ⁝
Always train correctly in being mindful, careful, and
   conscientious. ⁝

In particular, for accomplishing the state of emancipation, ҉
With the recognition and remembrance that all of samsara ҉
Is like a fiery pit, a garden of razors, or a forest of swords, ҉
Arouse again and again the intense and genuine attitude ҉
Of desiring to be quickly freed from the three sufferings. ҉

At some point, when you understand that all samsaric grandeur ҉
Is impermanent, inconstant, and illusive, ҉
Fascination with even the splendor of Brahma and Indra ҉
Will have no occasion to arise for as much as an instant. ҉

While truly perceiving the Three Precious Ones, the Roots, and
    the guardians of the Dharma ҉
To be the unfailing and permanent protection, ҉
Regard them respectfully as your refuge until enlightenment ҉
In order to free yourself and others from the terrors of samsara. ҉

Using your own experience as a measure, ҉
Arouse the bodhichitta of aspiration ҉
Through the four immeasurables of love, compassion, joy, and
    impartiality ҉
In order that your mothers, all beings, may have happiness and
    be free from suffering. ҉

With the intent of pursuing complete enlightenment solely for
    the sake of others, ҉
Give away, like grass, your body and possessions, ҉
And give the relief of protection to those disturbed by dangers. ҉
Practice the Dharma yourself and establish others in it. ҉

With the intention of renouncing, a thoroughly delighted frame
    of mind, ҉
Constrain yourself from committing the negative misdeeds of
    your three doors. ҉

Practice the conditioned and unconditioned virtues as much as
   you can, ⁝
And motivate yourself to carry out all your deeds for the sake of
   sentient beings. ⁝

In order never to be overcome by harmdoers, ⁝
Cultivate patience through mindfulness of the demerits of
   anger. ⁝
Joyfully undertake hardships for the sake of the Dharma, ⁝
And be unafraid of the profound emptiness. ⁝

By awakening a courageous fortitude for what is virtuous, ⁝
Don the armor of tirelessly engaging in bodhisattva deeds. ⁝
Exert yourself without distraction throughout day and night, ⁝
And cast away weariness when achieving the welfare of others. ⁝

With the thorough intention to calm your mind, ⁝
Take the mundane dhyanas as the foundation. ⁝
Through fully accomplishing samadhi with vipashyana, ⁝
Enter the domain of the experience of the tathagatas. ⁝

By means of the intelligence that fully discerns phenomena, ⁝
First comprehend the words of all teachings through learning. ⁝
Next seek an understanding of their meaning through
   reflection, ⁝
And finally realize the meaning through meditation. ⁝

Having ripened your own being, gather followers through
   generosity, ⁝
Delight them with pleasing words, and comfort them by being
   consistent. ⁝
Through counseling them in meaningful conduct, fully establish
   them, temporarily and ultimately, ⁝
In the splendor of benefit and well-being. ⁝

13

As the essential point, take upon yourself the burden ⁞
Of all the miseries of sentient beings. ⁞
Give away your happiness and virtue to the six classes of
    beings, ⁞
And train in compassion and bodhichitta without being carried
    away by difficulties. ⁞

In particular, external objects grasped by fixation ⁞
Are all unreal and appear like an illusion. ⁞
Not permanent, yet their transiency is able to function. ⁞
They are not singular, since a variety emerges and changes. ⁞
They are not independent, but follow the karmic deeds. ⁞
They are not particles, since partless atoms do not exist. ⁞

If they did exist, gross things could not be assembled. ⁞
If they had parts, this would contradict the assertion of
    partlessness. ⁞
They are nothing but a nonexistent and false appearance, an
    interdependence, ⁞
Like dreams, magical illusion, and the reflection of the moon in
    water. ⁞
Regard them as a city of gandharvas and as a rainbow. ⁞

The mind that observes is also devoid of an ego or a self-entity. ⁞
It is neither seen as something different from the aggregates ⁞
Nor as identical with these five aggregates. ⁞
If the first were true, there would exist some other substance. ⁞

This is not the case, so were the second to be true, ⁞
That would contradict a permanent self, since the aggregates are
    impermanent. ⁞
Therefore, based on the five aggregates, ⁞
The self is a mere imputation by the power of ego-clinging. ⁞

As to that which imputes, the past thought has vanished and is
    nonexistent. ⁑
The future thought has not occurred, and the present thought
    does not withstand scrutiny. ⁑

In short, understand the twofold self, the perceiver and the
    perceived, ⁑
To be totally quiescent, like the sky, and devoid of arising, ⁑
And also that this nonarising is beyond the domain of conceptual
    mind. ⁑
Since even the Omniscient Ones find no words for this, ⁑
This absence of mental constructs is called the Middle Way. ⁑

Having realized this, rest in equanimity, ⁑
Free from conceptual activity, in the state devoid of fixation. ⁑

Thoughts then subside, and the natural state of the essence is
    seen. ⁑
Hereby you accomplish the virtues such as the eyes,
    superknowledges, and dharani-recall. ⁑

The causal vehicle of the paramitas ⁑
Is to gradually attain the paths and bhumis. ⁑
On the path of fruition, you should still regard ⁑
The practice of unified emptiness and compassion as the basis of
    the path. ⁑

THE COMMENTARY

ༀ༎ བླ་མའི་ཐུགས་སྒྲུབ་རྡོ་རྗེ་དྲག་རྩལ་ལས། ཞལ་གདམས་ལམ་རིམ་ཡེ་ཤེས་སྙིང་པོའི་འགྲེལ་པ་ ཡེ་ཤེས་སྣང་བ་རབ་ཏུ་རྒྱས་པ་ཞེས་བྱ་བ་བཞུགས་སོ༎

The Light of Wisdom

by JAMGÖN KONGTRÜL

A Commentary on the Wisdom Essence
of Oral Instructions in the Stages of the Path,
according to Lamey Tukdrub Dorje Draktsal,
The Guru's Heart Practice of Powerful Vajra Wrath,
entitled *Fully Spreading the Light of Wisdom*

Section One

PROLOGUE AND TEACHINGS
ON THE TITLE, THE SIGN SCRIPT,
AND THE HOMAGE

– 1 –

Homage and Prologue

At the feet of the glorious Mahasukha Padmasambhava, the essence of all the buddhas of the three times, I bow down and take refuge with deep respect of body, speech, and mind. With your great compassion, please accept me and grant your blessings at all times and in all situations.

You are the source of inconceivable life examples, unfathomable
    like the nature of space.
The immortal vajra play of your great bliss benefits others as far
    as space pervades.
Guru and consort together with devas, dakinis, and Dharma
    protectors, your kindness is incomparable.
By recognizing the view of same taste, I salute your single
    wisdom that manifests in manifold ways.

As the drama of the magical net endowed with spontaneously
    completed qualities of fruition,
The perfection of enlightened conduct,
You spread the great light endowed with the seven transmissions
    for the teachings and beings.[28]
Padma Ösel Do-ngak Lingpa, to you I bow down.[29]

Charioteer of activity of the Victorious One of Uddiyana
   [Orgyen],
You are supreme [Chokgyur] among all treasure revealers.
Sporting in the delight of changeless great bliss [Dechen],
May you, endowed with the name Sanctuary [Lingpa], accept
   me constantly throughout the three times.[30]

For the sake of embodying all the Buddha's teachings
Solely into the practice of the stages of the path,
Garlands of volumes of scriptures of Sarma and Nyingma,
   extensive and subtle, common and special,
Have filled the entire Land of Snow.[31]

In harmony with all these, yet most excellent among them,
I shall here open up, as the wealth that delights all worthy ones,
An unprecedented jewel treasury, which completely and clearly
   shows the path of the summit of vehicles
And makes you realize the primordial view within a single
   lifetime.

I will now explain the root text *Wisdom Essence,* the excellent
speech of the sacred Dharma that is the supreme and most eminent
among all topics of knowledge endowed with the goodness of beginning, middle, and end. It belongs to the profound Vajra Vehicles that
take the fruition as path and are more exalted, by means of four
special qualities, than the extensive Philosophical Vehicles that take
the cause as path. Among the outer and inner Vajrayana, *The Wisdom
Essence* unifies the profound meaning of the three sections of the
Inner Yoga Tantras.[32]

Within the Land of Snow, the activity of the buddhas was first
carried out by the khenpo, the master, and the Dharma king.[33] Having gathered one hundred incarnated translators and panditas, the
teachings translated in this early propagation are renowned as Nyingma, the Old School. The Nyingma School possesses the three great

transmissions of the extensive Kama, the profound Terma, and the short lineage of Pure Vision. Of these, the root text *Wisdom Essence,* graced with the splendor of blessings and vajra words, is a profound teaching endowed with the three special qualities of a terma revelation: not constructed by intellectual reasoning, not corrupted by ordinary words, and not repeating what is said by others.[34]

What is the meaning explained in *The Wisdom Essence?* Generally, there are three kinds of teaching:[35] the tantras that manifest as the natural sound of dharmata from the Lord of the Circle and are like a treasury of jewels contained within the chest of the six limits and four modes;[36] the statements by the lords of the ten bhumis that clarify the meaning of the tantras, fully disclosing their secret significance, and are like the key to the treasury;[37] and, finally, the instructions in the key points of the tantras by the accomplished vidyadharas that condense them to be applicable for worthy people and are like one's heritage placed in the palm of one's hand.[38] Of these three, *The Wisdom Essence* is an instruction text, a teaching in the key points. It teaches, clearly and without concealment, the nature of the ground, path, and fruition, as well as the entire practice of the general and special stages of the path.

How will this text be explained? There exist numerous systems of the learned and accomplished great beings who have upheld the tantric and instructional traditions of Sarma and Nyingma. Among them, I have taken as the basis the character of the root text, which was taught for the unelaborate type of person, with the intent to condense spiritual practice to the essentials. Not following the textual traditions of intellectuals, with expositional phrases, elaborate quotations and reasoning, or critical evaluations of contradictions and proofs, I will phrase the explanation plainly so as not to waste the excellent fortune of having personally obtained the nectar of oral teachings of the supreme vidyadhara, the lord guru. By clarifying the meaning of the text word for word, I will explain the secret and profound significance of this most eminent text to the extent and ability of my faithful and devoted intellect.[39]

This oral instruction in the stages of the path is the heart essence of Padmasambhava, the knower of the three times. It is the "background teaching" of the Four Profound Cycles of Guru Sadhana that lucidly shows, in their entirety, the complete stages of the view, meditation, and action of the Three Yogas, and is equal to receiving teachings directly from the great master of Uddiyana, who is the Second Buddha.[40] I will now explain it under the following four headings:[41]

1. Teaching on the title in order to easily understand the main text.
2. Restating the sign script that is an authentic source and paying homage to the special object.
3. Explaining the actual text endowed with this title and meaning.
4. Concluding with words that establish the main text.

— 2 —

Teaching on the Title

TEACHING ON THE TITLE IN ORDER TO EASILY UNDERSTAND THE MAIN TEXT

This has three points: stating the actual title, explaining the meaning, and defining the scope of the scripture from the title.

STATING THE ACTUAL TITLE

The *Lamrim Yeshe Nyingpo* root text says:

> *The Heart Essence of Padmasambhava According to The Guru's Heart Practice of Dorje Drakpo Tsal, Powerful Vajra Wrath. The Wisdom Essence of Oral Instruction in the Stages of the Path.*

EXPLAINING THE MEANING

This has two parts: the general explanation of the literal meaning and the detailed explanation of the special meaning of the title.

GENERAL EXPLANATION OF THE LITERAL MEANING

In general, it is well known that the tantras are the basis of the oral instructions, the oral instructions are the basis of the sadhanas, and the sadhanas are the basis of the applications. Within these categories, countless sadhanas of the Three Roots have been taught, each of which again has many sadhana versions that are general or specific, root or branch, and intended to be temporary or ultimate.[42] Among them, *The Wisdom Essence* is the quintessential extract of the most pithy teachings of all the instruction tantras that explain the foundation of the *Magical Net of the Vidyadharas,* the *Root Tantra of the Assemblage of Vidyadharas,* and other scriptures.[43] It is a means of accomplishing chiefly the guru, the root of blessings, and epitomizes the realization of the victorious ones throughout all directions and times. It is the core of practice for all vidyadharas in the three times, the vital core of the wisdom sphere extracted from the expanse of Guru Rinpoche's mind, and a crucial means of accomplishing the most profound essence. Thus it is called the *Guru's Heart Practice.* The *Sheldam Nyingjang* says:

> This most profound Heart Practice
> Spontaneously manifested from the expanse of realization of
>   myself,
> The Self-Born Padma.[44]

And,

> I, Uddiyana, did not expound this
> As a commentary based upon
> Other tantras, statements, and instructions,
> But as the true meaning of the tantras, statements, and
>   instructions,
> The essential extract of the essence.

> Fully present as the essence of my heart,
> When it manifests as the natural sound of dharmata,
> It is especially exalted by not being in conflict with the tantras,

By being in accordance with the statements,
And by possessing the experience of the instructions.[45]

Of the Four Profound Cycles of Heart Practice, this teaching was revealed within the *Teaching Cycle of Dorje Drakpo Tsal, Powerful Vajra Wrath,* the means of accomplishing the guru according to the innermost way. He taught orally in the manner of instructions and advice, considering all worthy followers with loving kindness. Lucid and appropriately detailed, it possesses the complete stages of the path for accomplishing the unified state within one lifetime. It is entitled *Yeshe Nyingpo, The Wisdom Essence.*[46]

DETAILED EXPLANATION OF THE SPECIAL MEANING OF THE TITLE

This has two points: explaining in terms of the four modes[47] and explaining in terms of the meaning of ground, path, and fruition.

Explaining in Terms of the Four Modes

Basing the explanation on the particular title, *Wisdom Essence,* separate from the general title, I will now explain it according to the literal meaning.

In the general sense, considering the broad scope of the word "wisdom," *yeshe* or *jnana,* the root meaning of *jna,* which means "understanding," is applicable to both the objects known and to the subject, the consciousness.[48] The *Accomplishment of Means and Knowledge* explains:

Consciousness fully discerns the known object.
Having fully discriminated through joining,
All phenomena are devoid of a self-nature.
That itself is called wisdom.[49]

Here, the wisdom of the buddhas is described as knowledge that has fully discarded defilement. All the qualities of perfection result exclusively from the play of the wisdom of the victorious ones.[50] As the regent Maitreya revealed:

> From the buddhas comes the Dharma, from the Dharma appears the noble assembly.[51]

The word "wisdom" therefore describes the identity of what is characterized. The word "essence," *nyingpo* or *garbha,* means "the nakedly extracted essence devoid of covers." It refers to the extracted essence of the profound meaning of the teachings of Sutra and Mantra, free from the covers of words and constructs. The word "essence" therefore describes how the special characteristic is. Thus, *Wisdom Essence, Yeshe Nyingpo,* means "the essence of all the sacred teachings of the most perfect wisdom."[52]

When explaining the general meaning according to the sutras and the common teachings, "wisdom" means knowledge (*prajna*) that is primordially free from defilement, the basic state of emptiness. The word "essence" or *hridaya* means "extract" or "supreme," and is therefore compassion, the supreme path that is indispensable for accomplishing buddhahood. The *Five Hundred Thousand Scripture* says:[53]

> From the wish-fulfilling tree of emptiness
> Appear the fruits of nonconceptual compassion.
> This is the root of all the awakened ones.
> From this they emerge, there is no doubt.[54]

Therefore, *Wisdom Essence* means the "supreme path of emptiness endowed with a core of compassion."

Next, related to the general meaning of Mantrayana, "wisdom" is the support, the mandala, while "essence" is the supported, the circle of deities. This is explained in the *Two Segments:*

> The center describes the essence.
> This bodhichitta is the great bliss.

Taking hold of it is the mandala.
Their merging expresses this mandala itself.[55]

The meaning of that describes the path of the development stage as well as its associated points.

According to the hidden meaning, "wisdom" is the support, the syllable E of primordial great emptiness. "Essence" is the supported, the VAM syllable of great bliss. The *Exposition Tantra of Guhyasamaja* states:

Since omniscience abides
In the magical display of the two letters E and VAM,
E and VAM are fully explained
At the beginning of teaching the sacred Dharma.[56]

The *Vajra Garland* adds:

E is emptiness, it is taught.
Likewise, VAM is compassion.
The bindu results from their union.
This union is the supreme marvel
Embracing the 84,000 Dharma teachings.
In short, it is the seal of the Dharma.[57]

As thus stated here and in countless other places, the two syllables E and VAM provide the setting for teaching all the sutras and tantras, and therefore the profound and vast meaning can be elaborated from them.[58]

According to the hidden conventional truth of the system of Phak-shab, E and VAM mean the body of unity that manifests from luminous wisdom as its essence after the stages of illusory body have been perfected.[59]

According to the concealed teachings on passion, when following what has been taught in the *Ocean of Magical Display* and elsewhere, the nadi-wheels are the syllable E and the bindus are the syllable VAM, and thus they apply to the liberation of the upper gate. Moreover, the lotus of the consort is E and the lord's vajra is VAM, and thus they apply to the secret lower gate. The meaning of these points will be explained in this text.[60]

According to the ultimate meaning, "wisdom" is the original space of primordial purity, and "essence" is spontaneous presence, the "vajra chain of awareness." Thus they mean the indivisible unity of space and awareness, the ultimate realization of the Original Protector. Also these points will be understood from the following sequence of teachings.[61]

Explaining in Terms of Ground, Path, and Fruition

Ground. First, applied to the ground in the general way, "wisdom" means the basic dharmakaya, the ultimate nature of undivided space and wisdom that encompasses all phenomena and is present like the all-pervading sky.[62] The noble Nagarjuna said:

> As water within the earth remains free from defilement,
> The wisdom within emotions likewise dwells undefiled.

The *Sambhuti* states:

> Utterly free from all concepts,
> The great wisdom dwells in the body.
> It encompasses all things.[63]

As for the meaning of "essence," the *Tantra That Prophesies Realization* says:

> "Essence" is this pure nature of the buddhas,
> The experienced meaning of Mantra,
> The enlightenment of all experience;
> It is most eminent experience.[64]

Thus *Wisdom Essence* means that the ultimate wisdom is present as the essential quality in all of samsara and nirvana. The victorious Maitreya has said:

The suchness is in everything, pure without any distinction.
All beings therefore have the essence of the tathagata.

The *Radiant Lamp* explains:[65]

The abode of the victorious ones is all sentient beings
Because they are of the essence of the tathagatas.

In this way, the "essence of wisdom" indicates the basis for purifying defilements, the natural state of the sugata essence.[66]

According to the uncommon Mahayoga, *Wisdom Essence* means the superior dharmakaya of the indivisible two truths. According to Anu Yoga, it means the bodhichitta mandala of great bliss, the nondual space and wisdom that is primordially present as our natural possession.[67]

According to the system of the Great Perfection, [*Wisdom Essence* is described in the following way]. The primordial purity of the original ground that is inexpressible and inconceivable, indescribable and beyond the confines of mental constructs, is the universal ground of both confusion and liberation endowed with a threefold wisdom. Even when the seal of space broke open and samsara and nirvana separated with the unfolding of the manifestation of outward brilliance, this universal ground is still present as a temporary ground in all sentient beings as their essence.[68] The *Six Spheres* describes:

Devoid of constructs, the primordially pure nature
Is the pure natural face, the essential ground.[69]

This quote indicates the original ground of primordial purity. These points of the basic nature will also be taught within this text.

Path. When applying the meaning of *Wisdom Essence* to the path, "wisdom" means knowledge, *prajna.* "Essence," as the word *sara,* means the "root" or "source" from which manifold things unfold.[70] Thus it is the means, *upaya,* of the accumulation of merit from which originate the manifold excellent results, both temporary and ultimate. According to the ordinary paths, these two, means and knowledge, are merit and wisdom. According to the extraordinary paths, they are the development stage and completion stage; and in the case of the special paths, they are bliss and emptiness, space and awareness, and so forth. Thus they can be combined with the meaning of all the dual aspects of the path. The accomplishment of buddhahood requires that means and knowledge be united without one-sidedness. The *Lamp for the Path of Enlightenment,* which is a summary of the meaning of the sutras, makes this clear:

> Knowledge devoid of means as well as means devoid of
> knowledge
> Is in all cases taught to be a fetter; therefore, do not abandon
> either of the two.[71]

Since the details of the stages of the path of unity are taught here in *The Wisdom Essence,* the root text says,

> *This path of the wisdom essence, the epitome of all . . .*

Fruition. When combining the meaning of *Wisdom Essence* with the fruition, the general way is as the *Ornament of the Sutras* explains:

> The classification of the kayas of all the buddhas
> Is the natural, the perfect enjoyment,
> And the body of emanation.
> The first is the basis for the other two.[72]

In this way, "the pervaded" is the rupakaya appearing symbolically for the welfare of others from the manifestation of wisdom. "That which pervades" is the dharmakaya for the welfare of oneself, the nature of the absolute essence. Thus *Wisdom Essence* means the two kayas to be attained.[73]

The nature of realizing the wisdom endowed with the twofold purity is the qualities of freedom. The manifested power of the essence through the developed potential is the qualities of maturation. Thus *Wisdom Essence* means the two qualities of freedom and maturation.[74]

"Wisdom" means all-pervasive, and "essence" means inexhaustible and unchanging and therefore everlasting. Thus *Wisdom Essence* also indicates the everlasting and all-pervasive activities.[75]

In the extraordinary sense, "wisdom" means space, and "essence" means awareness. Thus *Wisdom Essence* means to attain enlightenment as the indivisible unity of space and awareness. Alternately, the phrase "endowed with the essence of wisdom" indicates the unity of the kayas and wisdoms. In other words, the realization that awareness since the beginning, like the sun, is spontaneously present as radiant cognizance, clears away the clouds of temporary obscurations and causes immaculate knowledge to unfold as a mandala of all qualities. Since this is the essence of all the kayas, the kayas and wisdoms are an indivisible unity.[76] The *Tantra of Self-Arising Awareness* states:

> Without different natures or change,
> The wisdoms of the five kayas
> In actuality abide in the way in which
> The kayas and wisdoms are an indivisible unity.[77]

Thus *Wisdom Essence* directly identifies the kayas as the support with the wisdoms as the supported, while the activity of deeds is indirectly demonstrated. Hence the root text says:[78]

May the wisdom essence be accomplished within this lifetime.

DEFINING THE SCOPE OF THE SCRIPTURE FROM THE TITLE

As for "oral instruction," there are many kinds: urging beginners to the Dharma, giving extensive instructions with words, giving profound instruction in the meaning, instructing in practice condensed to key points, and giving the pointing-out instruction in the manner of placing something directly in the palm of one's hand.[79] Of these, *The Wisdom Essence* is an instruction in the profound and extensive practices that is condensed to the key points and placed directly in the palm of our hand. The root text describes this in the following way:[80]

> *This most eminent essence*
> *Of all the hundred million scriptures of profound and extensive*
>   *instructions,*
> *Which you have taught in the past,*
> *Is the complete and sublime path of the causal and the resultant,*
> *A quintessence that has rarely appeared and will rarely reappear.*[81]

This quote shows how *The Wisdom Essence* is praised again and again.

Concerning the "stages of the path," *lamrim*, there exist many general versions for the Sutra tradition, such as the *Stages of the Path of Enlightenment* according to the tradition of the glorious Atisha and also Rongzom Pandita's and Aro's *Yogas of the Greater Vehicle*. As well, there are also the special types of lamrim belonging to Kama and Terma, such as *Padmey Lamrim, Rinchen Drönmey,* and others. Among these kinds, the text here entitled *Lamrim Yeshe Nyingpo, The Wisdom Essence of* [*Oral Instructions in the*] *Stages of the Path,* is superior by numerous special qualities.[82]

Who bestowed the title? It was not given as an intellectual construct of an ordinary person, but rather manifested as the self-existing and spontaneous vajra sound from the secret treasury of great wisdom, the expanse of the realization of ever-excellent Padmakara. Thus it is indivisible from the vajra words of the tantras, such as *Guhyagarbha* and *Hevajra.*[83]

34

Titles given through intellectual constructs of ordinary persons can be given in terms of analogy, meaning, place, or circumstance.[84] Yet, as Dignaga stated:

> Prajnaparamita is wisdom devoid of duality.
> The name demonstrates the scripture as well as the path
> Because it contains the ultimate
> Of what the tathagatas accomplish.[85]

In this way, *The Wisdom Essence* appeared as the spontaneous sound of wisdom that interlinks the scripture and the path.

The purpose of the title is the following. For people of the highest capacity the meaning of the scripture is contained in its title so they will easily understand the entire meaning from top to bottom simply from the title. Those of the medium capacity will understand the general meaning of what the scripture contains, and those of the lowest capacity will be inspired to quickly understand a scripture with such a title and meaning.

— 3 —

Explaining the Sign Script and Homage

This has two parts: the reason for the sign script and the meaning of homage.

ༀ་མ་ནི་མ་ཧྤྲུ་མ་ཤྲི༔

The *Tantra of Secrets* states:

> Dakinis make use of symbols.
> They are skilled in symbols and symbolic replies.
> They link the ultimate essence to symbolism.
> Dakinis are the life-force of symbols.[86]

The dakini script that makes use of symbols is impossible to decipher by anyone other than a person who is of equal status to the dakinis. Since most of the profound teachings existing as terma treasures are encoded in symbolic script and therefore originate from the secret treasury of the dakinis, they do not lie within the reach of experience of the ordinary learned or accomplished masters of India and Tibet. A scripture says:

36

Treasure letters are the body of magical creation.
They are also speech to understand sounds and words.[87]

A person endowed with the karmic continuation and destiny will,
by means of a profound coincidence of place, time, and aspiration,
be able to decode the symbolic meaning of these treasure letters that
are nirmanakayas, the vajra forms endowed with all eminent aspects,
and establish them correctly in writing. To indicate this, seven symbolic letters have been placed at the beginning of this book.[88]

There are three reasons for this: (1) The seal of command of the
Second Buddha, the Master of Uddiyana, is directly represented by
symbolic signs, indicating that the transmission is not interrupted by
ordinary people and that the source is authentic. (2) It is a translation
of the secret code of the dakinis without altering the symbols, mistaking the words, or confusing the meaning, indicating that the scripture
is profound and has great blessing. (3) Like someone born blind trying to examine an elephant, people lacking the right fortune cannot
even partially comprehend the symbolic script no matter how sharp-
minded they may be. You can therefore trust that the treasure master
transcends the scope of commoners.[89]

THE MEANING OF HOMAGE

The *Lamrim Yeshe Nyingpo* root text says:

Homage to Dorje Drakpo Tsal, Powerful Vajra Wrath,
embodiment of the Three Roots.

Who is paying this homage? It is the wisdom dakini Yeshe Tsogyal, compiler of the teachings of the Great Secret. To whom is the
homage being paid? It is made to Master Padmakara, the lord who
embodies the gurus who are the root of blessings, the yidams who
are the root of accomplishments, and the dakinis who are the root of

activity. He is the emanator of mandalas and the expounder of teachings who, out of compassion, manifests in the wrathful form renowned under the secret name Dorje Drakpo Tsal, Powerful Vajra Wrath.[90]

What is the purpose of paying homage? Generally, for everyone who enters the path of Vajrayana, accomplishment depends upon the guru. Therefore, it is vital to remember him in all activities and practices. Temporarily, homage is made in order to avoid obstacles and to receive the blessings for composing the text. Indirectly, homage is made to instruct later followers who will teach, study, meditate upon, or practice this scripture.[91]

How is homage being paid? According to the expedient meaning, homage is made by the symbolic homage of showing deep respect in thought, word, and deed. According to the definitive meaning it is made by recognizing the ultimate view, the state of realization in which means and knowledge are of same taste.[92]

As for "Three Roots," just as the root is the cause or basis for trees and flowers to grow, the guru and so forth are the causes or roots for blessings and so on to occur.[93] Numerous treasure root texts mention:

> *Guru* The lord guru is the root of blessings.
> *Deva* The yidam deity is the source of accomplishments.
> *Dakini* Bless me fully, dakinis.

The Three Roots are therefore the especially excellent Precious Ones of Vajrayana. The guru's body is the Sangha, his speech is the sacred Dharma, and his mind is the Buddha. Peaceful, passionate, or wrathful—whatever forms the yidams manifest—their natures are sambhogakaya and nirmanakaya buddhas, and their tantras of Mantrayana are the extraordinary Dharma. The dakinis and Dharma protectors are the special sangha. Since the yidams and dakinis both appear from the guru's wisdom display, he is dignified with the title Lord of the Circle.[94] The *Body Tantra of the Assemblage of Realization* states:[95]

38

The essence is the guru, dharmakaya.
The nature is the yidam, sambhogakaya.
The capacity is the dakini, nirmanakaya.[96]

A qualified guru is therefore an embodiment of the Three Precious Ones and the Three Roots.[97] The *Vajra Mirror Tantra* declares:

As Vajrasattva, the chief figure of the mandala,
The guru is equal to all the buddhas.[98]

As shown by this and other quotes, this nature of the guru is universally recognized. In particular, Guru Rinpoche is the natural form of indestructible wakefulness, the embodiment of all buddhas. In his vajra words:

Meditate upon me and you will accomplish all buddhas.
See me and you will behold all buddhas.
I am the embodiment of all the sugatas.

There are innumerable other such statements.
As for the meaning of his name, *Vajra* is described in the *Samayoga Tantra*:[99]

Vajra means emptiness, it is taught.

And the *Mirror of Magical Display* states:

I proclaim that *vajra*
Is the undifferentiated nature itself.[100]

Thus *vajra* is the nature of emptiness, which cannot be divided into separate entities for each of all the phenomena of samsara and nirvana. Since this nature is inseparable from the dharmakaya of all the buddhas, the word *vajra* in this context describes the dharmakaya essence. This word is used because it resembles the qualities of the material vajra.[101] The *Peak Scripture* says:

> Solid, substantial, and without hollowness,
> Uncuttable and indestructible,
> Impossible to burn and imperishable,
> It is described as the vajra of emptiness.[102]

Great compassion manifests out of the state of dharmakaya in a fierce and wrathful form in order to tame the incorrigible beings who cannot be swayed by peaceful means. As the *Assemblage of Realization* states:[103]

> Gentleness does not benefit
> Extremely incorrigible and savage beings.
> Thus through the union of means and knowledge
> The tathagatas appear in wrathful forms.[104]

The word "powerful" means the power of might, strength, and capability and therefore means possessing the powerful force of might, strength, and capability that is completely superior to that of others.

When combining the words into one, just as the hundred-spoked vajra in the hand of Indra, the king of the gods, has the great power and force to destroy the armies of demigods with a single blow, his name Dorje Drakpo Tsal, Powerful Vajra Wrath, represents the totally unassailable Great King of the Wrathful Ones, who is the single embodiment of the power and strength of all wisdom, action, and mundane types of wrathful beings.[105]

Section Two

THE EXPLANATION OF THE
ACTUAL BODY OF THE TEXT

— 4 —

The Setting

The explanation of the actual body of the text has five points: (1) the setting for the talk: the causes for the teaching to take place, (2) the circumstances for beginning the teaching, (3) the result: the topics of instruction that are to be fully understood, (4) the reason for and the linkage of the instruction, and (5) giving directions to the retinue and entrusting the teaching.[106]

THE SETTING FOR THE TALK: THE CAUSES FOR THE TEACHING TO TAKE PLACE

This has five parts: teacher, retinue, place, teaching, and time.

THE TEACHER

The *Lamrim Yeshe Nyingpo* root text says:

> *The essence of all the buddhas of the three times, the supreme sovereign of all power-wielding vidyadharas, the all-encompassing lord of the ocean of peaceful and wrathful yidams, the chief of the gatherings of all the dakas and dakinis, the great being who by his splendor outshines all the vajra protectors of the Dharma and the haughty*

43

*forces of appearance and existence, is the one renowned throughout
the infinite realms of the teachers of the three kayas as Mahaguru
Padmasambhava.*

Padmakara, the King of Victorious Ones, is not an ordinary person
who entered the path, but is Buddha Amitabha and the Matchless
King of the Shakyas manifest in the form of a vajra master for the
sake of beings who are difficult to tame. In terms of the threefold
equality, he is equal to all the buddhas of the three times who have
appeared in the past, remain in the present, and will appear in the
future, and is therefore established as completely inseparable from
the essence of all the buddhas, just as space itself is devoid of any
divisions.[107]

Nevertheless, when he appeared as a nirmanakaya in the perception of other beings, he attained the vidyadhara level of Immortal
Life, perfected the Mahamudra vidyadhara level on the path of cultivation, and acted as someone dwelling in the position of being the
Sixth Buddha Regent, the vidyadhara level of Spontaneous Presence
on the path of consummation. Therefore, even the eight great vidyadhara receivers of the transmissions bowed at his feet. Thus he
remains in the position of the supreme sovereign of all masters who
have attained the vidyadhara levels and wield the great power of
wisdom.[108]

The aggregates, elements, and sense-bases, as well as the actions,
faculties, and objects, are by nature completely pure and self-manifest
as the display of dharmadhatu, the deity circle of the great Spontaneous Presence.[109] Therefore, he is the all-encompassing lord who emanates and absorbs the infinity of that which is manifest as the centers
and surroundings (mandala) of the great vajra space of the peaceful
ones and the complete assemblage of the great gatherings of wrathful
yidams.[110]

He has mastered all the inner places comprised of the structuring
channels, moving winds, and essences of bodhichitta purified within
the sphere of the great wisdom of luminosity. By the power of that,

he is the great chief who turns the wheel of gathering (ganachakra) in the outer sacred places and countries, together with all the dakas who engage in yogic discipline and the yoginis who miraculously move through the skies (dakinis). Since his expression manifests as the great display of kayas and wisdoms, he is the great being whose majestic splendor, the awesome bodily form of the Great Blazing Heruka, has the power to outshine all the Dharma protectors and guardians upholding the vajra samaya and functioning as the wisdom, action, or mundane [wrathful beings] comprised of the three classes. Likewise, he outshines all the haughty forces who are filled with the arrogance of being the great elemental spirits of appearance and existence, such as Palgön and the guardians of the directions. Merely by hearing his name, no one dares transgress his command, just as the king of beasts subjugates other animals.[111]

His one name pervades the realms of the ten directions and, within a single realm, he manifests under countless different names.[112] Mentioning just this buddha realm, the *Magical Net of Manjushri* says:[113]

> Glorious buddha lotus-born,
> Bearer of the treasure of omniscient wisdom,
> King and master of various miracles,
> Great buddha, retainer of knowledge mantras.

The first line clearly indicates the one whose name is Padmakara or Padmasambhava, who was born from a lotus flower in the perception of others, and who is inseparable from the glorious Original Protector Vajradhara, Buddha Amitabha, and the King of the Shakyas. The second line indicates Loden Choksey, the bearer of the treasure of the wisdom of knowing all phenomena. The third line indicates Padma Gyalpo and Nyima Öser, who is the master of various displays of miracles. The fourth indicates Senge Dradrok, who is endowed with the greatest power in the three levels of existence; Shakya Senge, who appeared in the manner of a second buddha, and Dorje Drolö, blazing in the special splendor of the power and force of knowledge mantras. In accordance with this clear prediction, he manifested as the regent of our Teacher [Buddha Shakyamuni] in the form of a great master who embodies all buddha families, the all-encompassing lord of the ocean of mandalas.[114]

Since he appeared chiefly in the lotus family of supreme speech and demonstrated a miraculous birth from a lotus flower, he is universally renowned throughout the infinite oceans of the realms of the teachers of the three kayas under the name Mahaguru Padmasambhava, meaning Lotus Source or Lotus-Born.[115]

In the dharmakaya realm of the Luminous Vajra Essence he is known as the original protector Changeless Light, self-awareness truly enlightened in the primordially pure ground of liberation.[116]

In the self-manifest sambhogakaya realm of Thunder of the Drum of Brahma, he appeared as the five wisdom families of Immense Ocean with the all-encompassing displays of the five certainties.[117]

From sambhogakaya, in the outwardly manifest and semi-apparent, natural nirmanakaya realms of Great Purity, he appears for all the lords of the ten bhumis through the boundless manifestations of the realms and bodily forms of the five buddha families. Since all these manifestations are nonetheless never anything other than the display of Guru Rinpoche's wisdom, he is called All-Holding Lotus.[118]

Therefrom, he appears in all the immeasurable realms of the ten directions as the magical displays of the nirmanakayas who tame beings.[119]

In particular, it is taught that simply within this Saha realm he illuminates fifty world-systems as one hundred teachers of Sutra and Mantra with definite names and that he emanates eight manifestations to tame beings into the worlds that are situated in the cardinal and intermediate directions of each of these world-systems.[120]

According to Yeshe Tsogyal's vision of his specific manifestations, she said that in the eastern direction, in each pore of Vajra Guru Immense Ocean, are one billion realms. In each realm are one billion world-systems. In each of these there are one billion gurus, each with one billion emanations, who each have one billion disciples. Similarly, in the center and the other directions are immeasurable manifestations of the four other families.[121]

Here on the Jambu Continent alone, in terms of merely one fraction of the nirmanakaya that tames beings, he was seen to appear in different ways corresponding to the different types of fortune and faculties of those to be tamed. The biography among the New Treasures entitled *Wish-Fulfilling Tree* states:[122]

> As perceived by some people, I appeared in the land of
> Uddiyana
> In Dhanakosha from the top of a lotus flower.
> As perceived by some, I was the son of Uddiyana's king.
> As perceived by some, I appeared as a lightning bolt
> On the Peak of Meteoric Iron—thus there were different
> versions.[123]

The majority of terma treasures mention only the life story of miraculous birth, but most Indian sources, such as the *Oral History of Kilaya,* say that he was born as the son of the king or a minister of Uddiyana. As can be understood from the above quotation, another story tells of his appearing as a lightning bolt on the Peak of Malaya, which is made of meteoric iron. Each style includes numerous, different, wonderful life-stories as described in these words:[124]

> For the sake of future people with pure samaya
> I wrote and concealed ten thousand nine hundred biographies.

As thus shown, this lies completely beyond the reach of an ordinary person's intellect. Padmasambhava's great qualities actually described here represent merely a fraction of what the intelligence of an immature being may understand, demonstrating the exaltedness of this master, who is the lord of the teachings.[125]

THE RETINUE

THE RETINUE

The *Lamrim Yeshe Nyingpo* root text says:

Invited by Manjushri's incarnation, the Dharma-upholding King Trisong Deutsen, . . .

The chief cause for this great master and emanation body of the buddhas to personally visit the land of Tibet was the Tibetan king prophesied by the Victorious One in the *Root Tantra of Manjushri*.[126]

In the successive occurrence of kings, it is universally known that Tori Nyenshel, an emanation of bodhisattva Samantabhadra, instigated the sacred Dharma. Songtsen Gampo, Avalokiteshvara in person, established its tradition. Finally, the great Dharma ruler, King Trisong Deutsen, the emanation body of noble Manjushri, made it spread and flourish. In order that the sacred Dharma flourish, this latter Dharma king invited from the Noble Land of India one hundred and eight great panditas such as the great scholar Shantarakshita, Vimalamitra, who possessed the vajra body, and in particular Padmakara, the great vidyadhara of immortality. He let the subjects with devotion be ordained and learn translation. He erected temples, established the Sangha, and founded the tradition for translating, expounding, and practicing the sacred Dharma. Thus his deeds in initially spreading the Buddha's teachings will never disappear, not even at the end of existence, and the signature and fame of this demonstrate the exaltedness of the patron of the teachings.[127]

THE PLACE

The *Lamrim Yeshe Nyingpo* root text says:

. . . he came to this snowy land of Tibet, the realm of the noble Great Compassionate One.[128]

As entrusted to him by the matchless King of the Shakyas, the noble Great Compassionate One accepted this snowy land of Tibet as his sphere of influence.[129] He also blessed the place, the outer vessel of material things, to be inseparable from Mount Potala, endowed with the four liberations, and manifested countless self-appeared proofs of that.[130] He planted the first seed of its inhabitants of human beings and emanated an uninterrupted stream of various displays of incarnations, such as kings; ministers; householders; and learned, accomplished, and realized spiritual teachers to influence whomever needed them. Thus, he bestowed his blessings so that even children barely able to talk could effortlessly utter the sounds of the Six Syllables. Manifesting out of this noble one's compassion, Guru Rinpoche also appeared as the single protector of the beings of Tibet.[131]

According to the Victorious One's prophecy that the teachings would spread further and further north, the precious Dharma of Statement and Realization later on moved from the Noble Land to this country of Tibet where, until the present time, it has remained without waning. Filled with innumerable special representations of body, speech, and mind, such as the Twin Buddhas, this land is in many ways most wondrous, for example, being covered with temples and congregations of the Sangha. This demonstrates the exaltedness of the land where the Buddhadharma is present.[132]

THE TEACHING

The *Lamrim Yeshe Nyingpo* root text says:

> *He placed all the vicious elemental forces under the majestic seal of his command, erected the triple-styled Unchanging and Spontaneously Perfected Temple, a palace with shrines, and strewed the flowers of consecration. He established the great tradition of expounding and practicing the entire doctrine of the Buddha and, in particular, he turned an infinite variety of the Dharma Wheels of the tantras, statements, and instructions of Vajrayana.*
>
> *He visited personally all the sacred places, the snow mountains, caves, and lakes, blessed them, and concealed innumerable named*

*and unnamed treasures. Thus his immeasurable kindness permeates
all of Tibet, both the central and surrounding lands, and will remain
right up to the last day of the final future age.* SAMAYA.

It is inconceivable how the buddhas act through mastering the
magical display of the fourfold conversion by means of the never-
ending adornment wheels of body, speech, mind, qualities, and activities. All these deeds are the exclusive domain of the tathagatas and
are nothing but the Wheel of Dharma to benefit others. I shall now
explain, as is generally agreed, how these deeds manifested to influence beings in this land of Tibet.[133]

When the great master nirmanakaya arrived in the Land of Snow,
his first act of opening the door of the Dharma was to tame the
uncontrollable elemental forces native to Tibet—all the vicious spirits
from Ngari to Dokham—by placing them under the powerful and
majestic seal of his command. By making obstacles for the Dharma
and for virtuous actions, they had until then made it impossible even
for Shantarakshita, a great bodhisattva dwelling on the bhumis, to
establish the law of the Dharma. Padmasambhava appointed the vicious spirits henceforth as guardians of the sacred Dharma and of its
practitioners, placed them under oath as servants, and made them
never transgress that oath.[134]

Taking as a model Vikramashila, the source of teaching and practice, he erected, in accordance with the king's aspiration, a great and
miraculous center for the Dharma shaped as Mount Sumeru, the four
continents, the sun, and the moon, with the surrounding iron wall.
Designed in three styles of architecture—the lower story Tibetan, the
middle Chinese, and the top story Indian—this triple-storied central
structure of glorious Samye, the Unchanging and Spontaneously Perfected Temple, was unequaled on the surface of the earth and below
the sun. Outwardly it was a celestial palace, and inside it contained
wonderful shrines with representations of body, speech, and mind
that transcended the imagination.[135]

Padmasambhava personally strewn the flowers of consecration, accompanied by the wondrous great magical display of wisdom beings visibly dissolving [into the shrine objects]. By establishing Samye as an object of faith for the whole world, including the gods, and by preserving and sustaining the precious teachings of the Buddha in Tibet up until the present time, he has bestowed the kindness of never-waning auspiciousness upon the world and its beings.

The precious teachings of the Buddha consist of Statement and Realization. The Dharma of Statement is included in the Three Collections (Tripitaka), and the aspect of Realization is comprised of the Three Trainings. At first Padmasambhava clearly foretold the lotsawas who were to translate the Dharma of statements into the Tibetan language and allowed for them to learn the topics of knowledge. Gradually, bringing lotsawas and panditas together, he created the chief circumstance for translating into Tibetan all of the sacred Dharma prevalent in the Noble Land.[136] He first instigated the river of the great tradition of expounding and studying the entire statements and realization of Sutra and Mantra as well as of applying, meditating upon, and practicing the Trainings. Upon the fortunate beings and disciples he bestowed, as the most sublime teaching, all of the ripening and liberating aspects of the Vajra Vehicles of Secret Mantra that through numerous special qualities are superior to the Philosophical Vehicles and give enlightenment within one lifetime. By turning an infinite variety of the Dharma Wheels of the tantras of Maha, the statements of Anu, and the instructions of Ati, as well as all the profound meanings of tantras, statements, and instructions that are successively present in each of these three yogas, he illuminated the essence of the Buddhadharma in a way that far exceeded even that of the Noble Land.[137]

Through the tremendous, miraculous display of pervading an ocean of realms with a single bodily form, he personally visited, accompanied by the incarnated retinue of the king, subjects, and companions,[138] the major sacred places of Tibet, primarily the four grand snow mountains, the eight great caves, the four renowned great lakes, the five lands, the three valleys, the secret countries, and the major districts.[139] He visited all of the land of Upper, Lower, and Middle districts of Tibet and Kham without omitting as much as the imprint of a horse hoof. By his miraculous power of transforming an instant into an aeon, he blessed each of these sites to make them inseparable from all the primordially perfect major sacred places by performing assembly sadhanas and turning the wheel of the Dharma for years and months at each place.[140]

Those who were his disciples at that time attained liberation simultaneous with realization, and those of lesser fortune were implanted with the seed by merely seeing his face.[141]

Considering with loving kindness the beings of future generations, he concealed countless profound terma treasures, such as image treasures, Dharma treasures, wealth treasures, substance treasures, and so forth.[142] These included named termas with description lists predicting the persons who would reveal them, as well as unnamed termas that were intended for any fortunate person.

By filling the land in this way with teachings, precious articles, and sacraments, he declared that he will accomplish the welfare of all worthy beings by means of terma treasures until the arrival of the victorious Maitreya, even though the teachings of Shakyamuni will disappear, and that he thus will remain to the last days of the final future age. Thus, the fact that he pervades all the central and surrounding lands of Tibet and Kham with his immeasurable kindness is experienced as evident by all wise people of these present times. This demonstrates the exaltedness of his Dharmic deeds.[143]

THE TIME

The time when the great Dharma doors of these inconceivable and wondrous, miraculous displays took place is indirectly demonstrated.[144]

— 5 —

The Circumstances

This has two parts: establishing the basis for beginning the teaching and the actual beginning of the teaching.[145]

ESTABLISHING THE BASIS FOR BEGINNING THE TEACHING

The *Lamrim Yeshe Nyingpo* root text says:

At that time and occasion, . . . in which the retinue is indivisible from the teacher.

THE ACTUAL BEGINNING OF THE TEACHING

The *Lamrim Yeshe Nyingpo* root text says:

Because of these marvelous and inconceivable deeds, . . . the stages of the path condensed to the essence. SAMAYA.

Fearing that there would be too many words if at this point the general meaning were to be expounded upon, and also as the meaning of the words is easy to understand, I did not elaborate further.

— 6 —

The Four Vajra Syllables

THE RESULT: THE TOPICS OF INSTRUCTION THAT ARE TO BE FULLY UNDERSTOOD

This has three parts: brief statements in terms of the meaning to be explained, unfolding the brief statement by explaining the extraordinary setting of the teaching, and expounding in detail the meaning of the words through explanation.

BRIEF STATEMENTS IN TERMS OF THE MEANING TO BE EXPLAINED

The *Lamrim Yeshe Nyingpo* root text says:

OM AH HUNG HO

ཨོཾ་ཨཱཿ་ཧཱུྃ་ཧོཿ

The explanation of the meaning has two parts: the general explanation of the emanation basis, the nature of the syllables, and the special teachings on the meaning of the four syllables emanated therefrom.

GENERAL EXPLANATION OF THE EMANATION BASIS:
THE NATURE OF THE SYLLABLES

This has five parts: identity, nature, definition, function, and divisions.

Identity

In the context of general designation, syllables are among the five aggregates defined as "nonconcurrent formations." Since they are the symbols or marks of the Dharma, they are defined as the Dharma seal of all the buddhas. Since deity and mantra are not different, they are defined as deities by all yogins. Since these marks have the ability to bless the mind stream of sentient beings, they are defined as buddhas. Since the blessings of the tathagatas are intermingled with the phenomena of karmic ripening, they are defined as appearance. Since the wisdom of the buddhas has blessed the syllables, they are defined as indivisible. Thus they are explained under six kinds of consideration, according to the differences of persons and contexts.[146]

Nature

The luminous nature of mind spontaneously manifests as the "cloud bank of the circle of syllables," and apart from that nature the syllables do not possess concrete existence.[147] The *Guhyagarbha Tantra* describes this:

The nature of the mind is syllables,
And syllables have no concreteness.

A sutra mentions:

Subhuti, syllables are in the ultimate sense unborn and thus the nature of A. That which is the nature of A is the nature of mind and thus completely transcends everything concrete and inconcrete.[148]

Definition

Effortlessly written by the subject, self-existing knowledge, on the object, dharmadhatu, syllables are named *akshara* because they are unchanging and spontaneously present since the beginning, *vyanjana* because they clarify all that is expressed, and *varna* because they possess the power of embodying meaning. The *Guhyagarbha Tantra* states:

> They are called "syllables"
> Because they are written by space out of space.

Function

Since the inconcrete syllables manifest as the various displays of the "cloud bank of the circle of syllables," they allow for the appearance of all the names that express an object's identity and of all the words that express an object's distinctions. Their combination expresses all the existing utterances of samsara and nirvana comprised of ground, path, and fruition. Thus, syllables are bearers of the activity that accomplishes the deeds of the buddhas. As is said:

> This basis that upholds all words without exception
> Utters and expresses a variety of vast meanings.

Divisions

The system of the great Omniscient Lord of Dharma divides syllables into four types.[149]

The Ultimate Syllables of the Natural State.   These are as the *Maya Tantra* expounds:

> The mind has the nature of syllables.
> Syllables are a wish-fulfilling cloud of jewels.

Thus, the naturally luminous mind-essence, self-existing wakefulness, devoid of permanence and discontinuance, coming and going, is the emanation basis for all the syllables of samsara and nirvana.

The Nadi Syllables Abiding in the Body. Within the left, right, and central channels, the three life-pillars of the four nadi-wheels of the body, dwell self-appearing white, red, and blue OM AH HUNG. They serve as the basis for manifesting, outwardly, the body, speech, and mind; inwardly, the three poisonous emotions; and secretly, the enlightened body, speech, and mind.

Within all the nadi-petals of the four wheels dwell the luminous manifestations [of OM AH HUNG], the vowels and consonants of means and knowledge, which altogether number 84,000 when counting their single forms, combinations, and subsidiary aspects. Outwardly these syllables serve as the causes for the arising of the aggregates, elements, and sense-bases, as well as for all utterances. Inwardly, they serve as the conditions for the disturbing emotions and conceptual thoughts. Secretly, they serve as the support for innumerable Dharma doors to manifest at the time of purification.

The Audible Syllables of Utterance. These are all the utterances and expressions of the voice. They appear because the syllables dwelling in the channels are moved by wind and meet with the conditions of location and effort through the manipulations of the tongue, the palate, and so forth.

The Final Syllables of Fruition. They are the clouds of syllables, which emanate from the syllables of the purified nadi-places of the sambhogakaya and cause the tones of Dharma to resound through space. The syllables, having turned into bodily forms, act for the welfare of beings. The nadi-syllables of both sambhogakaya and nirmanakaya are adorned with the lights of the five wisdoms and manifest as the sounds of Dharma endowed with the sixty aspects of melodious speech.[150]

The nadi-syllables of body appear from the natural radiance of the ultimate syllables of dharmadhatu. From their manifestations appear the audible syllables of utterance. When freed from obscuration, they transform into the syllables of fruition. Thus all four kinds are embodied in one essence.

SPECIAL TEACHINGS OF THE MEANING

These four syllables [of OM AH HUNG HOH], briefly explained here, are called "vajra syllables of the Great Secret" because they cannot be discerned by the intellect of scholars and shravakas. They are also called "syllables symbolizing the tathagatas," like the syllables E and VAM. Among the two kinds of symbols—the ultimate itself manifest as symbol or sign and a symbol labeled by convention—these syllables are not artificially made into conventional words, but are the ultimate nature, which is spontaneously manifest as symbols. This is perceived and clarified by the wisdom of omniscience. As the life-force or embodied essence of all phenomena of samsara, nirvana, and the path, they are the basis from which all things manifest, the basis for exposition, and the vital point of recitation and meditation, as well as the ultimate destination.

The brief explanation of the meaning of these four vajra syllables has five points: their source of origin, the reason, the essence of the four syllables, symbolism and function, and the fourfold qualities.

Their Source of Origin

In general, the wind of luminosity appears from the self-existing invisible sound of luminosity, which is inseparable from indestructible vajra wind. From that appears the wind of manifestation, and from that the ten coarse winds and so forth. All the syllables of verbal expression arise when these winds are incited by thoughts that apprehend a sound mingled with an object.[151]

In particular, the *Immaculate Light* mentions that all the topics that fully express mantras, such as the vajra body and so forth, appear from the fivefold great emptiness. Later, from the anusvara, two A syllables, two bindus, and the indestructible HA syllables, the vajras of body, speech, mind, and wisdom fully manifest. In this way OM appears from the combination of A, U, and M; AH appears from the combination of A, A, and HA; HUNG appears from the combination of HA, U, and M; and HOH appears from the combination of HA, U, and HA. Thus, each has the nature of three qualities.[152]

The Reason

Generally, the Ali Kali is the source of all secret mantras, knowledge mantras, and dharani mantras. They all appear from the single expression of the self-existing and indestructible essence bindu of luminosity that is indivisible from the syllable A.[153] The *Magical Net of Manjushri* says:

> A is the supreme syllable,
> The sacred syllable of all meaning.[154]
> Arising from within, it is without arising.
> Beyond verbal expression,
> It is the supreme cause of all expressions.[155]

The *Guhyagarbha Tantra* says:

> A manifests in various ways
> Such as the forty-two of HA and so forth.

The Essence of the Four Syllables

Although these syllables can mean each of the six designations mentioned above, here it should be understood, respectively, that the identity of OM and so forth is inseparable from the nature of body as perfect form appearance, the nature of speech as perfect sound image, the nature of mind as perfect emptiness, and the nature of the perfect wisdom of great bliss.

Symbolism and Function

For example, since the syllable A has a different form than other syllables, it is not identical with them. Since it intermingles and pervades them all, it is not different from them. Likewise, the natural bodhichitta of luminosity accompanied by the wisdom wind is in essence different from all phenomena comprised of both [samsara and nirvana], and is thus not identical with them. It is also not different from them, since it permeates all of samsara and nirvana.

In accordance with that analogy, OM symbolizes the nature of manifest form that is primordially present as the empty appearance of the mandala circle. AH symbolizes the nature of audible utterance, voice, and words that is primordially present as the empty resonance of the circle of the indestructible nada. HUNG symbolizes the nature of concepts and thinking that is present as all-pervasive primordial purity, the luminous essence of suchness. HOH symbolizes the nature of the root of existence and transference that is present as the changeless essence of great bliss. Moreover, these four syllables each have the nature of three qualities, and thus there are twelve aspects, symbolizing the progressive and reverse order of the twelve links of dependent origination, and by the fact that each of these four vajras has the nature of the three kayas.[156]

Since the manifestation of these syllables appears as body, speech, and mind, as well as the notion of union, they embrace samsaric forms.[157] By taking them as path by means of yoga they are the remedies that cut through the obscurations and let the four vajras be realized by purifying the temporary stains. Thus, they function as both liberation and confusion. The *Immaculate Light* states:

> The hooded place is OM,[158]
> The world of humans is AH,
> The higher abodes are HUNG.

Thus, the three syllables can be connected to the three doors and the concept of passion and so forth.[159] This is mentioned in detail throughout all the Sarma and Nyingma schools, but chiefly in the *Concise Practice Way of the Vajra Recitation*. According to the *Jewel Garland*:

> Buddha is taught as the letter HUNG.
> His speech is said to be the letter AH.
> The Sangha is the letter OM.

Thus they are combined with the Three Precious Ones. The *Samaja Root Tantra* teaches:

> In order to attain all enlightenments,
> Act by means of the wisdom vajra.[160]
> OM is the wisdom essence;
> The vajra body is that which attains it.
> AH, being the egoless enlightenment,
> Causes attainment of the vajra speech.
> HUNG, as the body, speech, and mind,
> Lets the undivided three vajras be attained.

The Fourfold Qualities

These four seed syllables demonstrate all the fourfold qualities of ground, path, and fruition.

Regarding the time of the ground, the syllable OM demonstrates the all-ground, the body, and the nadi-element; the syllable AH demonstrates the disturbed-mind consciousness, speech, and the wind (prana) element; the syllable HUNG demonstrates the engaging consciousnesses, the mind consciousness, and the essence element; and the syllable HOH demonstrates the all-pervasive awareness and the wisdom element.[161]

Regarding the objects of purification at the time of the path, OM symbolizes the waking state and bodily obscuration, AH symbolizes the dream state and verbal obscuration, HUNG symbolizes the state of deep sleep and mental obscuration, and HOH symbolizes the state of passion and the obscuration of transference.[162]

Regarding that which purifies, the syllables demonstrate successively the four ripening empowerments: the vase empowerment, the secret empowerment, the wisdom-knowledge empowerment, and the word empowerment; the four liberating paths or the four yogas: the development stage with marks, relative self-consecration, mandala circle, and ultimate Great Perfection; the four immeasurables of love, compassion, joy, and impartiality; the four aspects of approach, full approach, accomplishment, and great accomplishment; the four joys of joy, supreme joy, transcendent joy, and innate joy; and so forth.[163]

Referring to the time of fruition, the syllable OM is the nature of vajra body, nirmanakaya, the emancipation of wishlessness, and the all-accomplishing wisdom; the syllable AH is the nature of vajra speech, sambhogakaya, the emancipation of marklessness, and the wisdom of discrimination and equality; the syllable HUNG is the nature of vajra mind, dharmakaya, the emancipation of emptiness, and the mirrorlike wisdom; and the syllable HOH is the nature of vajra wisdom, svabhavikakaya, the emancipation of nonformation, and the wisdom of emptiness.[164]

— 7 —

The Five Perfections and Instruction
to Retain the Teaching

UNFOLDING THE BRIEF STATEMENT BY EXPLAINING THE EXTRAORDINARY SETTING OF THE TEACHING

This has two parts. The general: how the teachers of the three kayas turn the Wheel of Dharma. The specific: instruction to retain the teachings that are condensed within the oral instructions.[165]

THE GENERAL: HOW THE TEACHERS OF THE THREE KAYAS TURN THE WHEEL OF DHARMA

The *Lamrim Yeshe Nyingpo* root text says:

> *The essence of primordially pure space is Samantabhadra,*
> *The spontaneously present awareness is Padmasambhava,*
> *And their indivisible unity, Dorje Drakpo Tsal,*
> *Is the heruka, the supreme sovereign of all mandalas.*

In general, all the teachings of the Great Secret appear endowed with the five perfections. This has two aspects: the ordinary setting, indicating the appearance of the tantras of words and their instructions, and the extraordinary setting, indicating the appearance of the tantras of meaning and their instructions.[166] The *Tantra of the Union of Sun and Moon* explains:

> By possessing five perfections,
> All the tantras of the Great Secret
> Are the seeds of the settings
> That are ordinary and extraordinary.[167]

Of these two, the former has been dealt with above.[168] Here the latter is as stated in the *Talgyur Root Tantra:*

> The basis is of five aspects.
> The place is held to be of three kinds.[169]

As indicated here and elsewhere, each of the five perfections can be subdivided into the aspects of the three kayas of the victorious ones.

THE PERFECT TEACHER

The primordially pure and original real condition, the essence of space free from all constructs, is the dharmakaya teacher Samantabhadra. The spontaneously present and self-cognizant awareness, effortlessly liberated in the ground, is the self-manifest sambhogakaya teacher Padmasambhava. Essence and nature indivisible, the natural expression of compassion that is the unity of space and awareness, is the nirmanakaya teacher Dorje Drakpo Tsal, Powerful Vajra Wrath. As the emanator and absorber of the all-encompassing mandalas of peaceful and wrathful ones, this great heruka, the supreme or most eminent sovereign of all mandalas, accomplishes the deeds of the buddhas. The meaning of *heruka* here is as described in a tantra:[170]

> HE is the emptiness of cause and so forth.
> RU is the absence of abiding, destruction, and gathering.
> KA is the nondwelling on anything whatsoever.

In this way, the meaning applies to each of the three kayas, since it indicates the meaning of the three gates of emancipation.

THE PERFECT PLACE

The *Lamrim Yeshe Nyingpo* root text says:

> *In the realm of the great sphere, the all-pervasive dharmadhatu,*
> *In the sambhogakaya palace with the fivefold luminosity,*
> *And in all the indefinite places of nirmanakayas who tame*
> *beings . . .*

In the self-existing dharmakaya realm of the Great Sphere, the dharmadhatu that is all-pervasive throughout samsara and nirvana; in the palace of the five sambhogakaya families, densely arrayed with ornaments of the space manifestations of luminosity and endowed with the five natural wisdom lights; and in all the various places of nirmanakayas who tame beings, the indefinite displays of pure and impure realms and places.[171]

THE PERFECT RETINUE

The *Lamrim Yeshe Nyingpo* root text says:

> *For oceanlike assemblies of disciples possessing potential . . .*

The dharmakaya retinue is the ocean of self-manifest wisdom. The sambhogakaya retinue is the space-filling mandala of sugatas, bodhisattvas, and wrathful deities. The nirmanakaya retinues are the supramundane and mundane beings endowed with good fortune. In short, since the retinues of disciples and those possessing a potential corresponding to their individual fortune are inconceivable and uncountable, they are described by the word "oceanlike."[172]

THE PERFECT TEACHING

The *Lamrim Yeshe Nyingpo* root text says:

> *The wheel of Dharma of the inconceivable number of causal and*
> *resultant vehicles,*
> *In accordance with the various types of suitability and capacity of*
> *each individual.*

The dharmakaya teaching is the Great Perfection of natural luminosity. The sambhogakaya teaching is the great resultant, unexcelled greater vehicle. The nirmanakaya teaching is primarily the three causal vehicles. In short, the countless Dharma Wheels of the inconceivable number of greater and lesser vehicles taking the cause or fruition of buddhahood as the path appear in accordance with the various types of suitability and faculties of the individual fortunes of the disciples.[173]

THE PERFECT TIME

The *Lamrim Yeshe Nyingpo* root text says:

> *They turn throughout the three times . . .*

Dharmakaya manifests as the effortless great realization of equality in the inexpressible time of dharmata, the fourth time of equality. Sambhogakaya teaches the meaning through symbols without words or letters in the self-manifest time of spontaneously present wisdom. Nirmanakaya manifests the media that illuminate the Dharma in the time endowed with the threefold ripening of disciples corresponding to their particular fortunes. In short, since the three kayas of victorious ones have the nature of all-pervading and everlasting activity, they turn uninterruptedly throughout the three times the Wheels of the Dharma that influence those to be tamed.[174]

THE SPECIFIC: INSTRUCTION TO RETAIN THE TEACHINGS THAT ARE CONDENSED WITHIN THE ORAL INSTRUCTIONS

The *Lamrim Yeshe Nyingpo* root text says:

I will now teach to my closest disciples
The quintessence of all these condensed into one,
The essence of my heart, the ultimate counsel,
As a direct instruction that is easy to understand and simple to apply.
Don't let it dwindle away but practice one-pointedly.

Padmasambhava promised to teach the oral instructions, saying:

I will teach those who delight their master with the three kinds of pleasing actions, my disciples of closest heart sons, the gathering of the king, subjects, and the companion. I shall teach you the quintessence of the words and meanings of all these Dharma Wheels of the three kayas of victorious ones, the profound and vast causal and resultant vehicles, condensed into one, which is the heart essence of all the buddhas, the ultimate counsel of Guru Rinpoche. I shall teach it, not as a mere dry explanation of words, but as a direct instruction stripped to the essentials which, being lucid, is easy to understand by everyone of sharp or dull faculties and which, being moderately extensive, is simple to apply in practice. Such an instruction, profound, rare, and condensed to the essence, is difficult to obtain. Without letting it dwindle away from indifference, retain the words through learning, discern their meaning through reflection, practice one-pointedly through meditation training, and accomplish the welfare of self and others.

Thus, he instructed them.[175]

− 8 −

The Meaning of the Ground

This has two parts: a brief statement and a detailed explanation.

BRIEF STATEMENT

The *Lamrim Yeshe Nyingpo* root text says:

> *It has that which is to be understood, that which causes realization,*
> *and the final result.*
> *Thus it is demonstrated by these three aspects.*

The instruction Padmasambhava thus pledged to teach is comprised of three major summations: the ground, what is to be known; the path, what makes it realized; and the fruition, into what it is perfected. Thus, it is demonstrated by three aspects.

DETAILED EXPLANATION

This has three parts: a detailed explanation of the ground, the path, and the fruition.

68

THE GROUND

This has three points: the ground of the essence, the natural state; the ground of the imagined, the confused state; and concluding the chapter with a summary.

The Ground of the Essence—The Natural State

The *Lamrim Yeshe Nyingpo* root text says:

> *The ground to be understood is the all-pervasive sugata essence.*
> *Uncompounded, luminous, and empty, it is the natural state of*
> *awareness.*
> *Beyond confusion and liberation, it is completely quiescent, like*
> *space.*
> *Although it abides without separation in samsara or joining in*
> *nirvana . . .*

The victorious Maitreya said:

> Adorned with the immense light of knowledge resulting from
> learning,
> The wise will quickly engage in the domain of experience of the
> buddhas.[176]

Thus resolve what is to be known by means of the knowledge that results from learning before entering the path of accomplishing buddhahood. Nevertheless, in terms of direct instructions for practice, I shall now explain the concise key points about which one should not be ignorant.

The ground of all knowable things is called *sugata essence,* and it pervades all of samsara and nirvana just as space pervades all worlds and beings. It is endowed with these five special qualities: its essence is uncompounded; its mode of being is the empty and luminous natural state of awareness; at the beginning, it knows no confusion and at the end it is beyond liberation; it is totally quiescent like the sky, being devoid of the marks of mental constructs, such as arising, ceasing, and so forth; it abides utterly devoid of separating, growing distant by conceiving faults in samsara, or joining, drawing close by perceiving qualities in nirvana.[177]

To explain the meaning of this a little, here follows the reason why the sugata essence is the ground of all knowable things. The *Abhidharma Sutra* says:

> The space of beginningless time
> Is the basis for all phenomena.
> Because of possessing it, all beings
> Can also attain nirvana.

This space, without a beginning in time, is, when not divided into pure and impure, defined as the basis or ground of all the phenomena of samsara and nirvana. When divided, the temporary stains based on the all-ground consciousness are the defiled cause of samsara. The sugata essence, which is the nature of the all-ground, is the undefiled cause of nirvana.[178] The noble Nagarjuna said:

> When that which is the cause of samsara has been purified,
> That purity itself is nirvana and also dharmakaya.

These two aspects are related as "basis and what is based upon it," as the victorious Maitreya taught through an analogy beginning with this line:

> Like earth on water and water on wind[179]

All the scriptures discuss these two aspects using numerous terms, such as phenomena and dharmata, the extremes and the middle, appearance and emptiness, superficial and ultimate, and so forth. In this way the all-pervasive space of the sugata essence is illustrated by the special attributes of being uncompounded and so forth. The *Uttara-tantra* describes the way in which this nature is all-pervasive:

> Just as the sky is all-pervading,
> Having a nonconceptual nature,
> Likewise, the immaculate space of the mind's nature
> Similarly pervades everywhere.[180]

The general characteristic of the sky is that by nature it permeates all eminent, medium, and inferior forms. In the same way, it is taught that the characteristic of the dharmadhatu space is to naturally permeate all phenomena.

This dharmadhatu space is described with three words corresponding to three ways of functioning: as "potential" in the context of sentient beings obscured by temporary stains, as "dharmakaya" in the context of buddhas who are free from stains, and as "suchness" from the aspect of pervading the essence of both and being unchanging.[181] As is said:

> Its nature is dharmakaya,
> As well as suchness and potential.

All the sutras of the Intermediate Dharma Wheel describe this dharmadhatu space using the terms "emptiness," "suchness," and so forth.[182] The *Compendium* states:

> The suchness of the past is the suchness of the future.
> The suchness of the present is the suchness of arhats.
> The suchness of all phenomena is the suchness of the victorious
>   ones.
> These types of suchness of phenomena are all devoid of
>   difference.

The *Prajnamula* says:

> That which is the nature of the tathagatas
> Is the nature of sentient beings.

Thus the meaning of emptiness, the natural state of things, has been taught in these and other innumerable places.

The Final Dharma Wheel and elsewhere use widely the term "sugata essence." The *Sutra of the King of Samadhi* reveals:

> Pure, crystal clear, and luminous,
> Undisturbed and uncompounded;
> This, the sugata essence,
> Is the nature that is primordially present.[183]

All the profound tantras of Secret Mantra describe it using numerous terms such as E and VAM, vajra being, continuity, unchanging sphere, luminosity, self-existing wakefulness, and so forth.[184] The *Hevajra Tantra* says:

> The precepts of all buddhas
> Are fully present in the letters E and VAM.[185]

The *Sambhuti* explains:

> The great wisdom dwells in the body,
> Fully away from all thoughts.
> It dwells in the body, but is not produced by the body.

The *Samaja* says:

> Potential is explained with the word "continuity" [tantra],
> And this continuity is taught to be primordial.

Indestructible, beyond dwelling and arising,
This is proclaimed to be the sovereign lord.[186]

The general quotations for gaining trust that the sugata essence abides in sentient beings are as follows. A sutra expounds:

All sentient beings have the essence of the tathagatas.

And:

All sentient beings are pervaded by the sugata essence.
These beings are the source of buddhas.

And:

Shariputra, "ultimate meaning" is a term that describes the nature of sentient beings. "Nature of beings" is a term that describes the essence of the tathagatas. "Tathagata essence" is a term that describes the dharmakaya.

The special quotations are as follows. The *Hevajra Tantra* says:

This is the great wisdom
That always abides in the body of everyone.
This sovereign nature of the concrete and inconcrete
Dwells as dual and nondual
And pervades the animate and inanimate.

Among the unexcelled quotations, the *Tantra of the Mind Mirror of Vajrasattva* states:

The tathagata essence abides within all sentient beings of the
    world system
Just as sesame seeds are permeated by oil.

The *Tantra of Self-Arising Awareness* says:

> The mind of the perfect buddhas
> Dwells in the mind stream of sentient beings
> In the manner of kayas and wisdoms.

Thus has it been taught in these and many other places. The victorious Maitreya set forth three reasons to establish this:

> Because the body of complete buddhahood is all-pervasive,
> Because the suchness is indivisible,
> And because of possessing the potential,
> All beings are eternally endowed with the buddha essence.

Thus, [the three reasons are]: the dharmakaya of buddahood pervades and therefore is present in all sentient beings; the suchness of sentient beings and of buddhas is indivisible, like the space in an earthen pot and in a golden vase; and the mind stream of sentient beings possesses two types of potential that allow the three kayas of buddhahood to appear.[187]

The *Angulimaliya Sutra* shows in detail the possession of the sugata essence through this analogy:

> You can churn milk because it has butter; but you cannot churn butter out of water. If you want gold, you can dig in rocks, but not in wood. Likewise, since sentient beings possess a buddha nature, the pursuit of buddhahood is meaningful. Without this potential, such effort would be meaningless.

In short, the noble Nagarjuna said:

> When the potential is present, the effort carried out
> Makes the pure gold visible.
> When no potential is present, the use of any effort
> Produces nothing but exhaustion.

The *Glorious Garland Sutra* teaches using the opposite reasoning of the *Uttaratantra*:

> If you did not have the potential for awakening,
> You would not feel weary of pain.
> You would not desire nirvana,
> Nor would you pursue or even aspire for it.[188]

This scripture continues by positively establishing the reason:

> Perceiving the faults of suffering and the virtues of happiness
> Of samsaric existence and nirvana
> Results from having the potential.
> Because without potential, [sentient beings] would have no [such perception].[189]

Since the sugata essence does not have the character of being produced from causes and conditions, it is beyond the reach of concepts, such as continuous or momentary, permanent or impermanent and, thus, it is not subject to destruction. Moreover, it is taught to be unconditioned because it possesses the four qualities of being permanent, stable, quiescent, and unchanging. As is said:

> The nature of mind, like the element of space,
> Is devoid of causes and without conditions.
> It is not a gathering and has no arising.
> Also, it is subject to neither destruction nor subsistence.

It is also said:

> It is unconditioned since its nature
> Is forever beyond destruction.
> This indestructibility is stability,
> And thus it is taught to be stable and so forth.

There are many other such statements. Since in its real mode of being its essence is unborn, it is empty like space. Its nature is unceasing luminosity, and its expression of unity is the intrinsic state of awareness. The *Tantra of Self-Arising Awareness* explains:

> The essence of this space is like the sky, its nature is self-luminous, and its expression remains the essence of awareness. Thus, it is the basis for all qualities to arise.

That this [buddha nature] appears to be confused or liberated merely results from labeling on the part of sentient beings, while in fact it is subject to neither confusion nor liberation. Saying that space or the sun is obscured or unobscured by clouds refers merely to the mistaken perception of the samsaric beings on the ground, while both are beyond being or not being obscured. Similarly, it is stated:

> The luminous nature of mind
> Is changeless like the sky.
> These temporary stains, desire and so forth
> Resulting from incorrect thinking, cannot disturb it.

The *Guhyagarbha Tantra* expounds:

> The thoughts of believing in a self-entity
> Persistently tie knots in the sky.
> Beyond bondage and beyond liberation—
> These are the primordial attributes of the spontaneously perfect
> buddha.

This is because, like the sky, its nature is the Middle Way, free from duality and totally uninvolved in all constructed extremes, like present and absent, existing and not existing, permanent and annihilated, arising and ceasing, and so forth, just as the *Mahaparinirvana Sutra* says:

The buddha nature present in sentient beings is like the sky. As the sky has no past, future, or present, neither inside or outside, and is not comprised of form, sound, smell, taste, or texture, so also is the buddha nature.

The *Vajra Dome* states:

In the element of space, whatever exists
In the thousands of world systems,
The Awakened One, the Mahamudra of perfect great bliss,
Remains present, like the sky.[190]

This essence itself has neither samsaric defects to be discarded or cleared away, nor nirvanic virtues to be established or added. The *Uttaratantra* gives the reason:

Since the faults are temporary
And because the virtues are naturally present,
Its characteristic is that of being unchanging;
It is the same after as it was before.

Both the *Uttaratantra* and the *Ornament of Realization* agree:

From this there is nothing whatsoever to remove,
Nor even the slightest thing to add.
Look truly into the true.
To see the true is total freedom.[191]

Therefore, with no concepts of samsara and nirvana being good or bad, to be accepted or rejected, it is free from partiality and is all-pervasive, like the sky. The *Uttaratantra* describes:

Just as the sky is all-pervading,
Of a nature free from thought,

The stainless space of the mind's nature
Similarly pervades everywhere.

The Ground of the Imagined—The Confused State

The *Lamrim Yeshe Nyingpo* root text says:

> *Due to the great demon of coemergent and conceptual ignorance,*
> *From the solidified habitual patterns of grasping and fixation,*
> *And the different perceptions of worlds and inhabitants,*
> *The six classes of beings appeared as a dream.*

Within this naturally luminous essence that is like the sky appeared the obscuring temporary veils, like clouds rising. In other words, coemergent ignorance arose simultaneously with the pure nature, without being before or after, like gold and slag. Conceptual ignorance means conceptualizing that something exists while it does not exist, the temporary confusion appearing as subject and object. These two are the basis from which all confusion arises and are the great demon that creates all kinds of faults. Their nature not being recognized, the habitual tendencies of thinking in terms of the duality of perceived object and perceiving mind gradually increased and solidified. From this appeared the different kinds of deluded experiences of [dualistically] grasping at and fixating on the various outer vessel-like worlds and inner contentlike sentient beings—the six classes of beings with different kinds of environments, sense objects, status, bodily forms, and actions—without a single one of them actually existing, just as in a dream after having fallen asleep.[192]

In order to explain the meaning of this a little, there are five points.

The Ground of Confusion. Confusion arising from the presence of a basis is like the cognitive act that apprehends a mottled rope to be a snake, because of the existence of snakes. Confusion arising from no presence is like seeing an apparition of hair in the sky. Confusion arising from indivisibility is like camphor, the identity of which has two abilities and therefore can be a medicine for the disease of heat or a poison for the disease of wind.[193]

The Causes of Confusion.   The *Guhyagarbha Tantra* states:

> The defects of the root of existence spread from the notion
> of a self.

Thus, the general cause of all samsaric phenomena is precisely the concept of a self-entity. In particular, the indirect cause is the "single-nature ignorance" that remains present as the subtle lack of recognizing the naturally pure and innate sugata essence. The concurrent cause is the ignorance that is coemergent with this innate nature and remains present as the potential for confusion to arise when meeting with the right conditions. The cooperating cause is the conceptual mind consciousness, the conceptual ignorance that is the mind apprehending itself as being subject and object. The perpetuating cause is karmic tendencies, the creation of which have the definite power to yield their respective results.[194]

The mind consciousness can be divided into two aspects: the disturbed mind, which fixates on the all-ground by thinking "I am," making cognition disturbed; and the subsequent mind, which is the six sense cognitions that create the flow of arising and ceasing, and place the karmic powers in the all-ground. The support for these two aspects and the retainer of all the habitual tendencies and seeds is the basis for using the label "confusion," and therefore all the scriptural traditions define it as the all-ground consciousness.[195]

The Conditions.   The conditions for taking rebirth in the higher, lower, and upper realms are the three kinds of karmic action: meritorious, nonmeritorious, and nontransferring. The activators of these karmic actions are the five disturbing poisons.[196]

When these causes and conditions come together, the result is the great wheel of samsara. There is never any impurity in the empty aspect, the nature of the sugata essence, but the cognizant aspect has the ignorance of not recognizing its own natural face. In the first instant, the mind that creates formations stirs and conceptualizes a perceiver as being separate from the perceived. From that results the consciousness that perceives objects, and therefrom comes the sensations that arise by conceptualizing what can be accepted or rejected. From that come the conceptions that apprehend objects as having defining attributes, and through the solidifications of the tendencies thereof, physical forms arise, and thus the five aggregates are formed.[197]

Just as in the example of outer dependent origination uninterruptedly arising through the six related causes, such as those of seed, sprout, and so forth, and the six related conditions of the five elements and the changes of time, in the same way, we circle throughout the three realms due to the inner dependent origination, the twelve links of ignorance giving rise to formation and so forth.[198]

The Creator.   The *Threefold Knowledge* states:

> The instant that has continuity
> Is described as the creator of karma.

In this way, the unfabricated continuous instant is the creator of both samsara and nirvana. In particular, the creator of samsara is the continuous instant of confused thinking that apprehends the nondual as being two. Its power becoming increasingly stronger, it connects confused cognitions into a chain and thus creates this endless samsara.[199]

The Result.   Because of the causes and effects of karmic deeds and disturbing emotions, spinning like on the rim of a water wheel, one experiences the vessel-like world due to the general apparent karma and the contentlike sentient beings due to the specific experienced karma as well as their ripenings. The meaning of this is as explained in the *Guhyagarbha Tantra:*

> Emaho, from the sugata essence,
> Emanated by the karma of one's thinking,
> The places and the sufferings and so on
> Are individually apprehended as me and mine.

The luminous Great Perfection teaches that Samantabhadra's enlightenment in the original ground of liberation is to recognize the natural face, thus dispersing the direct causes for the eight consciousnesses into dharmadhatu the very moment the ground-appearance of the spontaneously present nature manifests from the sugatagarbha, the ground of the primordially pure essence. When this ground-appearance is obscured by coemergent ignorance and conceptualized into perceiver and perceived, the eight gates of outward luminosity manifest, like a dream, from the precious sphere of Spontaneous Presence, and confusion into samsara is unceasing. This is what is called "sentient beings."[200]

Concluding the Chapter with a Summary

The *Lamrim Yeshe Nyingpo* root text says:

> *Although this is so, you have never moved and will never move*
> *From the original condition of the essence.*
> *Endeavor therefore in purifying the temporary stains.*

Although this is how samsara and nirvana have been conceptualized, as being two, and confusion has continued since time without beginning, so, just as the sky is never moved by the configurations of clouds, the original sugata essence of primordial purity cannot possibly change from its basic condition into anything other than its own nature.

Consequently, up to now it has not changed into the attributes of samsara nor nirvana, and from now on it will not change, though one might circle in samsara endlessly. For this reason and because you will realize your natural face and awaken when the temporary stains of confusion are completely purified, exert yourself tirelessly in the means of purifying these stains. As the *Lelag* describes:

> Samsara and also nirvana
> Are both without existence.
> When thoroughly understanding samsara,
> That itself is called nirvana.[201]

The *Two Segments* states:

> All sentient beings are buddhas themselves.
> However, they are obscured by the temporary stains.
> When these are cleared away, they are enlightened.

Since the essence in itself is never tainted by the temporary stains, by purification one can become free from them. The *Guhyagarbha Tantra* says:

> Not fettered by anyone, it is unfettered.
> Nor is there something that could be fettered.

In terms of sentient beings in general it has been taught that samsara is without beginning and end; but in terms of the individual in particular, the *Abhidharma Sutra* says:[202]

> Although without beginning, it has an end.

In this way, you will reach nirvana by purifying the stains through the path and, having purified them, the result will not reverse into the cause, just like a person who has recovered from smallpox. Thus it is reasonable to exert yourself on the path.

Section Three

PATH

EXPLANATION OF THE PATH
THAT CAUSES REALIZATION

There are two parts: a short statement by means of a summary and the detailed explanation of that.

SHORT STATEMENT BY MEANS OF A SUMMARY

The *Lamrim Yeshe Nyingpo* root text says:

> *The stages of the path that bring about realization are innumerable.*
> *Purify your being, sow the seeds, and cultivate them.*
> *Remove the hindrances, and likewise bring forth enhancement.*
> *Thus enter the correct path through these five aspects.*

An inconceivable number of stages of the paths of Sutra and Mantra have been taught as the methods that bring about realization of the inseparability of ground and fruition. Yet, when condensing these into one vital essence, the way to purify your being is like tilling a hard virgin field; the way to sow the seeds of ripening and freeing is like planting grain free from defects; the way to nurture them is like the endeavor of farming, such as giving water and fertilizer; the way to remove the hindrances of the path is like the exertion in protecting against hailstorms and the like; and the way to bring forth the enhancement of qualities is like applying the means for improvement, such as bringing rain and so forth.[203]

Therefore, thoroughly enter the correct path by training correctly in the path through these five aspects, and thus you will realize the fruition of liberation, like fully ripened crops.

DETAILED EXPLANATION

This includes five steps: purifying your being, sowing the seeds, cultivating them, removing hindrances, and bringing forth enhancement.

PURIFYING YOUR BEING

This has two points: the way to follow a spiritual guide, the root of the path; and, having followed him, the way of mind training.

– 9 –

How to Follow a Spiritual Guide

THE WAY TO FOLLOW A SPIRITUAL GUIDE— THE ROOT OF THE PATH

This has four parts: the characteristics of the master to be followed, how to follow a master, the characteristics of the disciples who follow him, and, having followed him, how the oral instructions should be taught.

THE CHARACTERISTICS OF THE MASTER TO BE FOLLOWED

The *Lamrim Yeshe Nyingpo* root text says:

> *First of all is to purify your mind and being.*
> *The vajra master, the root of the path,*
> *Is someone who has the pure conduct of samaya and vows.*
> *He is fully adorned with learning, has discerned it through reflection,*
> *And through meditation he possesses the qualities and signs of*
>   *experience and realization.*
> *With his compassionate action he accepts disciples.*
> *Serve a master endowed with these characteristics . . .*

Having understood the ground, now, for embarking on the stages of the path in order to purify the temporary stains, it is first of all necessary to thoroughly train your stream of being to tame its unsuitability caused by having fallen under the power of the unwholesome mental habit of deluded thinking. I shall now explain how to do that.

Since immature beings are unable to journey even in the direction of the correct path through their own mental power, it is necessary from the very first to examine properly and then follow a qualified vajra master, who is the root of all the teachings of the buddhas, in general, and of correctly entering and fully traversing the path, in particular. A master is indispensable, like a well-informed guide when you embark upon an unknown path, a powerful escort when you travel through a dangerous area, or like a ferryman when you cross to the other side of a river. Although all the sutras, tantras, and instructions have extensively discussed the characteristics of a master, they are in short as follows.

His being is perfectly pure, and he has abandoned wrongdoing, because he is untainted by flaws or downfalls in the conduct of whatever samaya or vow he has taken among the three sets of precepts, which are the foundation of all good qualities.[204]

He is beautified by not being ignorant about anything and by his life-style, which is free from falling into extremes due to his great learning in the Sutra system and in the tantras, statements, and instructions of Mantrayana. By having resolved the meaning of what he learned through reflection, he can distinguish the differences of the six limits and four modes. By taking this meaning to heart through meditation training, his qualities of experience and realization have grown like the waxing moon, and he is endowed with the signs of progress of having advanced through the paths and bhumis. Thus he has perfected the benefit of self by means of learning, reflection, and meditation.[205]

Through his fully bloomed power of immaculate knowledge resulting therefrom, he possesses the kindness of accepting destined disciples with his compassionate action, which is not conceptual and not aimed at gain, honor, or reputation.

Moreover, he is able to cut through misconceptions with his oral

instructions; he can make realization arise by pointing out the meaning; he can halt impure perception through the power of blessings;
and he can clear away hindrances to experience and bring forth enhancement of realization. In short, he is endowed with all the characteristics of spontaneously accomplishing the welfare of others by
means of his knowledge, compassion, and ability.[206]

Regarding quotations on the necessity of first following a spiritual
guide, the *Gandavyuha* states:

> Omniscience depends upon the oral instructions of a
>   spiritual guide.

The *Compendium* declares:

> The Victorious One, who possesses the supreme of all virtues,
> Has taught that you should follow a spiritual guide [to attain]
>   enlightened qualities.

The *Mother Scripture (Prajnaparamita)* states:

> The bodhisattva who desires to attain true and complete enlighten-
> ment should first of all serve, follow, and venerate spiritual guides.

Also it is said:

> Without a steersman to hold the oars,
> A boat will not reach the other shore.
> Though you may possess all learning,
> Without a master, samsaric existence never ends.

Innumerable quotations, reasons, and examples have been given
in this way.

HOW TO FOLLOW A MASTER

The *Lamrim Yeshe Nyingpo* root text says:

> Serve a master endowed with these characteristics by means of the
>   three pleasing actions,
> And do not commit the displeasing ones for even an instant.
> Take the pledge to accomplish whatever he commands
> By the skill of correctly training in his thoughts and deeds.

The way to follow a master endowed with these characteristics
once found is described in the *Ornament of the Sutras:*

> Attend the master by means of material things,
> By service, and by means of accomplishment.

Thus, the best way is the service of accomplishment, practicing
the meaning of his oral instructions, and doing as he commands. The
next best is to serve and attend him to the best of your ability in
thought, word, and deed. The least best is to venerate him and offer
all material things in your possession. By means of these three types
of pleasing action, regard him as a wish-fulfilling jewel, the medicine
that revives one from death, or as the heart in your chest, and then
follow him persistently and with boundless devotion and respect.[207]

Do not commit the actions that displease him for even an instant,
such as wrongdoing in thought, word, and deed, or the manipulative
deception of expecting rewards.

Since the depth of the profound teachings and the intention and
conduct of the sublime beings is difficult to fathom, be careful and
agreeable. By being skilled in correctly training in the behavior of
the three secrets, see whatever he does as perfect and whatever he
says as authentic. Again and again, take the firm promise or pledge,
which is unshakable in the face of adverse circumstances, to fulfill
whatever he commands and thus apply it in practice.[208]

The *Assemblage* declares:

> Son of noble family, all the tathagatas and all the bodhisattvas
> Regard the master as being the indestructible mind of
> enlightenment.[209]

The *Tantra of Self-Arising Awareness* states:

> Thus, the master of Secret Mantra
> Should be served with your body, with precious things,
> And with all that is extremely rare.

A sutra teaches:

> By serving a spiritual friend, you will attain the enlightenment of all
> the buddhas.

The present age makes it difficult to find a master endowed with all the qualities mentioned here. Even when finding a master, beings with impure personal perception will see him as having faults. Therefore, follow someone who predominantly [seems to] have good qualities. This is discussed in *Approaching the Ultimate*.[210]

> Due to the age of strife, the masters have mixed qualities and
> faults.
> There is no one who is always free of any misdeed.
> The disciples should therefore follow someone
> Who has mostly good qualities and has been carefully examined.

THE CHARACTERISTICS OF THE DISCIPLES WHO FOLLOW HIM

The *Lamrim Yeshe Nyingpo* root text says:

> . . . *Of the disciple who has faith, renunciation, and compassion,*
> *And who has sharp faculties, intelligence, and discipline.*

To what kind of disciple should a qualified master then give the instructions? It is said:

Impart to one with faith, diligence, and discipline.

The *Guhyagarbha Tantra* instructs:

Teach the worthy one of excellent character.
Give to the one who can surrender his body and possessions.[211]

To possess the roots of all the virtuous qualities of admiring, longing, and trusting faith; to have the attitude of renouncing samsaric existence by realizing samsara to be like a fiery pit or a prison; to be endowed with the compassion of delighting in benefiting others because of perceiving sentient beings as one's own parents; to have the sharp faculty of correctly understanding the meaning merely by hearing it, due to the awakening of one's potential through former training; to have the great intelligence of being able to accommodate without doubt the view and conduct of the extensive Mahayana and the profound Secret Mantra; to possess the courageous discipline to engage in any practice without feeling intimidated or discouraged— since these six virtues embody all good qualities, a qualified master should accept a disciple endowed with them.[212]

HAVING FOLLOWED HIM, HOW THE ORAL INSTRUCTIONS SHOULD BE TAUGHT

The *Lamrim Yeshe Nyingpo* root text says:

The master should give the teachings suited to the mind of the disciple . . .
He should not give instructions that are inappropriate for the recipient.

When in this way the connection between master and disciple has been well formed, the master should carefully examine the disciple's mind and give the teachings of either the lesser or greater vehicles that are suited to his mental capacity. Other than that, a master should not give what is inappropriate to the level of the individual, such as profound and extensive teachings to someone with lesser intelligence or Hinayana teachings to someone of higher capacity. Doing so does not benefit the recipient of the Dharma teaching, and the teacher himself will be at fault because of creating the defects that the person of lesser intelligence feels afraid of the profound or extensive teachings and therefore turns back from the path, while the person of higher intelligence, not being satisfied with the view and conduct, discards the steps of the path. The *Vajra Garland Tantra* explains:

> Just as the milk of a lioness
> Should not be placed in an earthen vessel,
> Likewise the tantras of the great yoga
> Should not be given to unworthy people.
> There will be disaster in both this and future lives
> If the unworthy is given the oral instructions,
> And the master's attainments will degenerate.

The *Bodhicharya Avatara* further states:

> Do not apply the teachings for lower people
> To someone suitable for the extensive teachings.

As for how to apply the teachings to the recipient, it is said:

> Detached conduct for the lower person.
> For the vast, the paramitas.
> For the profound, the vehicle of Mantra.

The *Vajra Dome* declares:

> For the lower ones, the Action Tantra
> And the Yoga of Nonaction.
> The superior people who are above Yoga Tantra,
> Should be given the Unexcelled Yoga.[213]

— 10 —

The Four Mind Changings

THE WAY OF MIND TRAINING

This has two topics: the preliminaries and the main part.[214]

THE PRELIMINARIES

This has two sections: the preliminaries for the session and the preliminaries for the instructions.

THE PRELIMINARIES FOR THE SESSION

This has two points: the remote preliminaries and the close preliminaries.

The Remote Preliminaries

The *Lamrim Yeshe Nyingpo* root text says:

> *For the way of guiding gradually in accordance with the types of*
> *mental capacity,*
> *First, keep far away from places of disturbance*
> *By going to a place of solitude and giving up worldly activities.*

As for the way of giving oral instructions in accordance with the different types of intellect or mental capacity, when you specifically know how to guide the gradual type of person, you will automatically also understand how to guide the instantaneous type of person.

In general, without ascending through the stages of the path you cannot suddenly jump to the higher levels, and without the lower qualities of the path having arisen you cannot attain the higher qualities. The manner of traversing gradually is therefore essential.[215] The *Nirvana Sutra* declares:

> Just as the steps of a staircase,
> You should also train step-by-step
> And endeavor in my profound teachings;
> Without jumping the steps, proceed gradually to the end.
>
> Just as a small child
> Gradually develops its body and strength,
> The Dharma is that same way,
> From the steps of entering in the beginning
> Up until the complete perfection.

The way of guiding step-by-step on the path is as follows. The person who wishes to enter the path should first of all remove himself from and keep far away from places of mundane disturbance that cause physical and mental distraction. Going to the sacred remote hermitages extolled by the victorious ones, he should be content with simply having the immediate necessities. Thus, giving up all activities that conform with worldly people, such as unvirtuous or indifferent actions of body, pointless chatter of speech, and mentally pursuing disturbing emotions or confused thinking, he should one-pointedly exert himself in practicing the sacred Dharma.[216]

The *Sutra to Inspire Superior Intention* teaches that being distracted by distractions causes twenty defects, including that your three doors remain uncontrolled, that you are interrupted by Mara, and that concentration and discriminating knowledge do not arise. The *Sutra of the King of Samadhi* and other scriptures teach that compared to making numerous kinds of offerings for aeons to all the buddhas there is greater merit in taking seven footsteps toward a hermitage, with the attitude of renunciation. You will then achieve all the qualities that are the opposite of the above faults of distraction. In particular, for the beginner who has not attained mental stability, it is essential to adhere to a secluded place.[217] This is stated in the *Ratna Karanda Sutra*:

> The beginner should remain in a secluded place in order to pacify his mind and fully tame it.

The Close Preliminaries

The *Lamrim Yeshe Nyingpo* root text says:

> *Sit on a comfortable seat, straighten your body, and expel the stale breath.*
> *Supplicate the Three Jewels and generate devotion to your guru.*
> *Apply mindfulness and reflect in the following way.*

By sitting on a soft and level comfortable seat in a secluded place, a cave, or a meditation hut, you can remain seated for a long time. By straightening the body posture, the channels and winds remain in their natural mode, and thus confused thoughts will diminish. By expelling the stale breath three times, the impurities of disturbing emotions within the channels are purified. By supplicating the Three Jewels to be able to reach perfection in the sacred Dharma, you will have no obstacles. By generating the devotion of perceiving your master as a buddha, your three doors are blessed. By applying a natural mindfulness that is not overcome by adverse circumstances, you will be able to remember the meaning of the meditation practice. Therefore, apply correctly what is explained here, and reflect on the mind training in the following way.[218]

THE PRELIMINARIES FOR THE INSTRUCTIONS

There are three points: the stages of the path common for people of lesser capacity, common for people of medium capacity, and common for people of superior capacity.

The Stages of the Path Common for People of Lesser Capacity

This has three parts: reflecting on the hard-to-find freedoms and riches, on death and impermanence, and on the causes and effects of karmic actions.

Reflecting on the Hard-to-Find Freedoms and Riches. The *Lamrim Yeshe Nyingpo* root text says:

> This bodily support adorned with the perfect freedoms and riches,
> Like the udumbara flower, is extremely hard to find.
> If you skillfully take advantage of it,
> Then this find has great value, exceeding that of a wish-fulfilling
>   gem.
> Therefore follow spiritual guides and virtuous friends
> At all times and on all occasions.
>
> Giving up concerns for this life, and for the sake of the future,
> Exert yourself quickly to take advantage of it, for if you don't [it
>   will not last].

This has four topics: the identity of this support, the reason it is difficult to find, how this find has great value, and instruction in the need to take advantage of it.[219]

The Identity of This Support. The identity of the support is the freedoms that are the opposite of the eight unfree states. The five riches from oneself resemble a body with beautiful ornaments, while the five riches from others resemble this body when it is especially illuminated by daylight and are thus showing its special features. The precious human body adorned with such perfect qualities is the indispensable support for attaining enlightenment.[220] The eight unfree states are described in these words:

> To be a hell-being, a hungry ghost, or an animal,
> A barbarian, or a long-living god,
> To have wrong views, be deprived of a buddha,
> Or to be a mute—these are the eight unfree states.

The five riches from oneself are:

> To be a human, centrally born, with intact sense-powers,
> To have unperverted livelihood, and faith in the right place.

The five riches from others are:

> A buddha appeared and he taught the Dharma,
> The teaching remains and it has followers,
> And [teachers] who compassionately benefit others.

The Reason It Is Difficult to Find. The difficulty of finding it in terms of the cause means that you will obtain the freedoms and riches if you have accumulated a vast amount of virtuous karma, such as keeping discipline and having connected it with aspirations. Yet, Shantideva said:

> By such behavior as mine
> I will not obtain a human body.
> And if I do not obtain a human body,
> There will be only misdeeds and no virtue.

Thus, only few people accumulate merit.

The difficulty of finding it in terms of analogy means that the support of the freedoms and riches is like the udumbara flower, renowned to be as extremely rare as the appearance of a buddha in the world.[221] Moreover:

> It is extremely difficult to find a human form,
> Like a turtle happening to stick its neck through the hole of a
>   yoke
> Tossed about on the ocean.

A sutra points out the obvious difficulty of obtaining it when thinking of the numbers:

> Hell-beings are as numerous as dust motes on a large plain, hungry ghosts like snowflakes in a blizzard, animals like husks in a barley brew, but gods and humans are as few as the dust motes remaining upon one's nail.

How This Find Has Great Value.   It is said:

> By means of the boat of a human body
> You can cross the great river of suffering.
> Since such a boat will be hard to find later on,
> At this time of delusion, do not fall asleep.

If you are skilled and careful in the means of crossing over the samsaric ocean of suffering with the boat of the human body, and thus take advantage of it by gathering the jewels of the permanent goal, this finding of what is difficult to find has extremely great value, even exceeding a poor person finding a wish-fulfilling jewel. According to Chandragomin:[222]

> Having obtained it, it can bring you to the end of the ocean of
>   rebirths,
> And you can plant the virtuous seed of supreme enlightenment.

Having once obtained a human form—superior in qualities even
  to a wish-fulfilling gem—
Who will let it remain fruitless?

Instruction in the Need to Take Advantage of It.   Once you obtain what
is difficult to find you have achieved something of immense value.
You must therefore constantly, at all times and on all occasions, follow spiritual guides and friends with a virtuous view and conduct
who can show the correct path of how to take advantage of the
freedoms and riches. This is as written in the *Letter to a Friend:*

Follow a spiritual friend, abide by pure conduct
Fully and completely, since the Muni has so taught.
You should follow the spiritual friend
Since many have attained peace after having followed a spiritual
  friend.

Conversely, you must abandon someone who leads your mind
toward the path of nonvirtue, an immoral teacher or an evil companion who makes you waste the freedoms and riches. The *Sutra on the
Application of Mindfulness* declares:

An immoral companion is a cause of all attachment, aggression, and
delusion and is thus like a poisonous tree.

The *Jewel Mound Sutra* agrees:[223]

What is a sinful companion? It is someone who decreases virtue and
links you to what is unvirtuous. Do not approach, do not follow,
and do not look upon such a person.

Moreover, all this life's experiences are short lasting and substance-
less, just like the good or bad dreams during a single stretch of sleep.
Therefore, completely give up all worldly aims and, in order to ac-

complish the permanent goal of benefit for the next life and onward, immediately exert yourself to quickly take advantage of these freedoms and riches. For if you do not, know it is uncertain how long you will live. As is said:

It is uncertain which one will arrive first—
Tomorrow or the next world.
It is therefore logical not to endeavor in plans for tomorrow,
But to .endeavor in what is of benefit for the future.

Reflecting on Death and Impermanence. The *Lamrim Yeshe Nyingpo* root text says:

Like the rising and setting of the sun and moon, composite things
*   are impermanent.*
The time of death lies uncertain, like a flash of lightning in the sky.
At the time of death nondharmic things are of no help at all,
So practice the sacred and sublime Dharma correctly.

In general, all that appear as world and beings are composite phenomena produced through the interdependence of causes meeting with conditions, and therefore not a single one is permanent. A sutra says:

Monks, all composite things are impermanent.

How are they impermanent? This is described in the *Udana Varga:*[224]

The end of gathering is depletion.
The end of rising is falling.
The end of meeting is parting.
The end of living is death.

Not beyond these four limits of impermanence, gross impermanence is the changes of the world and beings, creation and destruction, years and months, and the four seasons. Subtle impermanence
is the moment-to-moment aging and changing, just like the instantaneous movement of the rising and setting of the sun and moon. In
particular, the human life span is indefinite, so the time of death lies
uncertain. There are many causes for death, making it sure that we
will die. A human life is similar to a flash of lightning in the sky fading
away the moment it has appeared. The *Vinaya Scripture* describes this:

> Like the mountain river flowing into the ocean,
> Like the sun or moon approaching the western mountain,
> Like day and night, hours and minutes quickly go by;
> The lives of people pass in this same way.

When you die, nothing besides the sacred Dharma, such as high
mental capacity, friends, servants, or wealth, will be of any help whatsoever. Casting away mundane and superficial aims as though they
were spittle, engage in the correct practice of the sacred Dharma as
it has been taught by the victorious ones and their sons.

Reflecting on the Causes and Effects of Karmic Actions. The *Lamrim Yeshe
Nyingpo* root text says:

> *The root of practicing the sacred Dharma is the law of karma.*
> *Through evil deeds and nonvirtues you will go to the three lower
> realms.*
> *By virtuous actions you achieve the higher realms and liberation.*
> *Therefore confess evil deeds and make the wholehearted vow to
> refrain from them.*
>
> *Diligently take up the roots of virtue.*
> *Prostrations and circumambulations purify the wrongdoings of your
> body.*

Reciting and reading the Buddha's words purify the obscurations of
  your speech,
And supplicating the Three Jewels pacifies the faults of your mind.
Always train correctly in being mindful, careful, and conscientious.

The root or basis for accomplishing the sacred Dharma of emancipation is to correctly abandon evil deeds and adopt virtuous actions with trust in the Buddha's teachings about the ripening of the effect of intended mental and enacted physical or verbal actions.[225] As described in the *Jewel Garland*:[226]

Attachment, anger, and delusion
And the actions created by them are unvirtuous.
From nonvirtue comes suffering
And likewise all the evil states.

Nonattachment, nonanger, and nondelusion
And the actions created by them are virtuous.
From virtue come the happy states
And happiness in all rebirths.

The ten evil and unvirtuous actions of the three doors, as well as their sub-aspects, motivated by the disturbing emotions in great amount, will result in the hells; in middling amount result in the worlds of hungry ghosts; and in small amount result in the animal realms. Thus, they make you go to the three lower realms and be tormented by intense miseries.[227]

By committing the ten virtuous actions that are in accord with merit, as well as by performing their sub-aspects, you will be reborn in the higher realms and experience pleasant results. By performing the virtuous actions embraced by renunciation or bodhichitta that are in harmony with emancipation, you will attain one of the three types of emancipation.[228] According to the *Sutra of the King of Samadhi:*

Committed actions never disappear.
They ripen in samsara into white or black results.[229]

Thus the ripening of actions never fails, and the effects of virtue and evil deeds will unmistakenly ripen upon their doer. Since the karmas can be increased, even a small cause can yield a large result. The formerly committed misdeeds along with their sub-aspects that can be divided into the four types of impelling and completing, performed and accumulated, should therefore be confessed before a sublime object. With determination, make the wholehearted vow henceforth to not commit them again. You must joyfully undertake the roots of virtue as well as their sub-aspects, even down to the tiniest, with great endeavor and without belittling them.[230]

The conditioned and general virtuous actions of prostrating to and circumambulating the representations of the Precious Ones will purify chiefly the misdeeds of the three kinds of physical nonvirtues. Reciting incantations and essence mantras and reading the sutras of the words of the Victorious One and the profound tantras will chiefly purify the obscurations of the four kinds of verbal nonvirtues. Turning your thoughts onto the path of virtue, such as supplicating the Three Jewels and the Three Roots, motivated by admiring, yearning, and trusting faith, will chiefly purify the faults of the three kinds of mental nonvirtues.

Both virtue and evil depend upon your attitude. As the *Clouds of Precious Jewels (Ratnamegha)* states:

All virtuous and all unvirtuous actions
Are created by the mind.[231]

Therefore strive to control your mind at all times. Shantideva taught how:

All who desire to control their minds
Should guard themselves with effort at all times

Through being mindful and conscientious.
I will join my palms for that.

Thus, always train yourself correctly in being mindful, which means an unwavering watchful attitude; in being conscientious, which means to notice whether or not faults have arisen in your stream of being; and in being careful, which means to be cautious about what should be done or avoided in any action.

The Stages of the Path Common for People of Medium Capacity

This has two parts: how to train your attitude, and the measure of having trained.

How to Train Your Attitude. The *Lamrim Yeshe Nyingpo* root text says:

> In particular, for accomplishing the state of emancipation,
> With the recognition and remembrance that all of samsara
> Is like a fiery pit, a garden of razors, or a forest of swords,
> Arouse again and again the intense and genuine attitude
> Of desiring to be quickly freed from the three sufferings.

The conceptions common for the people of lesser capacity are indeed a correct view. But, in order to attain what is superior to that, the state of unexcelled emancipation and peace, the attitude of renouncing all of samsara is essential.

The characteristics of samsara are described in the *Scripture on Discernment:*

> As filth has no sweet fragrance,
> The six kinds of beings have no happiness.
> As there is no coolness in a fiery pit,
> The states of existence have no joy.

No matter where you are reborn within the higher or lower realms of existence, there is an exclusively painful quality, like staying naked in a pit of fire, walking barefoot in a garden of sharp razors, or climbing undressed in a forest of swords. A sutra describes the nature of samsara:

> Due to craving, becoming, and ignorance,
> All beings helplessly circle through the five kinds of
>   transmigration
> Among humans, gods, and in the three lower realms,
> Just like the spinning of a potter's wheel.

Since we, in this way, circle without beginning or end, first understand this fact, and then continuously motivate yourself with unwavering mindfulness. The sufferings of samsara can be condensed into the following three types.

The suffering of suffering means that the truth of suffering is established as soon as the five perpetuating aggregates are apprehended and, in addition, all the major sufferings then arise. This is like having boils in addition to leprosy. The main bases for these characteristics are the heat and the cold of the hell-beings, the hunger and thirst of the hungry ghosts, and the stupidity and muteness of the animals. But also the eight sufferings of human beings, as well as the unsatisfied desire of the gods and the fighting of the demigods and so forth, belong to this category.[232]

The suffering of change means that all samsaric happiness and splendor are impermanent and fleeting by nature, as when being suddenly crushed by sickness or enmity while living happily. All the gods and humans, though they live in seeming happiness, are not secure for long, but change and transmigrate.

The all-pervasive suffering of formations means that all samsaric phenomena comprised of the five aggregates arise and cease moment to moment. Although ordinary beings do not realize that, noble beings perceive that samsaric phenomena are painful because they are always transitory formations. The *Treasury Commentary* explains:

> A single strand of hair lying in the palm of the hand
> Will create discomfort and pain
> If it enters your eye.
> Immature beings, like the palm of the hand,
> Do not realize the hair of the suffering of formations.
> Noble beings, like an eye,
> Perceive that these formations are painful.

When your body and mind cannot bear the painful experiences of illness or enmity even for one instant, how can you expect to tolerate keeping constant company with the three dreadful sufferings in the beginningless and endless realms of samsara? Thinking carefully about this, generate from the core of your heart again and again the strong attitude of wanting to be quickly liberated from these miseries, with an intense yearning that is not just a temporary contrived impulse. The *Bodhicharya Avatara* says:

> Though countless buddhas have passed away
> After benefiting sentient beings,
> Due to my own demerits
> I was not within their reach of healing.
> If I act again in this same way,
> It will be like that over and over.

The *Vinaya Scripture* declares:

> I have taught you the means of emancipation.
> But exert yourselves, since emancipation depends upon
>   yourself.

Think about how this is.

The Measure of Having Trained.   The *Lamrim Yeshe Nyingpo* root text
says:

> *At some point, when you understand that all samsaric grandeur*
> *Is impermanent, inconstant, and illusive,*
> *Fascination with even the splendor of Brahma and Indra*
> *Will have no occasion to arise for as much as an instant.*

By having clearly understood this painful nature of samsara and
having generated a strong weariness and renunciation, you will at
some point realize that all things, all the seemingly superb wealth
and grandeur, from here up to the summit of samsaric existence, are
impermanent, like a magical illusion, because of being composite;
inconstant, like an autumn cloud, because of being transient; and
illusive, like a water bubble, because of being devoid of substance.

Through such understanding, the attitude of fascination with and
clinging to even the splendor and wealth of those who are renowned
as foremost within the realms of samsara—such as Brahma endowed
with the bliss of detachment, Indra who is the king of all the gods,
or the universal monarch who is the ruler of men—will have no
occasion to arise for as much as an instant. As the regent Maitreya
taught:

> Due to realizing that the gods have the pain of death and
>   transmigration and that humans suffer from striving,
> The intelligent person has no desire for even the eminent might
>   of gods and men.
> Thus the wise and the followers of the teachings of the Tathagata
> Perceive what is suffering, what is its cause, and what is its
>   cessation.[233]

— 11 —

Taking Refuge

This has two parts: taking refuge, the entrance of the path; and generating bodhichitta, the main part of the path.

TAKING REFUGE—THE ENTRANCE OF THE PATH

The *Lamrim Yeshe Nyingpo* root text says:

> *While truly perceiving the Three Precious Ones, the Roots, and the*
> *guardians of the Dharma*
> *To be the unfailing and permanent protection,*
> *Regard them respectfully as your refuge until enlightenment*
> *In order to free yourself and others from the terrors of samsara.*

Through these stages of the path, you will have given rise to the attitude of renunciation, the desire to be quickly liberated from the three realms without letting the freedoms and riches go to waste.

Next, it is logically confirmed that you cannot by yourself transcend, needless to say, the terrors of samsara, being incapable of transcending even the fears of this lifetime. Therefore, you need to take refuge in the objects of refuge that can protect you from such fears. These objects are the Three Jewels—the Buddha, Dharma, and Sangha—as well as the Three Roots—the guru, yidam, and dakini, together with their retinues of the wisdom guardians of the Dharma.

Having relinquished all their faults of imperfection, these objects of refuge are liberated from the fetters of samsaric existence, and through possessing immeasurable qualities, they are capable of protecting others. Thus they are always an unfailing and permanent protection. Perceiving them as such while truly understanding these reasons, take refuge in them with the intention quickly to deliver and free yourself and all others, your parentlike sentient beings filling space, from the tremendous terrors of samsara, from this moment and until attaining the great enlightenment, with respectful body, with yearning speech, and with one-pointed devotion of mind.

To explain this in slightly greater detail, there are seven points: the reason for taking refuge, the objects of refuge, the manner of taking refuge, the way in which one is protected, the measure of having taken refuge, the trainings, and the benefits.

THE REASON FOR TAKING REFUGE

The lord Atisha declared:

> Although you may have taken all the precepts,
> You do not possess them without taking refuge.

According to his statement, taking refuge is the indispensable foundation for all Buddhist precepts. Taking refuge marks the difference between being a Buddhist or a non-Buddhist. And without depending upon the protection of these objects of refuge, there is no way to attain emancipation from samsara.

THE OBJECTS OF REFUGE

Between the two types, causal and resultant objects, the causal objects of refuge are the Three Jewels and the Three Roots comprised

of the stream-of-being of others. The greater and lesser vehicles identify the Three Jewels in different ways, but the following accords
with the system of the Unexcelled Greater Vehicle.[234]

The Buddha is the nature of the four kayas and five wisdoms endowed with the twofold purity and the perfection of the twofold
welfare.

The Dharma is what is expressed—the unconditioned truth of
total purification, comprised of cessation and path; and that which
expresses—the two aspects of statement and realization appearing as
the names, words, and letters of the teachings.

The Sangha consists of the actual Sangha, the sons of the victorious
ones abiding on the noble bhumis, who are endowed with the qualities of wisdom and liberation; and the resembling Sangha, who are
on the paths of accumulation and joining, as well as the noble shravakas and pratyekabuddhas.

According to Mantrayana, in addition to the above, the special
Precious Ones are the guru, the object of receiving the blessings; the
yidam, who is the object of attaining the siddhis; and the dakini and
Dharma protectors, who are the companions for accomplishing the
activities.

Although the guru embodies all the Precious Ones, since the
yidam is the Buddha, and the dakini and Dharma protectors are the
Sangha, they are regarded as distinctive objects of refuge.

The resultant object of refuge is your own mind, which is the
unity of being empty and cognizant abiding as the identity of essence,
nature, and capacity, and thus it is of the nature of the Three Jewels.

Moreover, the causal way of taking refuge means accepting something as an object of refuge in order to attain the result of taking
refuge therein. The resultant way of taking refuge means to engage
in the cause in order to realize that your mind is the enlightened
state, or chiefly to rest in the natural state without searching for it
elsewhere because it is spontaneously present within yourself.[235] This
is stated in the *Accomplishment of Wisdom:*

To wish for perfect happiness elsewhere,
Through the lords of the Three Jewels,
Is called aspiring for the cause.
To realize that the luminous mind itself
Is the lord of the three mandalas
And to rest one-pointedly in evenness,
Is taught to be the foremost of fruition.

THE MANNER OF TAKING REFUGE

The visualization is as found in the individual meditation manuals. The attitude, the time, and the method are as plainly stated in the root text.

THE WAY IN WHICH ONE IS PROTECTED

You are protected by requesting the Buddha to be the ultimate refuge and teacher, by requesting the Dharma to be the path for transcending fears through practicing the meaning of what he taught, and by requesting the Sangha to be companions who guide you along on the path. The master of Secret Mantra performs singly the activities of the Three Jewels and therefore embodies all of them. According to the *Samvarodaya:*

The guru is the Buddha, the guru is Dharma,
Likewise, the guru is the Sangha.
The guru is glorious Vajrasattva.

THE MEASURE OF HAVING TAKEN REFUGE

This refers to possessing these four special qualities: understanding the qualities of the Three Jewels, understanding the refuge for self and others and the differences between the Three Jewels, resolving to take refuge after having understood those things, and not searching for another refuge even at the cost of one's life.

THE TRAININGS

The trainings are the six categories of what should be avoided and adopted, together with their sub-aspects.[236]

THE BENEFITS

The *Sutra of the Sublime Victory Banner* describes the benefits:

Because of protecting from all harms,
From fear, and from the lower vehicles,
They are taught to be a sublime refuge.[237]

And:

The one who goes for refuge to these three
Will quickly attain the state of a buddha.

There are innumerable other such quotations.

– 12 –

Conventional Bodhichitta of Aspiration

EXPLAINING THE MAIN PART
OF GENERATING BODHICHITTA

This has two points: generating conventional bodhichitta and generating ultimate bodhichitta.

GENERATING CONVENTIONAL BODHICHITTA

This has two parts: generating bodhichitta of aspiration and generating bodhichitta of application.

GENERATING BODHICHITTA OF ASPIRATION

The *Lamrim Yeshe Nyingpo* root text says:

> *Using your own experience as a measure,*
> *Arouse the bodhichitta of aspiration*
> *Through the four immeasurables of love, compassion, joy, and*
>   *impartiality*
> *In order that your mothers, all beings, may have happiness and be*
>   *free from suffering.*

Using as a measure your own experience of never wanting suffering and of desiring immense happiness, all the six classes of beings, who have been your own fathers and mothers, are also the same in desiring those things. This being so, you should resolve to take upon yourself to endow them with physical and mental well-being and the cause of happiness, which is the creation of merit, and to free beings from suffering and the cause of suffering, which is karmic actions and disturbing emotions.

In order to do that, resolve to practice love, recognizing them as your own mothers and so wishing to cherish them; to practice compassion, recognizing that they suffer in the states of existence and so not being able to bear to forsake them; to practice joy, taking delight in their attainment of the happiness of gods and of buddha-hood; and to practice impartiality, devoid of attachment to near ones or aversion to distant ones.

These four are called "to pledge the cause," and they become immeasurable by taking the beings pervading space as your focus. They are called "to pledge the effect" by means of the four samadhis. Thus generate the bodhichitta of aspiration by means of the attitude of wanting to establish them all in the state of buddhahood.[238]

To explain the meaning in a little more detail, there are the following seven points: the essence of generating bodhichitta, the different types, the focus, the way of generating it, the ritual, the trainings, and the benefits.

The Essence of Generating Bodhichitta

The *Ornament of Realization* says:

Generating bodhichitta means for the sake of others
To wish for the perfect and complete buddhahood.

Thus, it means the wish to personally awaken to complete enlightenment in order to establish all sentient beings in the state of buddhahood. This results from four principles, such as the strength of the cause, the strength of the helper, and so forth. The "helper" means to possess courageous strength, the superior intention to, solely by oneself, carry the great responsibility for the welfare of all sentient beings without exception. The essence is the desire to attain complete enlightenment that is able to liberate all beings.[239]

The Different Types

There are four different types of stages, from the devoted engagement of ordinary people up through buddhahood. Although twenty-two types are taught using analogies in terms of their characteristics, the following two divisions are easy to understand and more well known.[240]

The bodhichitta of aspiration, resembling the wish to travel, means desiring to attain buddhahood. The bodhichitta of application, resembling actually traveling, means exerting oneself in the two kinds of bodhichitta, the methods for attaining buddhahood. The *Bodhicharya Avatara* teaches:

> In short bodhichitta should
> Be understood as being of two kinds:
> The attitude of aspiring toward enlightenment
> And the application toward enlightenment itself.

> Like understanding the difference between
> Wishing to travel and actually traveling,
> The wise should likewise also
> Understand the different grades of these two.

The Focus

According to the *Bodhisattva Bhumi:*

> Generating bodhichitta is to focus on enlightenment and to focus
> on sentient beings.

In that way, it is to focus on pursuing the wisdom of the Greater Vehicle and the focus on the four immeasurables.

The Way of Generating Bodhichitta

This is as the root text precisely teaches. To explain that, the identity of the four immeasurables is as follows. Love means wishing that all sentient beings may meet with new and unprecedented happiness and virtue. Compassion means wishing that they may be free from the suffering they possess and henceforth bring its cause to cessation. Joy means filling one's mind with delight and rejoicing in all sentient beings' possession of such happiness. Impartiality means the special frame of mind which, guided by those three, remains at the same time unattached and free from aggression. Thus their identity is to discard each of their adverse factors.

The meaning of the word "immeasurable" is used because of taking as the focus sentient beings who reach as far as space pervades and are not limited to a certain number or category.

The *Supreme Essence Sutra* explains the different kinds:

> Love and the other three when not embraced by generating bodhichitta are merely causes for happiness within samsaric existence and are therefore called the Four Brahma Abodes. When embraced by the bodhichitta resolve these four are causes for nirvana and therefore called the four immeasurables.

Generating bodhichitta has four conditions. The naturally present potential is the causal condition. The spiritual friend is the ruling condition. Cognizing the respective objects is the objective condition. Perceiving the benefits and disadvantages is the subsequent condition.

They arise in the following way. The *Bhumi Sections* and the *Ornament of the Sutras* teach that the four immeasurables arise based on sentient beings together with their individual focus, and that based on dharmata these four arise without focus as the realization that their nature is unborn.[241]

The *Medium Prajnaparamita* gives their order:

> A bodhisattva mahasattva should cultivate great love, great compassion, great joy, and great impartiality.

The *Two Segments* agrees:

> As the first, cultivate love.
> Secondly, cultivate compassion.
> As the third, cultivate joy.
> At the end of all, impartiality.

Thus the sutras and tantras teach harmoniously.

The Ritual

Various rituals originate from the traditions of the Lineage of the Profound View, the Lineage of the Vast Conduct, and the Special Tradition of Mantrayana.[242]

The Trainings

In general, all the teachings to be practiced are considered trainings in generating bodhichitta. But, in particular, the trainings in the bodhichitta of aspiration are not to abandon concern for sentient beings through keeping their benefit in mind, to gather the accumulations and cultivate the four immeasurables, and to adopt the four white and avoid the four black deeds.[243]

The trainings in the bodhichitta of application come in detail below: the way of training in the six paramitas and the four means of attraction, comprised of three kinds of training.

The Benefits

It is needless to mention the instance of not trying to attain buddhahood, but bodhichitta is indispensable as soon as you pursue enlightenment. In the Buddha's words and in the treatises, both belonging to the Greater Vehicle, it is repeatedly said that the virtues of bodhichitta are immeasurable. In short, according to a sutra:

> Were the merit of bodhichitta
> To have a physical form,
> It would fill the entire realm of space
> And be greater even than that.

– 13 –

Conventional Bodhichitta of Application

Arousing the Bodhichitta of Application

This has three parts: training in the six paramitas to ripen oneself; training in the four means of attraction to ripen others; and the way of mind training, condensing these practices to their essence.

Training in the Six Paramitas to Ripen Oneself

With the attitude of personally pursuing true and complete enlightenment solely for the sake of establishing all other sentient beings pervading space in the state of buddhahood, train in applying the six paramitas. A sutra teaches:

> Subahu, in order to awaken to true and complete enlightenment, a bodhisattva mahasattva should always and continually train in these six paramitas.

Thus it has been taught extensively in this and other scriptures.

Generosity

The *Lamrim Yeshe Nyingpo* root text says:

> *With the intent of pursuing complete enlightenment solely for the sake of others,*

Give away, like grass, your body and possessions,
And give the relief of protection to those disturbed by dangers.
Practice the Dharma yourself and establish others in it.

The essence of generosity, the first of the six paramitas, is to earnestly give away belongings with a completely unattached frame of mind. The motivation is to be intent on pursuing complete enlightenment for the sake of others, as explained above. The objects to be given can be divided into three: the generosity of giving material things, of bestowing fearlessness, and of giving Dharma teachings.

For the first, while being free from the four impure and endowed with the four pure aspects of intention, material, recipient, and method, fully give away without stinginess, like giving grass, and with perfect thought and deed regarding the four special types of objects, all your possessions—inner things included in your body and outer things, the wealth and enjoyments belonging to yourself.[244]

For the second, depending on your ability, give any appropriate means of protection to those disturbed by the dangers of tyrants, carnivorous animals, enemies, bandits, thieves, fire, water, sickness, harmful influences, and so forth, and thus relieve them from those fears.

For the third, in order to inspire faith in others and not to corrupt yourself, practice the sacred Dharma personally by discarding the impure aspects and possessing the pure aspects of thought, word, and deed, and thus become worthy of being a spiritual friend. Thereby others will respect you, and the auspicious link between vessel and contents will be arranged. Thus establish those who long for the Dharma in the teachings of the greater and lesser vehicles that are suitable to the recipient and in which you have personally trained, while possessing the skillful methods for teaching the Dharma and with the frame of mind that is free from the turbulence of material craving.[245]

DISCIPLINE

The *Lamrim Yeshe Nyingpo* root text says:

> *With the intention of renouncing, a thoroughly delighted frame of*
> *mind,*
> *Constrain yourself from committing the negative misdeeds of your*
> *three doors.*
> *Practice as much as you can the conditioned and unconditioned*
> *virtues,*
> *And motivate yourself to carry out all your deeds for the sake of*
> *sentient beings.*

The essence of discipline is to possess the four qualities comprised of taking and observing, to keep the intention of renouncing personal defects, and to have a frame of mind that is thoroughly delighted and interested in the trainings while retaining the attitude of seeking deliverance.[246]

These trainings can be divided into three: the discipline of exercising self-control, of cultivating virtuous qualities, and of acting for the welfare of sentient beings.

For the first, carefully observe the general seven types of Individual Liberation and the specific trainings of bodhisattva precepts that stem from the traditions of the Two Chariots and thus henceforth to constrain yourself from committing the misdeeds of your three doors by interrupting negative conduct.[247]

For the second, practice as much as you can the conditioned virtues that are not embraced by discriminating knowledge and that are chiefly connected with actions of body and speech, as well as the unconditioned virtues that are embraced by discriminating knowledge and are chiefly connected with the samadhi of mind.

For the third, although the *Bodhisattva Bhumi* has taught eleven types, such as helping in meaningful actions and so forth, in short, motivate yourself with the superior intention to carry out all your deeds, whatever you do with your three doors, exclusively for the sake of other sentient beings. Then actually engage as much as you can in activities that are of benefit to others.[248]

PATIENCE

The *Lamrim Yeshe Nyingpo* root text says:

In order never to be overcome by harmdoers,
Cultivate patience through mindfulness of the demerits of anger.
Joyfully undertake hardships for the sake of the Dharma,
And be unafraid of the profound emptiness.

The essence of patience is to maintain the attitude of not taking offense, to be free from accepting or rejecting good and bad, and to cultivate a superior intention so that it becomes unswayable and never overcome by harmdoers, particularly such as ill-fitting ingratitude. Patience can be divided into three types: the patience of not taking offense at harmdoers, of undertaking hardships, and of having confidence in the Dharma.

For the first, be mindful of the demerits when you give rise to anger at harmdoers who are aggressive toward you, disturb, try to defeat, physically beat, or slander you or your party. As an example, it is said:

All good actions, whichever they may be,
Accumulated throughout thousands of aeons,
Such as generosity and offering to the sugatas,
Can be destroyed by one moment of anger.

Moreover, try to bear those harms, without taking offense, by means of the five notions and the nine considerations.[249]

For the second, gladly and with unwaning joy undertake whatever hardships or difficult deeds that may befall your three doors for the sake of the Dharma practices that accomplish enlightenment. For example, like following a rough cure in order to alleviate the pains of a severe illness, this patience is like a great warrior who turns back the army of samsara by defeating the enemy of disturbing emotions.

For the third, take delight in all the topics that transcend ordinary thinking such as the qualities of the Precious Ones and, in particular, be unafraid of, take interest in, and gain comprehension of the true thatness, the profound emptiness of the natural state free from constructs that is devoid of the two kinds of self-entity.[250]

DILIGENCE

The *Lamrim Yeshe Nyingpo* root text says:

> *By awakening a courageous fortitude for what is virtuous,*
> *Don the armor of tirelessly engaging in bodhisattva deeds.*
> *Exert yourself without distraction throughout day and night,*
> *And cast away weariness when striving for the welfare of others.*

The essence of diligence is to take delight in virtue free from laziness and to awaken an immense courageous fortitude for what is virtuous and wholesome, caused by the continuation of former good karma.

Such courageous effort can be divided into three types: the diligence of armor, of application, and of accomplishing the welfare of others.

For the first, don the armor of an attitude that is tireless in the face of long stretches of time or tasks that are difficult to achieve, thinking, "From this moment on and until all sentient beings have been established in unexcelled enlightenment, I will not abandon the bodhisattva deeds even for one instant!"

For the second, with a diligence that is constant and earnest, unshakable, unrelenting, and free from conceit, exert yourself in discarding disturbing emotions, in practicing virtue, and in benefiting others, without distraction for even an instant throughout day and night.

For the third, when able to achieve even the slightest aim that is of direct or indirect benefit for other sentient beings, abandon feelings of weariness or tiredness, even if you have to remain in the lower realms for aeons, and accomplish their welfare before anything else.

CONCENTRATION

The *Lamrim Yeshe Nyingpo* root text says:

With the thorough intention to calm your mind,
Take the mundane dhyanas as the foundation.
Through fully accomplishing samadhi with vipashyana,
Enter the domain of the experience of the tathagatas.

The essence of concentration, dhyana, is to remain one-pointedly directed inward to the nature of a virtuous mental state. Since one's mind with its movements is the root of all karmas and suffering, the application is first of all to achieve the prerequisites for dhyana, which entails keeping your body away from business and your mind from discursive thinking, harboring fewer desires, and remaining content, while keeping the intention of thoroughly desiring the happiness that comes from having calmed these thoughts; and then to adhere to the eight types of application that discard the five shortcomings as the prelude for the actual state of dhyana.[251]

Dhyana can be divided into three: the dhyana of abiding blissfully in this life, of accomplishing virtues, and of acting for the welfare of sentient beings.

For the first, based on the nine means of mental stillness and free from infatuation with and dwelling on tasting the bliss of physical and mental pliancy of the absence of all conceptual thinking, take the dhyanas that are common to the mundane paths as the basis, since they are the support for all the virtues to arise. Moreover, from the first state of dhyana to the fourth there are the special distinctions of the preparatory and main stages and so forth.[252]

For the second, in order to attain the main part of the first dhyana and upward, you must accomplish mundane vipashyana by means of the seven types of attention. This being so, with emphasis on the shamatha of the meditation state and the vipashyana of postmeditation, by fully accomplishing what is general for the shravakas, such as the ten totalities, the eight masteries and eight emancipations, and so forth, as well as what is not general but beyond the domain of experience of the shravakas and pratyekabuddhas, such as the emancipations and the countless samadhi doors, you will perfect the paths of accumulation and joining.[253]

For the third, that which attains the samadhi of noble beings on the path of seeing and onward is called undefiled dhyana or the dhyana that delights the tathagatas. By the power of that you can magically produce countless bodily creations and thus enter the domain of experience of the tathagatas, which entails the eleven ways of benefiting others.[254] The *Uttaratantra* points out:

> This way of the bodhisattvas
> Is in the postmeditation equal
> To the buddhas who perfectly liberate
> The sentient beings in the world.

All the foregoing paramitas should be embraced by the knowledge that does not conceptualize the three spheres and be free from clinging and expectation. Finally, they should be increased by nonconceptual dedication and endowed with the means that is purified by emptiness and compassion.[255]

KNOWLEDGE

The *Lamrim Yeshe Nyingpo* root text says:

By means of the intelligence that fully discerns phenomena,
First comprehend the words of all teachings through learning.
Next seek an understanding of their meaning through reflection,
And finally realize the meaning through meditation.

The essence of knowledge is intelligence that fully discerns all phenomena. Its actual form comprises the state of buddhahood, but here I shall describe how to develop knowledge through its cause, discriminating intelligence. According to Nagarjuna:

If you possess learning and reflection,
The two things that develop knowledge,
From that meditation will fully result,
And therefrom you attain unexcelled accomplishment.

Thus you should gradually develop the three kinds of knowledge of learning, reflection, and meditation.

For the first, by means of the knowledge of learning, gain an all-inclusive comprehension of the words and names of all the teachings about possible topics to be known. In brief, acquire impartial learning that is devoid of ignorance about any topic of knowledge: the mundane types of knowledge, such as language, logic, craftsmanship, healing, and so forth; and the supramundane knowledge, which is understanding the well-spoken Words of the Buddha and the treatises that explain their meaning. These are the causes that are named after their result.[256]

For the second, do not let this learning remain an acceptance with blind faith, but next, by the reflection of analyzing and minutely examining, strive to gain a correct understanding of the profound meaning, such as the two truths or the expedient and definitive meaning, by means of possessing authentic scriptural statements, factual reasoning, and noncontradictory proof, without leaving your learning behind as mere general ideas.

For the third, finally assimilate into your being this certainty you have gained through learning and reflection by means of adopting and avoiding [virtues and faults]. In particular, practice the meaning of that view through one-pointed meditation. Thus do not let it become mere words and speculations, but acquire true realization of the meaning of the natural state.

The details of these topics are found in the *Ornament of the Sutras* and in other texts. But, in brief, the definition of the six paramitas is this: any training practiced with bodhichitta accompanied by the attitude that accomplishes all virtues included in the six paramitas, such as generosity and so forth, which is endowed with the four special qualities. These four special qualities are: being free from their individual discordant factors; aided by the knowledge that does not conceptualize the three spheres; having the function of fulfilling the wishes of others; and after having done so, ripening the beings of those to be tamed into one of the three types of enlightenment by means of teaching the Dharma.[257]

The Different Types

Each of these six paramitas can be divided further into six of generosity and so forth.[258] Thus there is the generosity of each, such as the generosity of generosity, which means to establish other beings in the six paramitas, [the generosity of discipline] and so forth for the other six paramitas. Likewise, there is the discipline of each, which means practicing each paramita without being tainted by their individual discordant factors; the patience, which means practicing each by means of bearing their individual difficulties; the diligence, which means practicing each with joy; the dhyana, which means practicing each by means of not letting the attention wander elsewhere, by taking hold of it through this effort; and the knowledge, which means practicing each of the six paramitas by means of not conceptualizing the three spheres. Thus the *Ornament of Realization* teaches thirty-six types. Moreover, there also exist other divisions, such as the extensive classifications in the *Sutra of the Good Aeon.*[259]

The Definite Number

In regard to the fact that all the teachings practiced by bodhisattvas can be included within the three trainings, there is the definite number of six paramitas. Generosity frees one from attachment to wealth, and that results in perfect discipline. From that arises patience, because one thereby possesses the four attributes of a virtuous practitioner.[260] These three are included in the supreme training of discipline in terms of its cause, essence, and special quality. Dhyana is included within the supreme training of samadhi, and knowledge is included in the supreme training of knowledge, while diligence is the helper for them all. The *Ornament of the Sutras* states the way of practice:

> The generosity of not having expectation,
> The discipline of not desiring rebirth,
> The patience toward everything,
> The diligence of cultivating all virtues,
> The dhyana that is not the formless states,
> And the knowledge endowed with skillful means—
> Thus those who adhere to these paramitas
> Should practice them perfectly.[261]

They should all be put into practice while also possessing the six excellences: the excellent support is to possess bodhichitta; the excellent object is to be without partiality in generosity and so forth, but to embrace all objects; the excellent pursuit is to exert oneself for the welfare of all sentient beings; the excellent skillful means is to embrace the action with the knowledge that does not conceptualize the three spheres; the excellent dedication is to dedicate toward unexcelled enlightenment; and the excellent purity is to practice as a direct remedy for the two obscurations.

TRAINING IN THE FOUR MEANS
OF ATTRACTION TO RIPEN OTHERS

The *Lamrim Yeshe Nyingpo* root text says:

> *Having ripened your own being, gather followers through generosity,*
> *Delight them with pleasing words, and comfort them by being*
>   *consistent.*
> *Through counseling them in meaningful conduct, fully establish*
>   *them, temporarily and ultimately,*
> *In the splendor of benefit and well-being.*

Having fully ripened your being by training in the practices of application, you must now bring others to maturity. The four means of attraction are the chief of all techniques or methods for that. The *Ornament of the Sutras* states:

> To speak pleasantly, act meaningfully,
> And to be consistent with the meaning—
> That is regarded as being in harmony with generosity, giving
>   teaching, applying it,
> And following it oneself.[262]

In that way the order and number have been taught, and:

> They are called the four means of attraction
> Because of being the means for bringing benefit,
> Because of accepting and of causing to enter,
> And likewise because of causing to follow.[263]

Thus have their purpose, literal meaning, and so on, been extensively taught. In a similar way, the *Lotus Mound* advises:

Agreeably beckon them with the fan of generosity,
Welcome them with pleasantly spoken words.
Make them at ease with meaningful action,
And give them consistent advice.

As this teaching shows how to apply them, first of all fully attract
by means of giving any suitable material things to worthy recipients
who have not gathered among your followers. After they have been
gathered you should inspire them to the paths of emancipation and
omniscience by means of uttering pleasing words, talk that is relevant
and becoming to their minds. In order to prevent those who have
thus been inspired from falling back again but to make them follow
yourself and to encourage them, you should comfort them by being
tireless in acting consistently and without contradicting the meaning
of the teachings that you have explained to others. In accordance
with the different lower, medium, or superior dispositions and faculties of the disciples, teach them the individual Dharma doors of the
greater and lesser vehicles, counseling them in the permanent goal of
engaging in meaningful conduct.²⁶⁴

These four can, in short, be condensed to the generosity of material things and of teachings. By means of these two you should fully
establish all beings, both temporarily and ultimately, in the splendor
of immediate benefit and lasting well-being.

THE WAY OF MIND TRAINING—CONDENSING
THESE PRACTICES TO THEIR ESSENCE

The *Lamrim Yeshe Nyingpo* root text says:

*As the essential point, take upon yourself the burden
Of all the miseries of sentient beings.*

Give away your happiness and virtue to the six classes of beings,
And train in compassion and bodhichitta without being carried away
  by difficulties.

Condensing all the bodhisattva practices to their essential points, there are three topics: to train in the cause, cultivate deep-felt love and compassion; to train in the actual attitude, arouse bodhichitta throughout the six periods of day and night; to train in the conduct, exert yourself one-pointedly in dedicating the virtue to the welfare of others and in giving them your own happiness and taking their suffering upon yourself. About this Shantideva said:

One who desires to quickly protect
Himself as well as all others,
Should practice the secret excellence
Of exchanging himself with others.

In this way, practicing the profound mind training of exchanging yourself with others is essential. The reason for this is as he said:

Whatever happiness exists in the world
All results from wishing others to be happy.
Whatever suffering exists in the world
All results from desiring happiness for oneself.

Furthermore, he said:

Without fully exchanging
Your happiness for the suffering of others,
You will not accomplish buddhahood
And find no happiness in samsara.

In this way it has been taught both directly and in terms of the opposite. This point is also mentioned like this:

Give gain and victory to others.
Take loss and defeat upon yourself.

In accordance with the meaning of this, without hesitation, form the intention to happily and joyfully take upon yourself the burden of all the karmic deeds and disturbing emotions, the causes, accumulated since beginningless time, that exists in the mind stream of sentient beings pervading space, who have been your mothers, as well as all their painful sensations of body and mind, the results. Next, form the intention to give completely all the wholesome roots of virtue accumulated since beginningless time that exist in your own mind stream, as well as all the pleasant sensations of body and mind, their results, to each of the sentient beings in the six kinds of transmigration. The *Seven Points of Mind Training* teaches about this:[265]

Train alternately in the two aspects of giving and taking.
These two should ride on the breath.

Thus put them into practice. Whatever happens, such as good or bad health, joy or sorrow, high or low status, you should don the great armor of being not carried away by difficulties, train one-pointedly in conventional bodhichitta with compassion as its basis, and when it has arisen stabilize and increase it.

− 14 −

The View of Ultimate Bodhichitta

Explaining the Development of Ultimate Bodhichitta

This has three parts: resolving by means of the view, practicing by means of the meditation, and linking up by explaining the result.

RESOLVING BY MEANS OF THE VIEW

This has four points: establishing external perceived objects to be devoid of a self-nature, establishing the inner perceiver as well as the individual self to be devoid of a self-nature, establishing the examining mind to be devoid of a self-nature, and concluding the topic of the chapter.[266]

ESTABLISHING EXTERNAL PERCEIVED OBJECTS TO BE DEVOID OF A SELF-NATURE

The *Lamrim Yeshe Nyingpo* root text says:

In particular, external objects grasped by fixation
Are all unreal and appear like an illusion.
Not permanent, yet their transiency is able to function.
They are not singular, since a variety emerges and changes.

They are not independent, but follow the karmic deeds.
They are not particles, since partless atoms do not exist.

If they did exist, gross things could not be assembled.
If they had parts, this would contradict the assertion of partlessness.
They are nothing but a nonexistent and false appearance, an
interdependence,
Like dreams, magical illusion, and the reflection of the moon in
water.
Regard them as a city of gandharvas and as a rainbow.

Now follows the practice of the ultimate bodhichitta of knowledge (prajna), which is superior to the conventional bodhichitta of means (upaya). First of all, when closely examining through scriptures and reasoning all the seemingly real external objects grasped by means of fixation on self-entities, there is not even one that is real. They appear as illusory things conjured forth by a magician.

In other words, ordinary worldly people whose minds have not assumed a philosophical view cling to perceived objects as being real and permanent, while the tirthikas, who have adopted an erroneous philosophical view, believe in things being permanent, singular, independent, and so forth. These are, respectively, lack of understanding and misunderstanding.[267]

If something is a perceived object, it follows that it is not permanent because a permanent thing is devoid of action, as in the example of space.

If something is a conditioned object, it follows that it is impermanent because to a deluded mind it functions due to the change of its continuity, as in the example of a seed or a sprout.

If something is a permanent appearance, it follows that it is not singular because perceived things arise and change in manifold ways, as in the example of the different ways the six classes of beings perceive the same water.

It also follows that these manifold ways are in fact devoid of reality because they arise from conditions, as in the example of a rainbow.

If something belongs to the three realms, it follows that it changes involuntarily because of following karma, as in the example of the suffering of change.

If something belongs to karma, it follows that it is ultimately unreal because it cannot be established as being a concrete thing of substance or time, as in the example of something uncompounded.

When explaining this in a more understandable way, all composite things do not last. This is so because a permanent thing cannot possibly change into something else and is therefore nonfunctional, like the nature of space, which is completely unchanging. Composite things are impermanent because their continuity changes in the following instant and therefore function superficially, like the continuity of a flame or a sprout from a seed.

Well, can they be established as having impermanent existence? Such existence also cannot be proven, because both permanence and impermanence being mere words depend upon one another, and so dependent phenomena established through dependency are also unreal. As Phakshab (Nagarjuna) said:

> If a certain thing is established in dependency,
> That is itself also dependent.
> And if the dependent object is to be established,
> Then how can you establish the existence of something
>   dependent?[268]

Things are also not definite in being singular objects. If they were, then since singularity and plurality are contradictory, it would be illogical for things to appear in manifold ways. Just as the same substance of water is perceived as molten metal by a hell-being, as pus and blood by a hungry ghost, as something to drink by an animal, as a utensil by a human being, and as nectar by a god, it changes with and follows the karmic perceptions. This manifoldness is also unreal because the existence of a thing's specific attributes cannot be established when the existence of the singular object itself is not established, just as the existence of the specific attributes of being beautiful and so forth cannot be established when the basis for the special attributes, the child of a barren woman, is not proven to exist. Nagarjuna mentions this:

> All things are devoid of an essence because they change into
> appearing as something else.
> All things are devoid of an essence because they are emptiness.[269]

A so-called creator, such as Brahma, Indra, or Vishnu, who has independent control over the three realms, also does not exist, because if he did, it would be impossible to reverse after having attained peace, and all of them fall back into the three realms, dependent upon their white or black karmic deeds.[270]

Well then, can the existence of karma be truly established? Karma also cannot ultimately be truly established. Nagarjuna has stated:

> When all these phenomena are by nature devoid of coming and
> devoid of going,
> Then how can karmic deeds and the ripening of karmic deeds
> have any reasonable existence?
> Being nonexistent also in the ultimate sense, they have no going
> whatsoever.
> Conventionally, there is the teaching of entering the path as well
> as of the ripening of karmic deeds.[271]

The Shravaka Vaibhashikas,[272] who among the adherents of the Buddhist philosophical schools have partial realization, accept that since all perceived things are unreal although existing conventionally, the partless atom, which is the material finality that forms concrete things, has ultimate existence because it cannot be destroyed by a hammer or the like. As well, they accept that time ultimately exists because the partless moment that is the finality of consciousness cannot be divided by the intellect.[273] As the *Treasury* [*of Abhidharma*] teaches:

> When something can be destroyed, or eliminated by the
>   intellect,
> It will not be perceived by the mind.
> Like a jug or water, it exists conventionally,
> But ultimate existence is different from that.[274]

This position is, however, obscured by the darkness of [unfounded] belief because the atomic particle is not ultimate, since the existence of a partless atom cannot be established. If it could be established, just as partless space intermingles with space, everything would mingle into one spot and therefore be unable to form coarse concrete things. As stated in the *Twenty*:

> Since it is touched at six points,
> The most subtle particle has six parts.
> If these six were a single spot,
> Even a heap would be only the size of one particle.[275]

Since the particles have individual directions and therefore different parts by dividing them into east and so forth, this contradicts the former claim of partlessness. It also contradicts the belief that single particles remain while touching but not fusing with one another. Since it is impossible that particles of light or darkness would not interject between this touching without fusing, if such light or darkness is interjected, particles would fuse together without space in between. If light or darkness cannot be interjected, there would be no space in between, and so this would contradict the former claim.

The forming of time through a stream of instants is also a contradiction. If the former and following instants do not connect with each other, there would be no cause for the following consciousness, and therefore the former would not be a forming agent. If they do connect, everything would become simultaneous when three instants meet at the same time, and consequently an aeon would be nothing but a single moment. Were instants to meet alternately, there would be the former aspect of an instant that had ceased and the second aspect that was present and thus, having become two parts, this would damage the claim of partlessness.

This being so, the acceptance of substantially existent objects of knowledge in fact becomes the claim of an extreme view and is therefore the lowest of the Buddhist viewpoints. Thus they seem to have been taught merely to form a basis for characteristics.

Demonstrated indirectly through this indication, the Sautantrikas accept that all knowable objects are composed of hidden components and have merely imputed existence. The followers of the Mind Only School accept that all phenomena have true existence as being merely the manifestations of mind. They are all nevertheless philosophical schools that are exponents of concreteness, so refute them by means of scriptures and reasoning and enter the Middle Way.[276]

For these reasons, you cannot truly establish the existence of a single one of all the concrete appearances, so they are nonexistent while being perceived. While perceived, they appear falsely and unreal. These perceived appearances are perceptions that merely arise in dependent connection. If the existence of phenomena could truly be established on their own behalf, they would never lose their individual characteristics and therefore not be liable to arise, perish, and so forth. But because they cannot be so established, all phenomena arising in dependent connection can manifest unobstructedly. Emptiness is therefore not hindered by perceived appearances, and perceived appearances are not beyond the seal of emptiness. Nagarjuna declared:

> There exist no phenomena that do not originate in dependency.
> Therefore there exist no phenomena that are not emptiness.

These false manifestations that appear as mere interdependence are like the analogies for illusory nature: see them as a dream, not existing externally except as the manifestations of a confused mind; as a magical illusion, being mistaken for various kinds of appearances from the coincidence of causes meeting with conditions; as the reflection of the moon in water, being present anywhere due to circumstances; as a city of gandharvas, appearing individually without being fixed objects; as a rainbow in the sky, appearing as various colors with no real substance. Regard them in these ways as is taught:

> Like a star, an aberration, or a flame,
> Like a magical illusion, a dew drop, or a water bubble,
> Like a dream, lightning, or a cloud,
> Thus should you regard all conditioned things.[277]

ESTABLISHING THE INNER PERCEIVER AS WELL AS THE INDIVIDUAL SELF TO BE DEVOID OF A SELF-NATURE

The *Lamrim Yeshe Nyingpo* root text says:

> *The mind that observes is also devoid of an ego or a self-entity.*
> *It is neither seen as something different from the aggregates*
> *Nor as identical with these five aggregates.*
> *If the first were true, there would exist some other substance.*
>
> *This is not the case, so were the second to be true,*
> *That would contradict a permanent self, since the aggregates are impermanent.*
> *Therefore, based on the five aggregates,*
> *The self is a mere imputation by the power of ego-clinging.*

Although the outer observed objects possess no true existence, doesn't the inner observer, the mind, truly exist? No, it doesn't. The mind has no existence apart from imputing such an existence upon the perpetuating aggregates and holding the belief in an ego, with the thought "I am!" Since the two kinds of self-entity are not separate from that, neither can their existence be established when examined by correct discriminating knowledge.

When there is a belief in an "I" or a "self" it follows that its existence cannot be ultimately established, because it neither differs from nor is identical with the five aggregates. If, as in the first case, you could prove that there is a separately existing self, there would have to be a sixth aggregate of a substance different from the other five. Since such a knowable object is impossible, it would be like the name of the son of a barren woman. If the self were identical [with the five aggregates], then it would have to be of identical substance and, since the five aggregates have substantial existence while the belief in an "I" has imputed existence, their substances would be contradictory, like the concrete and inconcrete.

Again, to describe this in an easily understandable way: since the self cannot be observed as being some entity that is separate from the gathering of the five aggregates and also cannot be seen as being identical with them, the existence of the self cannot be established. In the first instance, [it is impossible for] the self to have any existence separate from the aggregates, because an additional sixth aggregate would then have to exist, because ego-clinging applies to nothing other than the aggregates. Moreover, as no concrete thing exists separate from the characteristics of the aggregates and, as an inconcrete thing cannot perform a function, the self cannot be established as existing separate from them.

Though the self does not exist separately in that way, can't its existence be established, as in the second case, as identical with the aggregates? No, it cannot, because their characteristics are incompatible. In other words, all the aggregates are conditioned and therefore proven to be impermanent. This is contrary to the self, which is held to be permanent, as in the case of assuming that one knows now what one saw earlier. Furthermore, the aggregates are composed of categories with many divisions, such as forms, sensations, and so

forth, while the self is believed to be singular, as in thinking "I am!"
And finally, the aggregates verifiably depend on arising and perishing,
while the self is obviously experienced to be independent, as in the
thought "I am!" The *Prajnamula* describes this:

> If the self were the aggregates,
> Then it would arise and perish.
> But, if the self is different from the aggregates,
> It would have none of the aggregates' characteristics.[278]

You may now wonder, "Though the self does not exist, its continuity is permanent and can be proven to exist." That is also not the
case. The *Two Truths* says:

> The so-called continuity or instant
> Is false, just like a chain, an army, and so forth.

While in reality possessing not even the slightest existence, the self,
the individual, and so forth, are merely imputations made by the
power of ego-clinging and are simply based upon the gathering of
the five perpetuating aggregates. *Entering the Middle Way* teaches:

> The self does therefore not exist as something other than the
>   aggregates,
> Because it is not held as anything besides the aggregates.[279]

And again, in the same text:

> When uttering such words as "the aggregates are the self,"
> It refers to the gathering of the aggregates and not to their
>   identity.[280]

The word "chariot," for instance, is merely a label given to the
gathering of parts, such as the wheels and the main beam of the char-

iot, while you find no basis for the characteristics of the chariot that is not the parts but the owner of the parts. In the same way, you cannot prove the basis for the so-called self besides the mere belief that the ego is the gathering of the aggregates. This is described in a sutra:

> Just as the name "chariot" is given to the gathering of all the
> parts,
> Similarly, the name "sentient being" is superficially used for the
> aggregates.

ESTABLISHING THE EXAMINING MIND TO BE DEVOID OF A SELF-NATURE

The *Lamrim Yeshe Nyingpo* root text says:

> *As to that which imputes, the past thought has vanished and is*
> *nonexistent.*
> *The future thought has not occurred, and the present thought does*
> *not withstand scrutiny.*

You may now wonder, "When in this way one can neither establish the true existence of the perceived objects nor of the perceiving mind, does the thought itself, that which imputes, really exist?" Does it or does it not possess the components of the three times? If it does not, it follows that since an instant is inconcrete, consequently any existent thought is inconcrete. And, if it does, the past thought previously arisen is nonexistent, having vanished and disappeared. The future one has not yet arisen and does therefore not exist. The present thought cannot examine or show itself, just as the eye cannot see itself and the edge of a sword cannot cut itself. The *Precious Garland (Ratnavali)* states:

> Just as with the end of an instant,
> You should also examine whether it has a beginning and a
> middle.

Similarly, because of examining these three aspects of an instant,
The world does not abide for one moment.[281]

CONCLUDING THE TOPIC OF THE CHAPTER

The *Lamrim Yeshe Nyingpo* root text says:

> *In short, understand the twofold self, the perceiver and the perceived,*
> *To be totally quiescent, like the sky, and devoid of arising,*
> *And also that this nonarising is beyond the domain of conceptual*
> *mind.*
> *Since even the Omniscient Ones find no words for this,*
> *This absence of mental constructs is called the Middle Way.*

To summarize the meaning of what has been explained: the two
kinds of self-entity of fixating on phenomena and the individual person, the perceived object and the perceiving mind, and the all-
ground upon which they are based are all devoid of true existence.
Therefore, you may now wonder whether their existence could be
established as inconcrete, and could they be labeled as such had they
earlier existed as true and concrete and later become unreal? But all
phenomena are by their very nature devoid of any established existence since the beginning. They are, therefore, beyond the extremes
of being existent or nonexistent. According to Saraha:

> Believing in concreteness is being like a cow,
> But believing in inconcreteness is being even more foolish.

The *Prajnamula* concludes:

> For this reason the learned abides
> Neither in existence nor in nonexistence.[282]

Accordingly, when you have understood through scriptures and
reasoning that all things are by their very nature primordially devoid

of arising and, like space, free from the swamp of fabrications, such as existence and nonexistence, and when your mind's activities of fixating on concreteness or inconcreteness have utterly subsided, you will realize that also this natural state of nonarising is inexpressible, inconceivable, and indescribable, and so transcends the realm of names, concepts, and intellect.[283] As the *Bodhicharya Avatara* states:

> When concreteness or inconcreteness
> Does not remain before the intellect,
> At that moment there is no other mental form,
> And so there is utter peace without conceptions.

This natural state cannot be demonstrated through descriptions, and so even the Moons of Speech, who directly perceive and see all objects of knowledge, seem to lack words to describe it when they explain this natural state directly. Thus, this inexpressible state, devoid of the constructs of the eight limits, is the Great Middle, the ultimate summit of the views of Mahayana. It is called "path" because of taking this Great Middle as path.[284]

— 15 —

The Meditation of Ultimate Bodhichitta and Its Result

PRACTICING BY MEANS OF THE MEDITATION

The *Lamrim Yeshe Nyingpo* root text says:

> *Having realized this, rest in equanimity,*
> *Free from conceptual activity, in the state devoid of fixation.*

When you have fully understood this view, the natural state devoid of constructs, and through the reasoning of analyzing the ultimate you have not found any constructed attributes whatsoever, you should then rest in the continuity of discriminating knowledge that has attained a penetrating certainty of the fact of the absence of extremes—free from all kinds of concepts of adhering to extremes, without clinging to anything whatsoever. Rest naturally, devoid of any corrective action by the inferential mind's reasoning, such as clinging to the emptiness of refuting a true or concrete existence, or the like—just as the fire produced from the rubbing stick, as well as its base, naturally vanishes after consuming both pieces of wood. The *Treasury of the Nonarising Jewel* advises:

Do not conceptualize and do not think of anything.
Nonfabrication is itself the treasury of nonarising.

The *Eight Thousand Verses* also states:

This cultivation of transcendent knowledge is to cultivate no
concept whatsoever.

Both the *Ornament of the Sutras* and the *Ornament of Realization*
state harmoniously:

From this there is nothing whatsoever to remove,
Nor even the slightest to add.
Look truly into the true.
To see the true is the total freedom.[285]

Thus one should continuously rest in equanimity. Concerning the
postmeditation state, the *Compendium* says:

I have no such pretense as settling in equanimity or emerging
from it.
And why, because of fully realizing the nature of phenomena.[286]

Accordingly, by having gathered the accumulation of merit to the
best of one's ability with the taste of understanding all phenomena to
be illusory, you will, when perfecting the highest stage of acquain-
tance, attain stability in the samadhis.

LINKING UP BY EXPLAINING THE RESULT

The *Lamrim Yeshe Nyingpo* root text says:

Thoughts then subside, and the natural state of the essence is seen.
Hereby you accomplish the virtues such as the eyes,
superknowledges, and dharani-recall.

The causal vehicle of the paramitas
Is to gradually attain the paths and bhumis.
On the path of fruition, you should still regard
The practice of unified emptiness and compassion as the basis
  of the path.

Having grown accustomed to the meditation in this way, all of the turmoil of conceptual thinking calms down and you are able to remain in your innate nature for as long as you desire, and thus your body and mind become pliable. In the manner of not seeing, you then clearly see and cognize the essence of perfect wakefulness.[287] The *Compendium* says:

Sentient beings exclaim, "I see the sky!"
But examine the meaning of exactly how the sky is seen.
This is how the tathagata describes the way we see phenomena.

The *Short Truth of the Midde Way* says:

The extremely profound sutras state
That not seeing is the true seeing.[288]

This path of the unity of means and knowledge annihilates the two obscurations. Thus you gradually accomplish all the temporary and ultimate qualities, including the five eyes, the six superknowledges, unforgetting recall, unimpeded courageous eloquence, the miraculous power of mastery over wind and mind, and the samadhi of the stream of Dharma. Successively journeying through all the five paths and the ten bhumis, you will attain all their qualities.[289]

In other words, the path of accumulation is to gather the accumulation of virtue conducive to liberation by endeavoring in the two accumulations, such as generosity, from the beginning of arousing bodhichitta up until attaining the wisdom of heat. Of the three levels [of the path of accumulation], one chiefly cultivates the four applications of mindfulness on the lesser path of accumulation, the four right endeavors on the middling, and the four legs of miraculous action on the greater path of accumulation.

Having fully completed the path of accumulation, you experience the four aspects of ascertainment—mundane wisdom resulting from meditation, which corresponds to the realization of the four truths. Thus, because this path "joins" you to the correct realization of the truths, it is called the path of joining.

The four aspects of ascertainment are the following four stages: the heat, which is the omen for perceiving the truths; the summit of mundane samadhi; the acceptance of the profound Dharma; and the stage of supreme mundane attribute. The former two are endowed with the five ruling faculties and the latter two with the five powers. Each of these four can be divided into a greater, middling, and lesser stage so that they then are renowned as the twelve aspects of ascertainment.

At the end of the stage of supreme mundane attributes, you experience the wisdom endowed with the nature of sixteen moments, arrived at by dividing each of the four truths by the cognition, ensuing cognition, acceptance, and ensuing acceptance of the Dharma.[290]

Thus, you relinquish all that is to be discarded through the path of seeing comprised of the three realms, and you see in actuality with the supramundane discriminating knowledge the nature that has not been seen before, the truths of noble beings. This is therefore called the path of seeing, and it is endowed with the seven bodhi-factors.[291]

Beginning from that point, the path of cultivation is so-called because one repeatedly makes oneself grow accustomed to the thatness which was previously realized. This path has the three aspects of higher, middling, and lesser and is endowed with the eightfold path of noble beings.[292]

In this way, when you have perfected the thirty-seven factors conducive to enlightenment comprised of the paths of training, the ultimate wisdom of realization after reaching the end of the path of cultivation and having relinquished all the most subtle discards without exception by means of the vajralike samadhi, that is the path beyond training, also called the path of consummation, and thus you have realized the ten qualities of the stage beyond training.[293]

There is the definite number of ten special levels of complete training in terms of defining "level" or "bhumi" as the basis for the qualities of each of these stages, as well as from the aspect of developing the bhumis above. On the path of seeing, one has attained the first bhumi of the Joyous; one is free from the five kinds of fear and has acquired the twelve times one hundred qualities.[294]

On the three parts of the path of cultivation, journeying from the second to the tenth bhumi, the special qualities of abandonment and realization are increased to a higher and higher degree until they are multiplied one thousand times one billion. On the eighth bhumi, you attain the ten masteries; on the ninth, the four right discriminations; and on the tenth, you receive the empowerment of the great rays of light. Thus you abide in buddhahood, the eleventh bhumi of Universal Illumination.[295]

Each of these bhumis is explained in terms of nine special qualities as elucidated in the root text *Ornament of the Sutras* and elsewhere.

In this way, having summarized the meaning taught in the paramita vehicle of taking the causes as the path, "bodhichitta of emptiness suffused with compassion" is the root of all the teachings. Consequently, also in the Vajra Vehicles of taking the result as the path, you must practice the emptiness of knowledge as united with the great compassion of means as the basis or foundation of the path. For this reason, I will here first of all explain this unity. According to the *Five Stages:*

The one who understands how to engage
In knowledge and compassion as one—
That stage, explained as "unity,"
Is the domain of the buddhas' experience.

The *Vajra Dome* agrees:

> The one who fully trains his mind
> In emptiness inseparable from compassion,
> Will demonstrate the buddhahood
> As well as the Dharma and Sangha.

Moreover, the *Lamp for the Path of Enlightenment* states:

> Knowledge devoid of means as well as means devoid of
> knowledge
> Are in all cases taught to be fetters; therefore do not abandon
> either of the two.

At this point, *Eliminating the Two Extremes* explains the meaning of the causal and resultant vehicles:

> Having fully turned the Dharma Wheel
> Of the causal teachings on applying the cause,
> [The Buddha prophesied] the short path of the resultant
> vehicle.[296]

In general, it is well known that the causal vehicles are so-called because of "being led along by means of this," while the resultant vehicles are so-called because of "being led right here."[297] Thus these terms are defined in the following way, according to the view of the omniscient Longchenpa:

> The causal vehicles are so-called because of accepting a sequence of cause and effect, asserting that buddhahood is attained by increasing the qualities of the nature of the sugata essence, which is merely present as a seed, through the circumstance of the two accumulations. The resultant vehicles are so-called because of asserting that the basis for purification is the [sugata] essence endowed with quali-

ties that are spontaneously present as a natural possession in sentient beings, just as the sun is endowed with rays of light; that the objects of purification are the temporary defilements of the eight collections,[298] like the sky being [temporarily] obscured by clouds; and that one realizes the result of purification, the primordially present nature by means of that which purifies, the paths of ripening and liberation. Besides this, there is no difference in sequence or quality.[299]

The *Two Segments* also asserts:

> All sentient beings are buddhas themselves.
> However, they are obscured by the temporary stains.
> When these are cleared away, they are enlightened.

The *Torch of the Three Ways* describes the difference between the two:

> Though of identical purpose, it is undeluded,
> It has many means and minor hardships,
> And is to be mastered by those of sharp faculties;
> Thus is the vehicle of Mantra especially eminent.

Although these two vehicles, the causal and the resultant, have the identical purpose of ultimate fruition, the Secret Mantra is especially exalted in four ways in traversing the path. The former is deluded by engaging in the outer paramitas and therefore obstructed by not reaching the ultimate even after a long duration. Mantrayana, on the other hand, is undeluded because of being capable of swiftly reaching perfection by means of the inner samadhi of united means and knowledge. The former must for a long time rely on partial and less profound means, such as hardships and vows, in order to purify a single disturbing emotion or to accomplish a single goal. Mantrayana, however, has methods that are both profound and manifold. One easily accomplishes the purpose even by each of the numerous types of development and completion, along with their subsidiary practices.[300]

Through the former you must gain accomplishment with great difficulties, because the means for accomplishing the results in the accordance with the intellectual capacities are scarce. Whereas through Mantrayana, the means corresponding to the special qualities of objects, time, situation, and mental faculties are easy, and even fetters can be transformed into something liberating. Since it is capable of easily attaining the results, it is free from hardships.[301]

The followers of the lesser vehicles are of dull faculties due to not knowing the means, and the paramita followers are of medium faculties because of mistaking the means. Whereas through Mantrayana, one is capable of transforming into enlightenment, by special means, even a karmic deed the engagement in which would otherwise cause rebirth in the lower realms.

In addition, through the former, one engages exclusively in dualistic thinking, accepting and rejecting, while through Mantrayana, one recognizes the world and the beings to be great purity and equality, the superior indivisibility of the two truths, without a perceiver and the perceived; and without accepting and rejecting, one can bring whatever is experienced into the path. For this reason, it is exalted by being for those of sharper faculties. Moreover, many other ways of being exalted, such as the six, seven, or twelve ways, are also explained.[302]

The reason for entering this path is as follows. The victorious ones, considering the remedies, have taught the 84,000 Dharma sections. They can be condensed into the twelve aspects of excellent speech or into the nine gradual vehicles. If they are again condensed, they can be included within the three or four Collections and so forth. In this way, regardless of the number of teachings given, all are steps for the paths of entering into this Unexcelled Yoga.[303]

That is to say, even all the shravakas and pratyekabuddhas who have reached perfection must, due to the great rays of light of the buddhas, at some point emerge from their state of cessation and then enter the Great Vehicle. Also, those who have journeyed to the stage of Great Regent on the tenth bhumi through the bodhisattva vehicle and the Three Outer Tantras of Secret Mantra, still must, for their attainment of the great enlightenment, relinquish from their very root not only the subtle conceptualization that ties one to samsara, but also the tendencies of the three experiences, also known as the habitual tendency of transference.[304] The remedy for relinquishing these tendencies is exactly the self-cognizant wakefulness of the path of the fourth empowerment, the unchanging great bliss of unity, which has not been taught anywhere else than in the Unexcelled Yoga.[305]

Consequently, not only must you eventually enter the path of the Unexcelled Yoga no matter which vehicle door you have entered, but also, the meaning of each lower vehicle is included within the following one. This vehicle of the Unexcelled Yoga is therefore the most eminent, the pinnacle of all the teachings and of all the gradual vehicles. According to the *Guhyagarbha Tantra:*

> This natural essence of secrets
> Has been definitively resolved as being the source
> Of all the Collections (Pitakas) and all the tantras.

Moreover, the *Exposition Tantra* states:

> As for this king of self-cognizance, the realization of the nature
>   of equality,
> Just as all rivers flow into the great ocean,
> All the infinite number of liberations and vehicles
> Are included within these great means of realizing the unexcelled
>   nature.

APPENDICES AND NOTES

DRAWN FROM

Entering the Path of Wisdom

by Jamyang Drakpa,
as recorded by Jokyab Rinpoche
Supplemented with clarifying remarks by
H. H. Dilgo Khyentse Rinpoche,
H. E. Tulku Urgyen Rinpoche,
and Chökyi Nyima Rinpoche

As an auspicious beginning for these appendices, I include the opening poetry from *Entering the Path of Wisdom* by Jokyab Rinpoche, alias Khenpo Pema Trinley Nyingpo.

Padmasambhava, lord of all mandalas,
You embody the wisdom of all the victorious ones in a single
    person,
And Mother Tsogyal, retainer of the secrets, compiler of the
    teachings,[306]
I bow to you by sporting in the dharmadhatu essence of
    awareness and emptiness.

Treasure-revealer Chokgyur Lingpa, emanation of Damdzin,[307]
Omniscient Do-ngak Lingpa, gentle King Trisong Deutsen,[308]
And Tennyi Yungdrung Lingpa, Vairochana;[309]
Three vajra masters, I venerate you at the crown of my head.

I revere as lords of the family all my gracious masters
Who found the treasury of oral instructions,
Conveyed to them, from mouth to ear, as a prophesied
    transmission,
And with deep joy I shall here gather the secret nectar of their
    words.

APPENDIX 1

The Six Limits and Four Modes

About these six limits and four modes, the *Galpo Tantra* says:

> There are six types of limit for detailed explanations:
> Expedient meaning, definitive meaning, and implied
>   exposition,
> The not implied and the literal,
> And explained in a not literal way.[310]

1. The expedient meaning. One vajra word demonstrates different meanings to two disciples—one who directly has and one who has not the fortune for the genuinely true, so that for the one who has not, the Victorious One will conceal it and, for instance, teach the subsidiary aspects of the development stage in order to lead the disciple to the real; that is teaching according to the expedient meaning.

2. The definitive meaning has two aspects: The "true definition" is in conformity with the development stage as taught in the *Vajra Wisdom Scripture,* as for instance that camphor is semen and so forth. The "true innate" is the continuity of cause, the natural and intrinsic belonging to the completion stage. That which teaches the meaning of these two is the definitive meaning.

3. The implied exposition. For those who desire the most emi-

nent, he teaches thatness; but in order to prevent them from practicing without a teacher, he speaks with contradictory sentences by means of what is despised by righteous worldly people, such as "You shall kill the living!" That is implied exposition. To kill the living implies stopping the wind of karma, and the contradictory sentences are for the purpose of converting slaughters and so forth. Moreover, implied exposition is what should be understood dependent upon the implied expressed meaning phrased in contradictory sentences, the same point of development and completion by means of different vajra words.

4. The not-implied exposition is what by means of the directly expressing teachings does not depend upon the implied expressed meaning. That is to say, the exposition that is not implied is to clearly teach that the nature of the phenomena of the development stage is empty and luminous and so forth to the people whose capacity for the implied exposition is dull.

5. The literal is the terminology and meaning taught with words universally known in mundane treatises and so forth and which is taught in conformity with the lower tantras, the extensive engagement in rituals of various activities, such as external mandalas, fire puja, torma offering, and so forth.

6. The not literal is what is not renowned in the mundane treatises and is phrased in the symbolism of the secret language of the tathagatas, such as the names of the ten winds being kotakhya and so forth—kotawa, kota, kotabashca, kotaraga, kolakhya, kolawa, kola, kolabashca, and kolasta—as well as the *Guhyagarbha Tantra* calling union and liberation "Ali Kali." These six are known as the six limits because all the secret words and meanings do not transcend them.

As for the four modes, the *Galpo Tantra* says:

I will teach to you the four modes of exposition.
There are the literal, the general, the hidden, and the ultimate.

1. The literal meaning is the explanation engaging only in the word-for-word meaning by means of the inflections and particles and

so on, and is stated in terms of the authoritative scriptures on grammar. The literal meanings are also known as the word-for-word meaning.

2. The general meaning has two aspects: the general meaning according to the sutras and the general meaning according to the development stage. First, to prevent regret of having entered the Sutra system due to the statement:

> One does not attain accomplishment
> Though endless vows of asceticism have been taught.
> But by relying on all the desirable objects
> One quickly attains accomplishment.

If one thus regrets, considering it to be unworthy to have entered the Sutra system or the Kriya or Charya systems prior to entering this easy and swift path of Inner Mantrayana, this path is not to be entered without practicing the Sutra system, such as renunciation for samsara and arousing the wish of bodhichitta, and they are all steps for this path. The same text therefore says:

> Although the levels have been stated,
> They are the path leading to the essence of secrets.

One sutra as well says:

> For the one who possesses the great means,
> The disturbing emotions become factors of enlightenment.

Thus, if one has sharp faculties and possesses special ingenuity, one single immense act of accumulation consummates the accumulation of many aeons. Since also the sutras maintain such an easy and swift path, it is called the general meaning.

Second, preventing the regret of having entered the Mantrayana system: The Buddha taught such topics as bathing, cleanliness, fasting practice, and so forth in the Sutra, Kriya, and Charya systems, so toward this [the system of the Three Inner Tantras], one may feel remorse, thinking that such practices are prohibited and that the Dharma practices, which are like pigs and dogs, making offering to the deities with feces, semen, and blood and also eating those things oneself, as well as asserting what harms, such as "union and liberation," to be a spiritual practice are nothing but the teachings of the tirthikas. These types of general meaning are therefore taught:

A. The general meaning for people of dull faculties is to teach that the bathing and cleanliness according to the systems of the tirthikas that lack the special ingenuity are prohibited; but the bathing and so forth that purify evil deeds and obscurations are also accepted here [in the inner tantras]. The eating of feces and so forth is practiced as the yoga of the thatness which is the one taste of sense object and faculty.

B. The general meaning for people of sharp faculties. The Kriya Tantra entitled *Arrangement of the Three Samayas* teaches that one attains accomplishment without adhering to asceticism and so forth; one does not realize the meaning of the Dharma without abandoning the clinging to purity and impurity; it is futile to cling to cleanliness and feel aversion toward dirt. Through that, one does not attain the wisdom of equality, so to practice same taste in order to abandon attachment is also accepted in the Sutra, Kriya, and Charya systems. It is permissible to engage in union and liberation with a virtuous attitude, such as killing Spear-Wielding Criminal, having intercourse with the chieftain's daughter, and so forth; one will not be tainted by infractions but accumulate boundless merit.[311] Since these things are common to all the [bodhisattva] trainings, they are called "general meaning."

C. The general meaning according to the development stage is, for instance, to explain the outer or general meaning of the development stage by teaching the people who are unsuited for the concealed teachings on passion to visualize the subtle emblems of the five families at the tip of one's "superficial nose" with statements such as:

> Always contemplate at the tip of your nose
> The precious gems of five colors.

Moreover, this includes all that is connected to the development stage, such as visualizing the basis, the celestial palace; and the based, the deities. Since that training is common to both development and completion, it is the general meaning.

3. The hidden meaning. Teaching plainly the rituals for the action seal (karmamudra) and union, the male and female yoga practitioners' engagement in the passion of intercourse, is unseemly and so inappropriate to express in verse. Therefore, this is hidden and is the concealed teachings on passion. The concealment of the relative is the completion stage of the channels, winds, and essences, the self-consecration, and so forth. Generally speaking, they are concealed because they are like the essence placed in the center of the two extremes.

The meaning of the higher, medium, and lower essence is as follows: According to the stages of illusory body, the higher essence covered by the thin manifest defilements is thus the concealment for realizing the relative truth. The cause of that, the wisdoms of appearance, increase, and attainment, is the medium essence covered by medium defilements. The cause of that, the secluded mind called vajra mind, the secluded speech called vajra speech, and the secluded body called vajra body, is the essence of the great defilement, the lesser natural state, and is therefore concealed. This explanation is also the explanation of concealment. In brief there are two aspects: the hidden and the concealed.

4. The ultimate meaning is the ultimate that pervades all of them—the completion stage of luminosity is the ultimate of the path, while the stage of the unity of the two truths is the ultimate of fruition. To explain these is the ultimate explanation. Since all four

modes must explain one single vajra word based on different mental capacities, it is the ultimate because it reaches to the end of all remaining meaning to be expressed about that word.

Again, [the four modes are]: to explain just in general the word-for-word meaning by means of the sense, grammar, and implication of the term; the general intent common to the sutras; the hidden and uncommon profound meaning of the Unexcelled (Anuttara); and in the manner of combining the ultimate to the unified level of training and beyond training.

Chagmey Rinpoche's statement that each word of the tantras should be understood according to the literal meaning, general meaning, direct meaning, and indirect meaning corresponds fairly well to what is meant here.

Without possessing these oral instructions, one will not be able to gain true knowledge, no matter how detailed the analysis of one's reflection may be. But when possessing the oral instructions, one will give rise to the flawless knowledge resulting from reflection when examining the ways of the sutras and tantras.

APPENDIX 2

The Four Noble Truths

The four truths are the truth of suffering, of origin, of the cessation, and of the path. There are twelve aspects when the four truths are multiplied by three each:

The truth of suffering is the vessel and its contents [the world and the beings]. The truth of origin is the karmas and disturbing emotions. The truth of cessation is the quality of having relinquished both the karmas and disturbing emotions along with their effects. The truth of the path is the paths and bhumis.

1. Describing their substance or essence: the truth of suffering is like a sickness, the truth of origin is the cause of the sickness, the truth of cessation is like having recovered from the sickness, and the truth of the path is like following a cure for the sickness.

2. Describing their functions: the truth of suffering, which is like a sickness, is what should be acknowledged; the truth of origin, which is like the cause of the sickness, is what should be relinquished; the truth of cessation, which is like having recovered from the sickness, is what should be realized; and the truth of the path, which is like a medicine, is what should be applied in one's being.

3. Describing the result: After having acknowledged the truth of suffering, which is like a sickness, it is not something to acknowledge again. After having relinquished the truth of origin, which is like the cause of the sickness, it is not something to relinquish again. After

having realized the truth of cessation, which is like having recovered from the sickness, it is not something to realize again. After having applied in one's being the truth of the path, which is like a medicine, it is not something to apply again.

The aspect of samsaric existence [the state of affliction] is two: the suffering [the effect of samsara] and the origin [the cause of samsara]. The aspect of peace and perfection is two: the cessation [the effect of nirvana] and the path [the cause of nirvana].

The sixteen aspects of the four truths:

Impermanence, suffering, emptiness, and selflessness.
Cause, origin, production, and condition.
Cessation, peace, excellence, and deliverance.
Path, knowledge, accomplishment, and liberating.

The four aspects of the truth of suffering: All composite things are impermanent. All samsaric phenomena are suffering. All outer phenomena are emptiness. All inner phenomena are devoid of a self-entity.

The four aspects of the truth of origin: Ego-clinging is the cause because it is the root of all suffering. It is the origin because from it all samsaric suffering arises. It is production because this forceful suffering produces immediate pain. It is the connecting condition because of experiencing suffering.

The four aspects of cessation: It is cessation because all causes and effects of suffering have ceased. It is peace because all the disturbing emotions of delusion have subsided. It is excellence because it is the most sublime and eminent quality. It is deliverance because it does not reverse and is definitive liberation from samsara.

The four aspects of the truth of the path: It is the path because it progresses higher and higher. It is knowledge because it serves as the antidote to the disturbing emotions. It is accomplishment because it is genuine achievement. It is liberating because it leads to perpetual emancipation and nirvana.

The *Uttaratantra* says:

> The sickness should be acknowledged and the cause of the
> sickness relinquished.
> While the medicine should be applied in order to attain the state
> of ease.
> Likewise, the suffering, its cause, its cessation, and the path
> Should be acknowledged, relinquished, realized, and applied.

APPENDIX 3

The Four Dhyanas and Formless States

The meaning of this, from the first dhyana to the fourth, is as follows. On the preparatory stage only the seven types of attention are important. The seven types of attention are, in summary: the attentions of characteristics, interest, seclusion, delight, discernment, basis of application, and result.

These seven types of attention are successively:

1. The attention that fully discriminates characteristics is, taking the example of the first dhyana, to focus the mind inwardly and put effort into fully training in that and then to exert oneself in developing the samadhi of the first dhyana, by means of the learning, reflection, and meditation of, first, regarding the Realm of Desire as being coarse because it has much pain and has many flaws, such as discomposure and so forth and, next, regarding the first dhyana as opposed to that, namely as having a pacified form.

2. The attention resulting from interest is, having trained in the former by means of the knowledge resulting from meditation, to give rise to the training in the samadhi of the first dhyana, which is beyond learning and reflection.

3. The attention resulting from total seclusion is, again after having cultivated as before, to give rise to the remedy for discarding, by means of the path of cultivation, the major discards of the Realm of

Desire, and then discarding the manifest disturbing emotions of the Realm of Desire.

4. The attention of taking delight is, by means of the lesser delight and bliss resulting from complete seclusion, that one delights in discarding what is coarse, and after seeing that as a benefit one keeps from time to time the attention of great delight. This will relinquish the medium disturbing emotions of the Realm of Desire.

5. The attention of discernment is, after having in this way relinquished most of the disturbing emotions with their remedies, to give rise to the notion "Are all the disturbing emotions not relinquished?" and then to apply the attention of discernment corresponding to the arising of disturbing emotions, in order to examine whether or not disturbing emotions arise.

6. The attention of the basis of application is, when examining in that way and seeing that disturbing emotions are arising, to give rise in one's being to the remedies against the lesser disturbing emotions of the Realm of Desire by means of cultivating the aspects of the pacified and the coarse as before.

7. The attention of the result of the basis of application is, by having cultivated the path above and what follows it, to apply the attention of experiencing their results.

In this way, the first dhyana and from the second up to the summit of existence are accomplished by means of the seven types of attention, regarding them [the dhyanas] as having the aspects of being pacified or coarse.

The individual path of the first attention is its *path of joining*. The three that are the attentions of complete seclusion, of taking delight, and of the basis of application are its *uninterrupted path*. The attention of discernment is its *special path*. And the attention of the result of application is its *path of liberation*.

The three that are the attentions of complete seclusion, of taking delight, and of the basis of application are lesser, medium, and greater aspects and thus are successively remedies against the lesser, medium, and greater disturbing emotions.

The capable preparatory stage is the seven types of attention in addition to the basis of the nine means of mental stillness.

Both the ordinary and special main part are as will be explained below.

It is taught that the mundane vipashyana should be accomplished by means of the seven types of attention. This means that the shamatha of the meditation state is the nine methods of mental stillness, and the vipashyana of the postmeditation state is the seven types of attention. By means of these two aspects, the causes and effects of all the dhyanas will arise.

The first dhyana is a state with both concept and discernment. The second dhyana is a state without concept but with just discernment. The third dhyana is a state without delight but with bliss. The fourth dhyana is a state of equanimity.

The four states of formless spheres are: the state of the sphere of infinite space, the sphere of infinite consciousness, the sphere of nothing whatsoever, and the sphere of neither presence nor absence, which is also called the sphere of neither absence of conception nor presence of conception.

The four states of formless spheres are:

1. The serenity of the sphere of infinite space is to have attained and not lapsed from the mental state of the fourth dhyana and, in addition, that the three of form [such as square and so forth], touch [of what is obstructible], and visual appearances [of white, yellow, and so forth] are blocked, and thus one has the complete meditation of thinking, "All phenomena are infinite, like space!"

2. The serenity of the sphere of infinite consciousness is, in addition to that, to have the complete meditation of thinking, "Just like space is infinite, consciousness is also infinite!"

3. The serenity of the sphere of nothing whatsoever is, after seeing that both of these have conceptual attributes, to have the

complete meditation of thinking, "There is nothing whatsoever to apprehend!"

4. The serenity of the sphere of neither absence of conception nor presence of conception is, after seeing that the three of them have conceptual attributes, to have the complete meditation of thinking, "Coarse conceptions are absent, and subtle conceptions are not absent!" This is the ultimate path of the summit of existence.

By means of having cultivated the causes, the dhyanas of serenity, one attains their result, the dhyanas of rebirth. For that, the eight aspects of the preparatory stage for the dhyanas of serenity explained above are the seven types of attention, in addition to the basis of the nine means of mental stillness—eight altogether—and these are preliminary meditations.

The eight aspects of the main stage of the dhyanas are the eight from the state with both concept and discernment to the state with neither absence nor presence of conception.

The special stage of dhyana is the perfection of the individual stages.

The results, the dhyanas of rebirth, are the gods of the seventeen abodes of the Realm of Form comprised of the Four Dhyana Realms. One is reborn within the Three Brahma Abodes in the First Dhyana Realm by cultivating the four immeasurables and the firelike concept and discernment. Being further accustomed to these states, one is reborn in the Three Abodes of Radiance within the Second Dhyana Realm, with its waterlike joy and bliss. Being further accustomed to these states, one is reborn in the Three Abodes of Goodness within the Third Dhyana Realm, with its windlike inhaling and exhaling of breath. Being further accustomed to these states, one is reborn in either of the three flawless abodes within the Fourth Dhyana Realm—Cloudless Light and so forth. By increasing an undefiled state by meditating on the fourth dhyana, one takes rebirth within the Five Pure Abodes, depending upon whether this cultivation is lesser, medium, great, greater, or extremely great.

The paramita teachings mention seventeen abodes, while some

other sources assert that there are eighteen. Nevertheless, the cause for taking rebirth as a long-living, conceptionless god stems from cultivating a conceptionless serenity after the third dhyana because of fixating on the cessation of notions and feelings as being nirvana. This abode is said to be situated near the god realm of Great Fruit, like a retreat place from a village, and is therefore not counted as a separate abode.

The abodes known as Immense Vista and Sublime Vision are held to be but different names for the same place, and thus it is also accepted that there are Sixteen Abodes of the Realm of Form.

The Formless Realm contains the gods in the four states of formless spheres.

APPENDIX 4

The Sugata Essence

In the context of the Three Turnings of the Wheel of Dharma, the First Wheel teaches emptiness indirectly and the latter two directly. That is to say, the First Dharma Wheel covers the vehicles of shravakas and pratyekabuddhas, as well as the philosophical schools of Vaibhashika and Sautrantika, while the Middle and Final Dharma Wheels cover the vehicle of bodhisattvas as well as the philosophical schools of Mind Only and the Middle Way. Adding these earlier and later schools together, they are known as the Four Philosophical Schools.

First, the basic position of the Vaibhashika School is that existence is the five aggregates and that the articles of existence are four: dwelling place, food, clothing, and medicine. They regard the noble potential as being the mental state of contentment that is detached from existence and the articles of existence.

Second, the proponents of Sautrantika regard the noble potential as being a mental seed, the potential for undefiled wisdom to arise.

Third, the Mind Only followers regard the noble potential to be a potential for developing the undefiled qualities, which is present in one's mental continuum since the beginning and which is a natural possession.

These three schools are systems that regard the sugata essence as being a conditioned phenomenon and are therefore known as systems that are Proponents of Concrete Existence.

Fourth, the followers of the Middle Way are for the most part alike in regarding the suchness as being endowed with impurity, although there are indeed many different ways in which they define that. Here, according to the uncommon Mahayana system, the mind-essence that is naturally pure since the beginning, the all-pervasive essence that is unobstructed emptiness and cognizance, the nature that is present without change or alteration, is called *sugata essence* in all the sutras of definitive meaning. The *Uttaratantra* says further:

> Because the body of complete buddhahood is all-pervasive,
> Because the suchness is indivisible,
> And because of possessing the potential,
> All beings constantly have the buddha essence.

By means of these three reasons, Maitreya taught that all sentient beings possess the sugata essence and furthermore established that through nine analogies with nine meanings. The nine analogies are, from the same text:

> Like a buddha statue within a lotus, honey in a beehive,
> A kernel within a husk, gold within filth,
> A treasure in the ground, the fruit of a bamboo shoot,
> A buddha image within tattered rags,
> A king in the womb of an inferior woman,
> A precious image covered in earth;
> Similarly this potential is present within all beings
> Who are obscured by the temporary stains of disturbing
>   emotions.

The same text states further:

> The meaning of this ultimate dharmadhatu space should be
>   known
> Through its essence, cause, result, function, endowments,

Its approach, phases, and all-pervasiveness,
And that it is forever unchanging and never separated from its
qualities.

This has been extensively explained by the ten presentations of the
intended meaning of the sutras.

At the time of the First Dharma Wheel, the seed of the Second
Dharma Wheel is present by stating simply the word "unconstructed" such as in the verse:[312]

I have found a nectarlike truth,
Profound, tranquil, unconstructed, luminous, and
unconditioned,
But whomever I teach, there is no one who will understand,
So I shall remain silent in the forest.

At the Second Turning of the Wheel of Dharma, numerous seeds
of the Final Dharma Wheel are present through such statements as:

Mind is devoid of mind because the nature of mind is
luminous.[313]

and,

It is not empty, it is not not empty, [and so forth].

The Final Turning of the Wheel of Dharma explains with great
clarity the entire meaning taught in the Unexcelled Tantras of Mantrayana, using such words as pure, crystal clear and luminous, or sublime purity, bliss, identity, and permanence.

The term "sugata essence" applies to the fact that the essence
mind, which is present as the indivisibility of the [two] truths, is itself
the identity of buddhahood. The term "naturally present potential"
applies to the essence of mind, which is present as the unobstructed

potential for the qualities of dharmakaya arising from its empty aspect and the qualities of rupakaya arising from its manifest aspect. It is also called "all-ground wisdom" because of being the ground from which both samsara and nirvana arise, and it is called "defiled suchness" because of being linked to defilement while in the state of a sentient being.

The *Three Stages* further explains:

> It is called "ground" because without exception it is the source
> Of all phenomena of the two denominations.[314]

The *Sutra of the Dense Array* states:

> The stainless all-ground will through merit
> Turn into the tathagata.

The *Scripture of the Compendium of Knowledge* says:

> It is courageous as it is the all-ground, the space of all.
> The vajra essence is extremely courageous.
> Courageous mind is the space of all buddhas.
> The courageous vajra mind is suchness.[315]

Furthermore, the *Uttaratantra* states:

> This potential is devoid of the temporary [defilements]
> Which bear the mark of being discardable.
> But it is not empty of the unsurpassable qualities,
> Which bear the mark of being intrinsic.

APPENDIX 5

Padmakara and the Four Vidyadhara Levels

The Second Buddha, Padmasambhava, should be linked to how the four vidyadhara levels of the path are attained. That is to say, he was born in the Milky Lake in the southwestern direction and became the adopted son of the king of Uddiyana. After renouncing the kingdom, he practiced in the eight charnel grounds headed by Cool Grove (Sitavana) and, at that time, manifested the vidyadhara level of Full Maturation.[316]

Although he was burned alive by the king of Sahor, he was unharmed and, transforming the mass of fire into a lake, he established the kingdom in the Dharma. Doing life sadhana in Maratika Cave with Mandarava, his consort for the path of longevity, he received the empowerment of immortality from Amitayus and at that time manifested the vidyadhara level of Life Mastery.

The levels of Full Maturation and Life Mastery both belong to the path of seeing.

When practicing the Vishuddha Essence of Great Bliss together with the Nepalese Shakya Devi at Yangleshö in Nepal, he manifested the vidyadhara level of Mahamudra, which belongs to the path of cultivation. When invited by the Tibetan king, he resided in the manner of a mahamudra vidyadhara on the path of cultivation.

179

Finally, when he departed for the land of rakshasas and resided as the chief of the gathering of vidyadharas, dakas, and dakinis in the Palace of Lotus Light, he manifested as abiding on the level of the Regent of Vajradhara, the vidyadhara level of Spontaneous Presence of the path of consummation, where his realization equals the Lords of the Three Families. This is the oral tradition according to the teachings of Jamyang Khyentse Wangpo. At this point, it is necessary to explain a suitable length of Guru Rinpoche's life story, combined with what is being expounded here.[317]

APPENDIX 6

Shakyamuni's Prophecy about Buddhism in Tibet

Flourishing in the Noble Land in the past, the teachings of the Buddha—the Three Collections, which are the Dharma of Statements, and the Three Trainings, which are the Dharma of Realization—were prophesied to spread further and further north. This is stated in the *Sutra of Prajnaparamita in Eight Thousand Verses:*

"Shariputra, later on these sutras endowed with the six paramitas, after the Tathagata has passed away, at the time when the sacred Dharma of the Vinaya teachings is being destroyed, will appear from the south when their essence is re-obtained. From the south they will appear in Baratani. From Baratani, they will appear in the north. Shariputra, at that time, the ones who memorize this Prajnaparamita, who retain it, read it, master it, read it aloud, teach it, explain it, give the reading transmission of it, make it their daily recitation, or even make it into a scripture and keep it, such noble sons or daughters will be considered by the Tathagata. They are known by the Tathagata. Shariputra, they are blessed by the Tathagata. Shariputra, they are perceived by the Tathagata. Shariputra, they are seen by the Tathagata with his buddha eye."

Shariputra asked, "Blessed One, will this profound Prajnaparamita spread to the lands in the north and the areas in the north in the future times later on?"

The Blessed One said, "Shariputra, in the lands in the north and the areas in the north, the ones who listen to this profound Prajna-paramita and make this profound Prajnaparamita their practice will make it spread. Shariputra, the bodhisattva mahasattvas who listen to this profound Prajnaparamita, write it down, memorize it, retain it, read it, master it, read it aloud, teach it, explain it, give the reading transmission of it, make it their daily recitation, train in suchness, cultivate suchness, or make suchness their practice, are suitable to enter perfectly the vehicle before long."

Shariputra asked, "Blessed One, in the lands in the north and the areas in the north, will there be few or even numerous bodhisattva mahasattvas who will listen to this profound Prajnaparamita, write it down, memorize it, retain it, read it, master it, read it aloud, teach it, explain it, give the reading transmission of it, make it their daily recitation, train in suchness, cultivate suchness, or make suchness their practice?"

The Blessed One said, "Shariputra, in the lands in the north and the areas in the north, there will be many and extremely numerous bodhisattva mahasattvas."

APPENDIX 7

The Five Aggregates

The divisions of the five aggregates are as follows:

1. The aggregate of consciousnesses, defined as the fully cognizing of objects.
2. The aggregate of forms, defined as physical forms.
3. The aggregate of sensations, defined as the experiencing of what is pleasant, painful, and neutral.
4. The aggregate of conceptions, defined as the apprehending of the concreteness of things and so forth (as attributes).
5. The aggregate of formations, defined as the fully forming [of attitudes] in regard to objects.

I. The aggregate of consciousnesses can be divided into eight:

1. The all-ground consciousness, like the pure surface of a mirror, is cognition that does not reach out toward an object, but forms the basis for cognition to take place.
2. The mind consciousness has as the object a general mental image and is the subsequent intellect that examines the object.
3. The disturbed-mind consciousness forms the cognitions that accept or reject.
4-8. The five sense consciousnesses are the five nonconceptual cognitions perceiving visual form and so forth.

That is to say, the five sense consciousnesses are nonconceptual in terms of seeing, hearing, touching, tasting, and smelling. The mind consciousness knows them individually, and the disturbed-mind consciousness accepts or rejects them. The five sense consciousnesses and the mind consciousness alone do not accumulate karma; karma is accumulated in the all-ground by the disturbed mind consciousness.

This all-ground is the basis for all of them and is nonconceptual as well as neutral. For instance, it is like the moment of consciousness resting in itself without examining anything and also without clear cognizance.

The all-ground consciousness is the moment of consciousness that is clearly cognizant, but not actively involved in an object.

The five sense consciousnesses are the clear perceptions of the objects.

The mind consciousness is merely the apprehending that can link outside and inside together.

The disturbed-mind consciousness is what gives rise to accepting and rejecting.

II. The aggregate of sensations has three types: feeling pleasure toward pleasant objects, feeling pain toward the unpleasant, and feeling indifferent toward the neutral.

III. The aggregate of conceptions has three types: engagement in an object that is vast, small, or intermediate.

IV. The aggregate of formations has the fifty-one mental states that are concurrent formations:

1–5. The five ever-present mental states are contact, attention, sensation, conception, and attraction.
6–10. The five object-determining mental states are adherence, intention, recollection, concentration, and discrimination.
11–21. The eleven virtuous mental states are faith, conscience, shame, conscientiousness, equanimity, commiseration, exertion, pliancy, nonattachment, nonaggression, and nondelusion.

22–27. The six root disturbances are attachment, anger, arrogance, ignorance, belief of the transitory collection, and doubt.

28–47. The twenty subsidiary disturbances are envy, stinginess, hypocrisy, pretense, self-infatuation, lethargy, excitement, lack of faith, laziness, distraction, heedlessness, forgetfulness, nonattentiveness, hostility, lack of conscience, shamelessness, fury, resentment, concealment, and spite.

48–51. The four variable mental states are regret, sleep, concept, and discernment.

Among them, the forty-nine excepting sensation and conception and the nonconcurrent formations, such as names and attributes, are what perform the function of producing samsara and nirvana.

The nonconcurrent formations that are neither matter nor cognition are: acquisition, serenity of cessation, conceptionless serenity, nonconception, life faculty, birth, aging, subsistence, impermanence, group of names, of words, and of letters, regular sequence, definitive distinctness, connection, link, number, sequence, location, time, and gathering.

V. The aggregate of forms can be divided into fifteen:

1–4. The four causal forms, which are the four elements of earth, water, fire, and wind.

5–9. The five sense objects of visual form, sound, smell, taste, and texture.

10–14. The five sense faculties of eye, ear, nose, tongue, and body.

15. Imperceptible form.

Imperceptible forms are five: form of particles, spatial form, form resulting from a fully taken promise, imagined form, and mastered form.

APPENDIX 8

Establishing the Basis
for Beginning the Teaching[318]

At that time, possessed of the five perfections such as teacher, retinue, and so forth, and on the occasion of intending to teach the stages of the path and to show the ripening and liberating Dharma doors, the basis for commencing the teaching is stated as follows.

When the Abbot, the Master, and the Dharma King were assembled, the moment had come for the ripening of the final result of actions conditioned by an impure intention, caused by perverted aspirations made through many series of former lifetimes.[319] These were expressed as the hostile and evil-minded ministers, such as Lhagong Lupal and others, and the Dharma King Trisong Deutsen's Queen Margyenma, the mother of the three princes, engaging through their three doors in various kinds of perverted and unwholesome thoughts and deeds due to these perverted causes and conditions.

In the presence of the great Dharma king and ruler of Tibet, they, the queen, and so forth, said the following words:

> This sorcerer and master of various illusions, a savage from the barbaric borderland of Mön who is adept in evil spells, has deceived the mind of you, the king Trisong Deutsen, who rules over the people

of Tibet, with all the kinds of deceit of his dishonest character, different types of trickery to fool others' minds, and various dazzling optical illusions. At worst, he will deprive you of your dear life. Second to that, he will rob you of all the kingdom, of both religious and secular power. At the least, if unable to do that much, he will make the people rise up in revolt against Your Majesty by spreading divisive slander between the ruling king, your subject ministers, and the governed queens. He should, therefore, before that happens, be thrown in the river Tsangpo before the very eyes of and directly perceived by the king, ministers, queens, and everyone else in the country.

As they repeatedly insisted in such a way, the king, Manjushri incarnate, became saddened with overwhelming compassion and related in detail to Guru Rinpoche of Uddiyana the story of what had earlier happened. "As a method for taming them, what will you yourself do about this type of perverted thought and deed?" he asked. Through the power of compassion, tears streamed forth, like the flow of a river, from his eyes, his wind (prana) reversed, and for a short while he fell unconscious, into a faint, from the intense fervor of devotion in thought, word, and deed. When he regained his senses after a few moments had passed, the great Guru Rinpoche laughed, and with a beaming smile on his face adorned with the major and minor marks, he said with his vajra speech in the utterly fearless tone of voice of a roaring lion:

Great king, you need not feel even the slightest bit disheartened about this story you have related to me. Formerly, Garab Wangchuk, who is the Mara of the gods in the Realm of Desire, the evil-minded Devadatta, and the six teachers of heretics, such as Kuntugyu Naglha Putra and others, also tried to compete with and harm our Teacher, the truly perfected Buddha Shakyamuni, but rather than causing even the most minute injury to the Three Jewels—the Buddha, Dharma, and Sangha—they could only reveal the example of his supreme enlightened virtues of having perfected abandonment and realization.[320] Likewise, as in that example, since within my mind I have attained mastery over the wisdom of the expression of awareness, I can outwardly transform all of the phenomenal world into whatever I desire. And since I have accomplished the indestructible vajra form of light, the unconditioned great transformation of the rainbow body, the four elements of earth and so forth definitely cannot inflict the least harm on me, such as burying me underneath the earth or the like. Even if all the three realms—the Realm of Desire, the Realm of Form, and the Realm of Formlessness—were to rise up simultaneously as an enemy toward me, Padmakara, the pandita of all the panditas and siddhas of the Noble Lands headed by Uddiyana and the person who is the successor of all, with no exception, the activities and qualities of the fathers, the victorious ones, and their spiritual sons, the bodhisattvas of the three times of past, present, and future; they will only help in revealing my supreme displays of the miraculous powers of the three secrets, and it is needless to mention that they would surely not find the slightest opportunity to cause me harm or even shake a fraction of the tip of my clockwise-coiled hair, an aspect of the major and minor marks of the body.

When Guru Rinpoche had spoken to the king in this way, the great king, who was deeply honored by the vassal kings of the border lands, felt even further deep devotion and rejoiced delightedly in his virtuous greatness. He prostrated respectfully numerous times and made this supplication in verse:

> Amazing, how wonderful, supreme nirmanakaya Guru Rinpoche! There is never at any time deception in whatever unfailing vajra words you utter with your voice, since you are present as the embodiment of the body, speech, and mind of all the root and lineage masters without exception, the great lord who has the nature of encompassing the encompassed, the ocean of yidams of the tantras, and since you are the compassionate chief of all the assemblies of the families of wisdom, action, and mundane dakinis.
> Please humble, daunt, and subdue the group of evil-minded min-

isters with malevolent karma and aspirations, thoughts, and deeds, by the inconceivable miraculous power over various skillful means of compassionate kindness for those to be tamed. And so, please do not withhold your miraculous powers in order that we, the king, subjects, and so forth, the assembled retinue of your devoted disciples, may rejoice in your deeds and be greatly inspired by your life example, and in order that the precious doctrine of the Three Jewels—the perfect Buddha, the Dharma he taught orally, and his retinue of listeners, the Sangha followers—may flourish further and further.

Since the king respectfully supplicated him in this way, Guru [Rinpoche] quite joyfully promised in his melodious tone of voice, "I will do that in accordance with the wishes of Your Majesty!" And in the center of the nine regions of Tibet and Kham, in the courtyard of Golden Orphan Temple among the three outer temples of the queens at Glorious Samye, which is rich with the splendor of vessels and contents [shrine halls and statues], he let his mind enter the samadhi that tames all the hordes of Mara, among his mastery over countless samadhis.[321]

During this time, in the middle of the great courtyard amidst his gathered retinue—learned panditas such as Vimalamitra, bilingual translators such as Vairochana, monks who had renounced samsara such as Namkhai Nyingpo, mantrikas who had reached perfection in the two stages such as Dorje Düdjom, the king such as Trisong Deutsen who was ruler of the two systems,[322] advice-giving ministers such as Pema Gungtsen of Gö, queens who are the source of the monarchy, and, as well, numerous common subjects—the precious and great guru, while remaining seated on his throne, performed in actuality a multitude of billions of, for a mundane person, unfathomable and miraculous displays to tame suitable beings with the methods that correspond to their needs, such as sometimes letting his body disappear and reappear, turning into many and into a multitude; at times becoming a blazing fire of wisdom, letting water issue forth;

making the earth quake in the sixfold ways; manifesting yidams with the nine peaceful expressions and herukas endowed with the nine wrathful moods—deities together with their assemblages of chief figures with many retinues; manifesting sounds with his audible and yet empty voice, filling boundlessly the expanse of the sky with the thousandfold thunderlike sounds of secret mantras, knowledge mantras, and dharani mantras all resounding simultaneously; elevating his body to the height of seven palm trees; soaring in the sky like a bird; moving freely through solid rock; swimming like a fish through water; teaching the Dharma in the language of each individual sentient being; letting the sounds of the Dharma resound from the material substances of the elements; emanating and reabsorbing billions of rays of light; and dispelling the sufferings of each sentient being.

At this time, all the classes of human as well as nonhuman maras were humbled and subdued and lost their power even to expect to inflict harm, to oppose, or to cause danger. The power of admiring, yearning, and confident faith among the five ruling faculties[323] was greatly opened for the first time in both the intermediate beings, the common subjects who were neutral as to feeling faith or aversion, and also the previously evil-minded ministers belonging to the side of nonbelievers. The already present faith and devotion of the believers, the Dharma ministers, and others were increased even further, just like the river Ganges in summertime, and they yearned constantly to see the mandala of his countenance endowed with the major and minor marks and to drink insatiably the nectar of his words. All the people whose minds were ripened, such as the translators, achieved the supreme siddhi of liberation, which is exalted above the common accomplishments, and the liberated ones, the king and the close disciples, attained the state of realization of the great Guru Rinpoche himself, in which the retinue is indivisible in quality from the teacher.

APPENDIX 9

The Actual Beginning of the Teaching

Because of these marvelous miracles and due to these inconceivable deeds, His Majesty the king felt even greater faith and devotion, which were totally unshakable by circumstances. In particular, at a time when the great Guru Rinpoche was staying in the Shining Turquoise Temple in the middle story of Glorious Samye, the king, thinking with compassion of all the future disciples born in the final age when the five degenerations are rampant, arranged upon a beautiful golden mandala plate shining heaps of precious turquoise resembling huge and radiant stars at dawn. The king and the princes, his sons, made numerous respectful prostrations and, together with the incarnated translator Vairochana, the Eye of the World, who was an emanation of Buddha Vairochana, and I, Yeshe Tsogyal, who was granted to be the spiritual consort of Guru Rinpoche, made this supplication simultaneously and with a single voice:[324]

> You are the fully perfected qualities of fruition, the virtues of the Five Never-Ending Adornment Wheels of body, speech, mind, qualities, and activities of all the buddhas and their disciple sons of the ten directions of east and so forth and four times of past and so forth. Your form is the supreme Lotus immortal and indestructible Vajra body, untainted by the defilements of a womb. Mahaguru, precious master, we prostrate respectfully at your feet.[325]

Protector of beings, equal in realization, qualities, and activities to all the buddhas of the three times, your kindness both direct and indirect toward all the sentient beings in general and especially in the Land of Snow is exceedingly great, surpassing even the Buddha.

In particular, by the power of our past wishes and aspirations, there exists elsewhere for us, the present gathering of king and subjects, no other crown jewel or object of refuge than you, the single lord of the family.

Your special, exalted display of great and wondrous feats of miracles has subdued and humbled the impure karmic aspirations of the hordes of Mara and evil-minded ministers.

Raising the victory banner of expounding and practicing the statements and realization of the Buddha's teachings impartially throughout the ten directions of the world, you have ripened and freed the fortunate destined ones and established them on the path of the three levels of enlightenment.

Your benefiting whoever is linked with you, be it in a good or evil way, is an inconceivable and amazing wonder. So for all of us assembled here, our former gathering of the two accumulations must be extremely great.[326]

However, later on, when in the future time the age of the spread of the five degenerations arrives, due to the small number of people practicing positive actions, the side of sustaining virtue will be feeble and, due to the large number of people performing negative actions, the evil forces of elemental spirits will be powerful and raised high.[327]

Just as the saying that a demon has entered each Tibetan's heart, with all the male and female violation-demons visibly possessing the people's hearts, their minds will change, and they will engage in various unvirtuous and perverted actions. With that as the cause and condition, Buddhism, comprised of statements and realization, which is the source of all happiness and goodness of both this and future lives, will degenerate. The Sangha members who are the doctrine holders of the two classes will become sectarian and will be like a mere reflection.[328] Nonsectarian great beings and holders of the teachings who are great masters will be rare, no more than a few, and their lives will be short. The immediate and lasting happiness of the inhabitants, the people and other beings, will be suddenly ravaged and destroyed. The elemental forces of the world and its inhabitants will rise up as enemies, and the eight classes [of gods and demons] headed by the mamos will be enraged, so, as the sign of the three poisons, the evil ages of plagues, famine, the warfare of invasion by foreign armies, and outer and inner conflict and strife will therefore simultaneously well up.[329]

As for a refuge and savior, protector and defender, since there will be no other object of refuge and hope than you, the Mahaguru Rinpoche, no matter where one searches, when this ocean of the threefold misery brims over and overflows the people of Tibet and Kham, we beg you to consider us with kindness and bestow, for our sake, the present king and subjects, and for all the later disciples of future generations yet to come, the quintessence of all the profound and vast instructions of the unexcelled Sutra and Mantra, far superior to precious stones because of fulfilling the wish for permanent happiness, which temporarily subjugates by wrathful means the outer maras with physical form and the inner maras without physical form, enables one to accept them by peaceful means, which effortlessly and spontaneously accomplishes the four activities of pacifying and so forth, and ultimately is the method for attaining the sublime sixteenth bhumi of Unexcelled Wisdom, endowed with the magical form of the unconditioned body of rainbow light, possessing the essence of the five wisdoms.

When we had made this supplication, Guru Rinpoche transformed himself and manifested in an instant in the form of the vidyadhara Dorje Drakpo Tsal and bestowed all the four ripening empowerments, the liberating explanations, and the oral pointing-out instructions. Following this, he displayed wondrous miracles, in the manner of totally filling up the space to pervade dharmadhatu, the miracle of emanating out and absorbing back in the time of a single moment infinite deities with retinues, sub-retinues, and assemblages, from the "approach" as the single mudra heruka of Guru

Drakpo with one face and two arms,[330] through those with the elaborations of heads and arms of the "full approach" of Guru Drakpo with three heads and six arms, the "accomplishment" of Guru Drakpo with nine heads and eighteen arms, and the "great accomplishment" of Guru Drakpo with twenty-one heads and forty-two arms.

Following that, through the great splendor of blessings of his vajra wisdom, he manifested everywhere throughout the central Dharma centers of Samye and so forth, and the surrounding areas in the cardinal and intermediate directions of the snowy land of the Central and the Tsang provinces of Tibet and the Upper and Lower Districts of Kham, the unprecedented various kinds of magical-showlike and miraculous displays, manifestations of his three secrets, of five-colored rainbows, beams of lights, rains of multicolored flowers, the six kinds of earth trembling, such as the east higher than the west, spontaneous sounds of dharmata and the self-resounding of musical instruments not being blown, played, or beaten by anyone, and of the vajra wisdom of the four empowerments in actuality and not in a hidden way descending into the minds of the fortunate destined disciples.

Once again, Guru Drakpo himself appeared in person vividly and majestically in the peaceful form of Mahasukha Padmasambhava, with the major and minor marks and of the nature of wisdom light, and uttered with his self-resounding vajra voice of dharmata this, the ultimate vajra speech, the unexcelled, profound, and extensive stages of the path condensed into one as the essence of oral instructions. Samaya is the commitment of teaching this to the worthy ones.[331]

The Sixty Aspects of Melodious Speech

The meaning of manifesting as the sounds of the Dharma endowed with the sixty aspects of melodious speech is described in both Sutra and Tantra. First, according to the *Sutra on the Inconceivable Secret:*

> Gentle, soft, appealing, and attractive,
> Pure, flawless, distinct, and captivating,
> Worthy, indomitable, pleasant, melodious, and clear,
> Not rough, not coarse, and extremely pleasing to hear,
> Satisfying for body, for mind, and delightful,
> Creating happiness, without sorrow, and instigating insight,
> Comprehensible, elucidating, and generating joy,
> Utterly enjoyable, bringing comprehension and full
>   understanding,
> Reasonable, relevant, free from the fault of repetition,
> Melodious like the sound of the lion, the elephant, and the
>   dragon,
> Like the naga king, the gandharvas, and the kalapinga bird,
> Like the melodious voice of Brahma and the shangshang bird,
> Majestic like the voice and the drum of Indra,
> Not boastful and pervading all sounds without utterance,
> Without corruption of words, without incompleteness,
> Not feeble, not weak, extremely magnificent,

Pervasive, free from rigidity,
Connecting interruption and perfecting all sounds,
Satisfying the senses, not inferior, and unchanging,
Not blurting and fully resounding to the assembly,
Endowed with the supreme of all aspects,
He teaches in the manner of the profound and vast teachings.

Second, according to Tantra, there are six categories: like the voice of Brahma, cymbals, singing, the kalapinga bird, thunder, and the sitar. There are sixty aspects when each of them is multiplied by these ten: generating understanding, comprehensible, respectable, without discord, extremely profound, acceptable, indomitable, pleasing to hear, unconfused, and extremely distinct.

Moreover, there are sixty aspects when these ten natures each have six occasions: being most resonant, all-pervading, immediately comprehensible, clearing doubts, commanding presence, showing immediacy, completely engaging, interesting, distinctive, and taming everyone.

Appendix 11

The Four Schools of Buddhist Philosophy

The Vaibhashika School

The followers of the Vaibhashika School explain that consciousness perceives an object in direct contact, and that the object is different from or apart from the consciousness. They take support from their authoritative scripture, the treatise known as the *Great Treasury of Detailed Exposition,* and accept that particles and consciousness are partless, ultimate, and true existence. Partless particles touch but do not adhere to each other, like pages in a book or grain in a heap, and are kept together by wind to avoid scattering.[332]

They hold the five bases of knowables to be real: physical forms, mind [primary acts of cognition], mental events, nonconcurrent formations, and unconditioned [phenomena]. As well, they claim the three times have substantial existence, that consciousness apprehends perceived objects without a mental image, and that this consciousness is ignorant of itself.

The three types of unconditioned [phenomena] are space, analytical cessation, and nonanalytical cessation.

Since the Vaibhashika's philosophical point of view is clearly detailed in the commentary itself, I see no need to elaborate further than this.

The Sautrantika School

The second of the four schools is Sautrantika, which holds that what appear as being external objects are nothing other than a mental image for the senses, rather than an experience of real objects outside. They take the support of the *Seven Sections of Abhidharma* as their authoritative scripture.[333]

Both schools accept fully the nonexistence of a personal identity, but are also alike in claiming that there are no Mahayana teachings.

Without directly asserting the existence of an indivisible particle, the Sautrantika School teaches that there does exist some unseen substance that acts as the forming agent of all our present experiences of sights, sounds, and so forth. The exact way this unseen substance exists is when one's eyes are directed toward a visual form—and similarly in the case of a sound, a scent, and so forth—the basis for that perceived object has a basis that is consistent with mind [the cognitive act]. While the object cognized remains unseen, the mental image [of the object] and consciousness are indivisible.

In detail, this school has three subdivisions: one is to hold that the myriad different experiences have the same identity as consciousness, another is to claim that there is a corresponding number of consciousnesses to the number of mental images, and the third is to maintain that the mental image and the consciousness are [two halves of one whole], like a split eggshell.

The Sautrantika's philosophical point of view is that physical forms, mind, and mental events do have ultimate existence, while nonconcurrent formations only exist as imputations. The unconditioned phenomena resemble identitylessness. The objects that produce all these are the "perceived," while the mental state that resembles what was produced is the "perceiver." Moreover, they assert that cause and effect have dissimilar features, and that consciousness is self-knowing.

THE MIND ONLY SCHOOL

Concerning the general Mahayana, there are numerous differences between the lesser and greater vehicles, but as a summary it is said that the difference lies in the bodhichitta resolve—that the Hinayana followers do not aspire to perfect buddhahood for the sake of others, while the Mahayana followers do.

In terms of appearances, Mahayana has the two divisions known as Mind Only and Middle Way.

The Mind Only adherents include all phenomena under the imagined, the dependent, and the absolute. Since they assert that appearances (snang ba) are only mind and that this mind has true existence as the self-aware, self-cognizant all-ground consciousness, this school is called Mind Only.

This understanding that mind is real, that [everything is] only mind, and the acceptance that consciousness has true existence is in accordance with the statement of the Buddha: "Listen, sons of the victorious ones; the three realms are mind only!" All that appears and exists, samsara and nirvana, is included within three principles called the imagined, the dependent, and the absolute, also known as the three natures.

The two aspects called "perceiver" and the "perceived," accepted by both the Vaibhashika and Sautrantika schools, are known as "mistaken dependent [phenomena]." The perceived objects believed to be separate from and other than mind are the "imagined [phenomena]." The knowledge that both of these, [the dependent and the imagined], are mind is the "absolute."

These three natures can be divided into the following: (1) The "imagined [phenomena] lacking attributes" is the appearance of the duality of self and other things, including visible forms, sounds, and so forth, which in fact does not exist.[334] (2) The "enumerated imagined [phenomena]" is the groups of names, words, and letters. (3)

The "impure dependent [phenomena]" is the manifold forms of objects and meanings of the outer world and its inner contents that
appear by the power of manifold habitual tendencies. (4) The "pure
dependent [phenomena]" is the pure kayas and wisdoms, buddhafields, and so forth. (5) The "unchanging absolute" is the dharmadhatu of the true all-ground of the natural state, the tathagata essence
that is by nature luminous [wakefulness]. (6) The "unmistaken absolute" is the undefiled path and fruition.

THE MIDDLE WAY SCHOOL

The Middle Way School accepts that all phenomena are included
within the two truths: that ultimately all things are free from the eight
limits of constructs, while conventionally they appear as dependent
origination, just like a magical apparition or a dream. Thus the Middle Way is the pinnacle of all views in that it accepts as well the
understanding that mind is devoid of true existence or that consciousness does not really exist. The Middle Way itself is as directly
stated in the *Lamrim* root text.

APPENDIX 12

The Bodhisattva Bhumis

The identity of a bhumi is as a "support for qualities to increase." The basis for being attributed a bhumi is "the means and knowledge within the stream of being of bodhisattva trainees." The definition of bhumi is "bhumi or stage is used because of gaining support and progressing further." The names of the bhumis are the Joyous and so forth. The meaning of the names are as described in the *Ornament of the Sutras:*

It is called the Joyous
Because you feel incredible joy
When approaching enlightenment
And seeing that you can accomplish the welfare of beings.

It is called the Stainless
Because you are free from the stain of immorality and ambition.

It is called the Radiant
Because you shine with the great light of the Dharma.

It is called the Brilliant
Because you are ablaze with the factors that are conducive to
   enlightenment.

5 It is called the Hard to Conquer
Because of fully maturing all sentient beings,
Because of guarding your own mind,
And because it is hard to conquer by wise beings.

6 It is called the bhumi of the Realized
Because of having realized both
Samsara and nirvana
By means of transcendent knowledge.

7 It is called the bhumi of Reaching Far
Because of being connected to the "single traversed path."

8 It is called the Unshakable
Because of being unswayed by dual notions.

9 It is called the bhumi of Good Intelligence
Because of possessing the eminent intelligence of the correct
    discriminations.

10 It is called the Cloud of Dharma
Because the two pervade the sky, like a cloud.

The ten bhumis are attained by means of their respective types of complete purification, and when that purification is completed, one moves on to the next bhumi.

The practices on the ten bhumis are the ten paramitas, such as chiefly the paramita of generosity on the first bhumi and so forth.

The person on the first bhumi is called the person of correct view because of having realized twofold egolessness; on the second, the person of pure discipline; on the third, the person of total composure because of boundless dhyana and samadhi; on the fourth, the person free from the conceit of contrasting phenomena because of being utterly free from fixation; on the fifth, the person free from the conceit of contrasting within his stream of being because of having gained equanimity of mind; on the sixth, the person free from the conceit of contrasting affliction (samsara) and perfection (nirvana) because of having purified their nature; on the seventh, the person who cultivates the factors conducive to enlightenment in each moment because of having calmed down attributes; on the eighth, the person of fully trained impartiality because of spontaneous perfection; on the ninth, the person skilled in bringing sentient beings to maturity because of mastering the four correct discriminations; and on the tenth, the person who receives empowerment from all buddhas and reveals magical emanations, such as great power, perfecting the body of the media of samadhi and retention, and remaining in Tushita, because of having attained the great superknowledges.

In terms of the three trainings, on the first bhumi one trains in the pure causes for the three trainings; on the second, in discipline; on the third, in mental stability; on the fourth, fifth, and sixth bhumis one trains in respectively the thirty-seven factors conducive to enlightenment, the [four] truths, and in the discriminating knowledge that understands dependent origination. As the result of these, on the seventh one accomplishes immeasurable wisdom; on the eighth, spontaneously perfect wisdom; on the ninth, the complete ripening of sentient beings; and on the tenth one accomplishes all the samadhis and retentions, dharanis.[335]

In terms of the [five undefiled] aggregates, having realized the nature of things directly on the first bhumi, one perfects the aggregate of discipline on the second bhumi; the aggregate of samadhi on the third bhumi; the aggregate of discriminating knowledge on the fourth, fifth, and sixth. As the result of these, on the seventh and so forth one perfects gradually the aggregate of liberation from the four obscurations, and on the stage of buddhahood is perfected the aggregate that sees the liberation from the cognitive obscuration and the wisdom of this freedom.

In terms of purification, by means of three causes—during many aeons to venerate the Three Jewels, to bring sentient beings to full maturation, and to dedicate the root of virtue to enlightenment—the virtuous roots become pure from the first to the tenth bhumi.

In terms of the different objects to be abandoned and realized on the bhumis, on the path of seeing 112 discards and on the path of cultivation 414 discards are abandoned. On the first bhumi one realizes the meaning of all-encompassing dharmata by understanding that dharmadhatu pervades all knowable things; on the second, the meaning of sublime phenomena; on the third, the meaning of causes conducive to realizing stable phenomena; on the fourth, the meaning of not fixating on singular identities; on the fifth, the meaning that the stream of being of self and other are not separate within the pure space of dharmadhatu; on the sixth, the meaning of twofold purity; on the seventh, the meaning that names of teachings including the sutras are not different; on the eighth, the meaning that disturbing emotions are beyond increase and decrease by means of attaining the acceptance of the nature of nonarising, or alternately, the meaning of mastery over the nonconceptual state and the transformation of the disturbed-mind consciousness, as well as mastery over purity and transformation of the sense consciousnesses; on the ninth, the meaning of the transformation of mind consciousness and mastery over the wisdom of correct discrimination; and on the tenth, one realizes the meaning of mastery over activity by means of producing magical emanation at will and thus accomplishing the welfare of beings. These are all described in the *Ornament of the Sutras* and in *Discerning the Middle and the Extremes*.

The objects to be abandoned by means of these ten bhumis are ten types of cognitive obscuration that are not disturbing emotions, so that in terms of being their antidotes, ten wisdoms are defined as the realization of the ten bhumis.

The twelve times one hundred qualities are described in the *Avatamsaka Sutra:*

The bodhisattva can see a hundred samadhi states and a hundred
  buddhas,
Journey to a hundred buddhafields, illuminating, and moving
  everywhere,
Purify a hundred sentient beings and establish them in the
  gateway to the Dharma,
Enter a hundred aeons and reveal himself in a hundred forms,
He can teach one hundred sons of the victorious ones,
And beyond that the strong and eminent aspiration knows no
  boundary.

Similarly, in a number that is twelve times one thousand on the
second bhumi, twelve times one hundred thousand on the third
bhumi, twelve times ten million on the fourth bhumi, twelve times
one billion on the fifth bhumi, twelve times one hundred billion on
the sixth bhumi, twelve times ten trillion on the seventh bhumi, a
number equal to the atoms in one hundred trillion worlds on the
eighth bhumi, a number equal to the atoms in one quadrillion worlds
on the ninth bhumi, and in a number that is indescribable on the
tenth bhumi—the bodhisattva can behold the countenance of buddhas, receive teachings, make worlds shake, illuminate them, journey
to these worlds, bring sentient beings to maturity, disclose the doors
to the Dharma, enter the state of samadhi, reveal a single instant for
numerous aeons, reveal numerous aeons in a single instant, perceive
unlimited past and future, magically transform his body into innumerable forms of the buddhas, and in each of these forms simultaneously teach the Dharma to their surrounding retinues.

Epilogue

As an auspicious conclusion, I include the colophon to Jokyab Rinpoche's (Khenpo Pema Trinley Nyingpo) *Entering the Path of Wisdom:*

> By the power of dedicating all virtuous actions to the great
> enlightenment,
> As exemplified by this effort and by the good deed of confessing
> my faults,
> May the light of the profound and secret tradition spread
> everywhere,
> And may the lotus flowers of auspicious goodness bloom.

The glorious Jamyang Drakpa was a sovereign of knowledge, compassion, and capability and a great guide of all beings. He had perfected an ocean of the virtues of learning, reflection, and meditation by gathering within the glorious knot of his heart all the streams issuing forth from the nectar of the speech and the extracts of the realization of the three great tertöns and vidyadharas. He was also chief among the direct disciples of the sun and moon pair of Jamgöns who, in accordance with the vajra prophecy, accepted the oath of carrying out the activity of linking one million eight hundred thousand [beings to this teaching].[336]

While being nurtured by his great kindness of being accepted with the nectar of his profound and vast speech, and having received the dust of his feet at the crown of my head, I was afraid to forget all the clarifications through the guru's oral tradition of what was taught in the authoritative commentary and, wanting to help people of inferior intellectual capacity like myself, I had taken down some notes. Later I was told to write them down in an assembled form by Samten Gyatso and his brother and was encouraged to do so with a present of writing paper. In response thereto, this ignorant Buddhist monk, Pema Trinley Nyingpo, who practices the essential yoga of the supreme vehicle as nothing but a mere wish, wrote this down at Mindröl Norbu Ling, the Mind Seat of Chokgyur Lingpa. May the virtue of this be a cause for the tradition of the Vajra Essence to spread throughout all times and directions. SARVADA KALYANAM BHA-VANTU.[337]

6/6/2012

Notes

1. These are the three primary teachings within the Nyingma tradition of terma treasures. Any major tertön must reveal a version of all three. Guru sadhana is the practice of approaching and accomplishing the body, speech, and mind of Padmasambhava. The Great Compassionate One is the practice and teachings of Avalokiteshvara. [TUR]

   The Eight Sadhana Teachings (sgrub pa bka' brgyad) are the eight chief yidam deities of Mahayoga and their corresponding tantras and sadhanas: Manjushri Body, Lotus Speech, Vishuddha Mind, Nectar Quality, Kilaya Activity, Liberating Sorcery of Mother Deities, Maledictory Fierce Mantra, and Mundane Worship. *See also* eight great vidyadharas. [EPK]

2. The *Ocean of Blessings* is the manual for the empowerment of Vajra Yogini Yeshe Tsogyal according to a terma revealed by Jamgön Kongtrül. [EPK]

3. Dharma treasures are the transmission-concealed teachings, hidden, mainly by Guru Rinpoche and Yeshe Tsogyal, to be discovered at the proper time by a *tertön,* a "treasure revealer," for the benefit of future disciples. [TUR]

4. The two lords of the Land of Snow mentioned here are Jamyang Khyentse Wangpo and Jamgön Kongtrül Lodrö Thaye. [TUR]

5. One list of the five tertön kings contains Nyang Ral Nyima Öser (1124–1192), Guru Chökyi Wangchuk (1212–1270), Dorje Lingpa (1346–1405), Pema Lingpa (1445/50–1521), and (Padma Ösel) Dongak Lingpa (Jamyang Khyentse Wangpo) (1820–1892). Sometimes

the list also includes the great tertön Rigdzin Gödem (1337–1408).
[EPK]

6. The manual for conferring the extensive empowerment of *Tukdrub
   Yishin Norbu,* composed by Jamgön Kongtrül. *Chokling Tersar,* vol. 29.
   [EPK]

7. Tsangpa Lhayi Metok is the initiation name of the Tibetan King Trisong Deutsen. [TUR]

8. The two great treasure revealers and all-encompassing masters and
   lords of the circle are Chokgyur Lingpa and Jamyang Khyentse Wangpo. The fourteenth Omniscient King of the Victorious Ones is the
   fourteenth Karmapa, Tekchok Dorje. He had two male relatives—
   Döndrub Tulku and Chöwang Tulku. Tsurphu is the seat of His Holiness the Gyalwang Karmapa, situated in the Tölung Valley in central
   Tibet. Dechen Chödrön was the consort of Chokgyur Lingpa. [TUR]

9. Tsewang Drakpa was one of the sons of Chokgyur Lingpa. His other
   name is Wangchok Dorje. [TUR]

10. The name *omniscient Jamgön Lama Rinpoche* ("precious master and gen-
    tle protector") refers to Jamyang Khyentse Wangpo who, as soon as
    the terma of *Lamrim Yeshe Nyingpo* had been revealed, bestowed an
    oral commentary including an outline of the subjects upon Jamgön
    Kongtrül. [TUR]

11. The *Key That Opens One Hundred Doors to Accomplishment* is Jamgön
    Kongtrül's index of transmission lineages for the *Rinchen Terdzö.* It is
    found in its second volume. [EPK]

12. *The Life and Teaching of Chokgyur Lingpa* (Rangjung Yeshe Publica-
    tions, 1988) contains more details about the other termas revealed by
    Chokgyur Lingpa, as well as further stories about Jamyang Khyentse
    Wangpo, Jamgön Kongtrül, and Chokgyur Lingpa. [EPK]

13. Rongmey Karmo Taktsang, the "White Tiger's Nest at Rongmey," is
    situated at Meyshö near the capital Derge in the eastern Tibetan prov-
    ince of Kham. It is one of thirteen Tiger's Nests—the places where
    Padmasambhava manifested in the wrathful form of Dorje Drolö.
    Today, only five of them seem to be known. [TUR]

14. *Clarifying the Aspects of the Auspicious Melody* is the extensive biography
    of Chokgyur Lingpa written by Könchok Gyurmey Tenpey Gyaltsen,
    alias Pema Künkyab Yeshe Dorje Nyingpo, the second incarnation of
    Chokgyur Lingpa at Kela Monastery. It is based on the *Auspicious Mel-*

ody, a supplication to Chokgyur Lingpa in verse form summarizing his life story by Jamgön Kongtrül. [EPK]

15. The *Garland of Jewels* is a detailed list of the contents and lineages of transmission of the *Chokling Tersar* written in 1946 by the third reincarnation of Chokgyur Lingpa at Neten, named Tekchok Tenphel, after he had received the *Chokling Tersar* from Jamyang Khyentse Chökyi Lodrö at Dzongsar Monastery in Kham. [EPK]

16. *Lamrim Yeshe Nyingpo* and its commentary also contain detailed teachings on the nature of empowerment, samaya, the ngöndro, the prerequisites for being a suitable vessel for Vajrayana, the practices connected with the four levels of empowerment, practices for dispelling obstacles, methods of enhancement, the final fruition, and the entrustment of the teachings. [EPK]

17. The collection of teachings famed under the name *Damngak Dzö* is one of the Five Treasuries of Jamgön Kongtrül Lodrö Thaye. Its thirteen volumes contain the most essential empowerments and instructions of the Eight Chariots of the Practice Lineage, the major lineages of transmission of Buddhism in Tibet: Nyingma, Kadam, Kagyü, Shangpa Kagyü, Sakya, Chö and Shijey, Jordrug, and Nyendrup. [EPK]

18. These are the notes presently included as the third part of this book. [EPK]

19. The full Tibetan title is ZHAL GDAMS LAM RIM YE SHES SNYING PO'I RNAM 'GREL RAB GSAL NYIN BYED SNANG BA. [EPK]

20. The full Tibetan title is ZHAL GDAMS LAM RIM YE SHES SNYING PO'I BSDUS DON. [EPK]

21. The supreme siddhi is the accomplishment of complete enlightenment. The common siddhis are usually eight types of miraculous powers. [TUR]

22. This figure was a terma image of Padmasambhava. [TUR]

23. *Dorje Ziji* means "Indestructible Majestic Splendor" and is one of the names of Jamyang Khyentse Wangpo. [EPK]

24. The Ngakso is often practiced as a seven-day group sadhana. [TUR]

25. *Rinchen Terdzö* is a collection of termas by Jamgön Kongtrül covering the Three Inner Tantras. [TUR]

26. The "I" refers to Yeshe Tsogyal, the compiler of this teaching. [TUR]

27. "Approach" and "accomplishment" are two aspects of sadhana practice, especially phases in the recitation stage according to Mahayoga.

There is also the well-known phrase "four aspects of approach and accomplishment" including approach, full approach, accomplishment, and great accomplishment. These are four essential aspects of Vajrayana practice, especially the recitation stage of yidam practice, but can apply to any level of meaning within the tantras. Their traditional analogy is to invite the ruler of a country, to present him with gifts and make a specific request, to obtain his permission to carry out one's aim, and to use one's authority to accomplish the welfare of self and others. In the context of recitation practice, approach is to visualize the yidam deity with the mantra in its heart center; full approach is the spinning garland of mantra syllables emanating light rays making offerings to all the buddhas in the ten directions; accomplishment is to receive their blessings, which purify all one's obscurations; and great accomplishment is to transform the world into the mandala of a pure realm, the beings into male and female deities, sounds into mantra, and all thoughts and emotions into a pure display of innate wakefulness. [TUR]

28. The seven transmissions are: (1) Kama, the Oral Transmission, the early translated Tripitaka and tantras passed on uninterruptedly from master to disciple; (2) Earth Treasure, revealed by the tertön; (3) Rediscovered Treasure, revealed for the second time from a past treasure; (4) Mind Treasure, revealed from the mind of the guru; (5) Hearing Lineage, received directly from an enlightened being; (6) Pure Vision, received in a pure experience; and (7) Recollection, remembrance from a former life.

   In the case of Jamyang Khyentse Wangpo, Kama is the Sutra Pitaka of the Early Translation School, Earth Treasure is *Lama Tennyi Korsum,* etc., Rediscovered Treasure is *Tsasum Drildrub,* etc., Mind Treasure is *Phagma Nyingtig,* etc., Hearing Lineage is *Phurpey Döntig,* etc., Pure Vision is *Kusum Rikdü (Zabtig),* etc., and Recollection is *Chetsün Nyingtig,* etc. [JOKYAB]

29. Padma Ösel Do-ngak Lingpa is the tertön name of Jamyang Khyentse Wangpo. [TUR]

30. Jamgön Kongtrül here plays on the meaning of Chokgyur Lingpa's full name: Orgyen Chokgyur Dechen Lingpa as meaning "Uddiyana Sanctuary of Supreme Great Bliss." [EPK]

31. For the Sarma and Nyingma schools, see also New Schools and Old School. [EPK]

32. Concerning taking either the cause or the result as the path, the *Heruka Galpo Tantra* says:

> The causal vehicles of philosophy
> Regard mind-nature as the cause of buddhahood.
> The resultant vehicles of Mantrayana
> Train in mind-nature as being buddhahood itself.
> Understand exactly what belongs to the causal
> And what belongs to the resultant.

The four special qualities are mentioned in the *Susiddhikara Tantra:*

> Though of identical purpose, it is undeluded;
> It has many means and minor hardships,
> And is to be mastered by those of sharp faculties;
> Thus is the vehicle of Mantrayana especially eminent. [JOKYAB]

Concerning the vehicles of philosophy, the causal vehicles of philosophy consist of the three (general) yanas: the lesser vehicle of shravakas, the medium vehicle of pratyekabuddhas, and the greater vehicle of bodhisattvas, which possesses the sevenfold greatness. [JOKYAB]

The sevenfold greatness of Mahayana mentioned in the *Ornament of the Sutras* is, according to Jamgön Kongtrül in his *All-Encompassing Knowledge:* the greatness of focus on the immense collection of Mahayana teachings; the greatness of the means of accomplishing the welfare of both self and others; the greatness of wisdom that realizes the twofold egolessness; the greatness of diligent endeavor for three incalculable aeons; the greatness of skillful means, such as not abandoning samsaric existence and enacting the seven unvirtuous actions of body and speech without disturbing emotions; the greatness of true accomplishment of the ten strengths, fourfold fearlessness, and the unique qualities of the awakened ones; and the greatness of activity that is spontaneous and unceasing. [EPK]

As for outer and inner Vajrayana, the resultant vehicles of Mantra have outer and inner sections, among which the Three Outer Tantras are Kriya Tantra, Charya Tantra, and Yoga Tantra, and the Three Inner Tantras are Father Tantra Mahayoga, Mother Tantra Anu Yoga, and Nondual Tantra Ati Yoga. [JOKYAB]

The *Tantra of the Mind Mirror of Vajrasattva* says:

> Development Mahayoga resembles the ground of all phenomena.
> Completion Anu Yoga resembles the path of all phenomena.
> Great Perfection Ati Yoga resembles the fruition of all
> phenomena. [JOKYAB]

Mahayoga means great yoga. Anu Yoga means subsequent yoga. Ati Yoga means sublime yoga. [JOKYAB]

33. Khenpo Bodhisattva, Master Padmakara, and Dharma King Trisong Deutsen. The one hundred incarnated translators were headed by Vairochana, Kawa Paltsek, and Chok-ro Lui Gyaltsen, while the one hundred incarnated panditas included Vimalamitra and Jinamitra. [JO-KYAB] [DKR]

34. Nyingma is also known as the Old School of the Early Translations. Although there were no new or old schools in India, these names are given to the early and later spread of the teachings in Tibet. Translations up to and including King Triral (866–901) are called the Nyingma School of early translations and later ones are known as the New Schools of Later Translations. Lord Atisha (982–1054) and Lochen Rinchen Sangpo (957/58–1055), respectively, are renowned as the first pandita and translator of the New Schools of Secret Mantra, and they are noted as being contemporaries of the lord Smritijnana. Ratna's *History of the Dharma* reports that Tsandraghirti (Chandrakirti) was the last translator of the Nyingma School, while Lochen Rinchen Sangpo was the first of the Sarma Schools. [JOKYAB] [DKR]

The Nyingma School possesses the three great transmissions of the extensive Kama, the profound Terma, and the short lineage of Pure Vision. The extensive Kama is also called the long lineage, the profound Terma is called the short lineage, while Pure Vision is the extremely short lineage. [JOKYAB]

According to the view of Rongzom Chökyi Sangpo, the Early Translation School possesses six superior qualities: the greatness of the benefactor who made the invitations, the greatness of the site where the teachings were translated, the greatness of the lotsawas who made the translations, the greatness of the panditas who clarified the translations, the greatness of the offerings and gifts, and the greatness of the translated teachings. The Nyingma School of Secret Mantra, exalted by these six special qualities, also possesses the three special qualities of transmission: the Kama lineage that is spoken orally, the Terma lineage that is bestowed subsequently, and the lineage of Pure Vision that is given as blessings. [JOKYAB]

The three special qualities of the terma treasures can also be: the terma teaching possesses the great warmth of blessings because of having a close lineage; it is a pure source because of having the scriptural proof of the terma letters; and it is a never-waning profound path because it appears at the appropriate time for those to be tamed. [DKR]

35. The three types of teaching are here called tantras, statements, and instructions. [EPK]

     The term "instruction" refers to the condensation of the meaning of the tantras into key points that are easy to apply and most effective. [TUR]

36. The six limits are the bounds of the expedient meaning, definitive meaning, implied, not implied, literal, and not literal. [JOKYAB]

     The four modes are the literal, general, hidden, and ultimate. [JO-KYAB]

     The tantras must be clarified by means of the six limits and the four modes. [DKR]

     For more of Jokyab Rinpoche's details, see Appendix 1, "The Six Limits and Four Modes." [EPK]

37. The "statements" here are the commentaries made by the bodhisattvas abiding on the ten bhumis, from the first bhumi of the Joyous to the tenth bhumi of the Cloud of Dharma. As will be explained in the chapter on the meaning of the title, these commentaries are, for instance, the *Trilogy of Commentaries by Bodhisattvas:* Vajrapani's commentary on the *Praises of Chakrasamvara,* Vajra Garbha's commentary on the *Two Segments* (of the *Hevajra Tantra*), and Kulika Pundarika's (Tib. Rigden Pema Karpo) commentary on the *Kalachakra Tantra* named *Immaculate Light.* [JOKYAB] [DKR]

38. The accomplished vidyadharas who received the transmissions for the Eight Sadhana Teachings are Hungchen-kara and so forth. [JOKYAB]

39. As for the systems of explanation, the New Schools of Secret Mantra, for instance, explain the twelve thousand [verses] of the *Kalachakra Tantra* by means of the commentary in sixty [chapters] by the Dharma King Suchandra (Tib. Chögyal Dawa Sangpo) as being like the embellishing eighty minor marks, while the embellished [basis] is eighty-one topics of presence, such as the kayas and so forth. The root tantra established by Kulika Manjushrikirti (Tib. Rigden Jampal Drakpa) as the *Condensed Tantra* is then explained as a summary by means of the *Immaculate Light,* the detailed commentary of Pundarika, the second Kulika, which is like the thirty-two major marks. [JOKYAB]

     In the case of the Old Mantra School, for example, the *Magical Net (Gyütrül)* and other texts are explained in great detail according to the system of Kadey Zurpa, in great depth according to the system of Rongzom Pandita and Longchenpa, as well as in many different ways according to the respective traditions of the Tantra Section and Sadhana Section. [JOKYAB]

According to oral information from Dakpo Tulku Rinpoche, the tradition of Kadey Zurpa originates from the three Zurpa masters and is the system of explaining the *Guhyagarbha* using other tantras. It was continued at Mindröl Ling Monastery by the illustrious Terdag Lingpa and his brother Lochen Dharma Shri. Comparatively, the system of Rongzom Pandita and Longchenpa placed emphasis on expounding the *Guhyagarbha* using oral instructions. [EPK]

Moreover, there are numerous sophisticated ways of scholarly exposition, heavy with loads of words, details of contradictions between or relations to authentic scriptures and to reasoning, or presentations of criticism against the sectarianism of philosophical views. Alternately, an explanation can demonstrate the actual nature of the vajra words of this root text, *The Wisdom Essence,* without placing emphasis on the dry words of elaborate dissertations, but rather by emphasis on combining everything into the essentials of simple practice. This is the nectar of the oral teachings of the supreme vidyadhara, the all-pervading lord guru Jamyang Khyentse Wangpo, also called Künga Tenpey Gyaltsen Pal Sangpo, which Jamgön Kongtrül Lodrö Thaye received personally from him. [JOKYAB]

The word "intellectuals" refers to the five types of non-Buddhist philosophers. [JOKYAB] Also known as the Five Sophistic Schools, they are the Samkhya, Aishvara, Vaishnava, Jaina, and the Nihilists. [EPK]

40. About the heart essence of Padmasambhava, "heart essence" in Sanskrit is *chitta tilaka,* and thus it means the purest and most essential extract of the mind of all the victorious ones. [JOKYAB]

The Four Profound Cycles of Guru Sadhana are the four termas revealed together by the two great tertöns Jamyang Khyentse Wangpo and Chokgyur Lingpa: the outer sadhana *Barchey Künsel,* the inner sadhana *Sampa Lhündrub,* the secret sadhana *Tsokye Nyingtig,* and the innermost sadhana *Dorje Draktsal.* [JOKYAB]

About the Three Yogas: for instance, the view of Mahayoga is purity and equality; the meditation is divided into development stage and completion stage, means and liberation; and the action is the yogic discipline that corresponds to one's level of progress. Similarly, the view, meditation, and action of Anu and Ati will also be shown. [JO-KYAB]

41. The two first headings are covered in Chapters 2 and 3. The third heading embodies the main part of this book, Chapters 4 to 15. The last will be included in forthcoming volumes. [EPK]

42. The Three Roots: The gurus of the three lineages are the root of the blessings of the four vajras. The yidams of the six sections of Tantra are the root of the supreme and common siddhis. The dakinis and wisdom protectors are the root of pacifying and the other activities. [JOKYAB] [DKR]

The gurus of the three lineages include the masters of the Mind Lineage of the Victorious Ones, from Samantabhadra down to Garab Dorje; the Sign Lineage of the Vidyadharas, from Garab Dorje down to Padmasambhava; and the Hearing Lineage of Great Individuals, from Padmasambhava down to the present day. [TUR]

In the case of the terma of Jamyang Khyentse Wangpo entitled *Lama Tennyi Korsum,* there is a general sadhana and also specific sadhanas for each of the three kayas. In the case of the terma of Chokgyur Lingpa named *Tukdrub Barchey Künsel,* the general is the root cycle of teachings, while the specific are the individual sadhanas for Dharmakaya Amitabha and so forth, as well as the application of the activities. As for root and branch, in the particular tradition of Chokgyur Lingpa, the root heart practice is *Gongpa Kundü,* while the branch heart practices are *Barchey Künsel* and *Yishin Norbu Sampa Lhündrub.* All of them condensed to the essential is the terma called *Lama Ngödrub Gyatso.* [JOKYAB]

The four activities and the eight accomplishments are intended to be temporary, while the fruition endowed with the three kayas and five wisdoms is the ultimate. [JOKYAB]

43. The *Magical Net of the Vidyadharas* is defined by Jamyang Khyentse Wangpo as one of the Eight Sections of Magical Net belonging to the Tantra Section of Mahayoga. The *Root Tantra of the Assemblage of Vidyadharas* is found in the *Nyingma Gyübum,* vol. 32. [EPK]

44. To explain this quote: "This most profound heart extract practice, more profound than any other profound teaching, spontaneously manifested from the wisdom expanse of realization of myself, the self-arisen and instantaneously born bearer of the name Padma, who is not dependent upon the causes and conditions of a father and mother." [JOKYAB] [DKR]

45. The scripture quoted from and referred to here is the *Sheldam Nying-jang,* the root tantra of the *Guru's Heart Practice, Barchey Künsel.* [TUR] To explain this quote:

> I, the great master of Uddiyana (Padmasambhava), did not expound this elaborately in terms of expedient meaning as a commentary that is based upon other tantras, statements, and instructions and then clarifies their intent; but I have taught it as the definitive meaning that is the essential extract of all the tantras, statements, and instructions, just like butter is the essential extract of milk that again is the essence of grass and plants. When this definitive meaning, which is always fully present as the dharmadhatu essence of my heart, manifests as the ineffable natural sound of dharmata, it is especially exalted by not being in conflict with the extensive chief Eighteen Tantras and so forth; it is especially exalted by being in accordance with the statements, the sadhanas, and empowerment manuals that unravel the meaning of the tantras; and it is especially exalted by possessing the direct experience of the profound instructions.

Thus Jamyang Drakpa has taught that it is endowed with three special qualities. [JOKYAB] [DKR]

About "instruction," the *Words of the Outcaste Rishi* mentions, "Philosophical scriptures elaborate on the tantras in great detail, while instructions condense them into key points." [JOKYAB] [DKR]

46. Jamdrak Rinpoche heard personally from Padma Ösel Do-ngak Lingpa that the *Teaching Cycle of Dorje Drakpo Tsal, Powerful Vajra Wrath,* consists of fifteen sections. [JOKYAB]

The phrase "appropriately detailed" means not too condensed as to be unclear and also not too extensive as to be difficult to comprehend. It is easy to understand for a simple person and possible to elaborate upon by the learned. [JOKYAB]

The unified state refers to the unity of kaya and wisdom in which kaya is emptiness endowed with the supreme of all aspects, and wisdom is the mind of unchanging great bliss. [JOKYAB]

47. The literal, general, hidden, and ultimate. For more details see Appendix 1, "The Six Limits and Four Modes." also, #36

48. The word "wisdom" can be applied to the objects that are to be known, both samsara and nirvana, as well as to the subject, the consciousness. [JOKYAB]

"Wisdom" is the English equivalent for the Sanskrit *jnana* and the Tibetan *yeshe*. Literally, *yeshe* means "original knowing." In this case both "objects known" and "consciousness" contain the Tibetan root *shes*, in Sanskrit *jna*. [EPK]

49. The *Accomplishment of Means and Knowledge,* which is one of the *Seven Sections of Accomplishment,* mentions, "The subject, consciousness, fully discerns the individual known objects. Having fully and correctly discriminated and analyzed through the joining together of the subject and object, the nature of all phenomena is devoid of a self-nature. That itself is called wisdom." [JOKYAB]

The *Seven Sections of Accomplishment* are seven scriptures composed by Indian mahasiddhas: *Accomplishment of Secrets,* written by Mahasukha Natha; the *Accomplishment of Means and Knowledge,* written by his disciple Yenlak Meypey Dorje; *Accomplishment of Wisdom,* written by Yenlak Meypey Dorje's disciple Indrabhuti; *Accomplishment of Nonduality,* written by Indrabhuti's consort Lakshmikara; *Accomplishment of the Innate,* written by Dombi Heruka; *Accomplishment of the Great Secret Thatness,* written by Darikapa; and *Accomplishment of Thatness to Clearly Encompass Reality,* written by Yogini Chito. [JOKYAB]

50. Defilement here means the fixation on dualistic experience that is a temporary (noninherent) delusion. [JOKYAB]

The qualities of perfection are the opposite of the state of affliction. [JOKYAB]

"Perfection" is synonymous with nirvana, while "affliction" corresponds to samsaric existence. [CNR]

51. To explain this quote: "From the buddhas comes the Dharma of the three vehicles, and from the Dharma appears the noble assembly of shravakas, pratyekabuddhas, and bodhisattvas." [JOKYAB]

52. "Wisdom" is the characterized, while "essence" is its special characteristic. [JOKYAB]

"Essence" is the English equivalent for the Sanskrit *garbha* and the Tibetan *nyingpo*. [EPK]

The word *garbha* sometimes means "the kernel or core that dwells within the covering husk" and sometimes "the nakedly extracted essence devoid of covers." The latter connotation is used here. [JOKYAB]

53. As for the *Five Hundred Thousand Scripture,* the *Hevajra Tantra,* the king of the Mother Tantras of knowledge, has extensive, medium, and condensed versions. The extensive is the *Seven Hundred Thousand.* The

medium is the *Five Hundred Thousand Scripture*. The condensed is called the *Two Segments*. [JOKYAB]

54. To explain this quote: "From emptiness endowed with the supreme of all aspects, represented in the form of the wish-fulfilling tree that encompasses all realms, appear the fruits of the twofold welfare (of self and others), the nonconceptual compassion, which is not a nihilistic void. This is the root that is the source of the kayas and wisdoms of all the perfectly awakened ones. From this unity of means and knowledge, emptiness and compassion, they emerge, there is no doubt." [JOKYAB] [DKR]

55. The following explanation relates *Wisdom Essence* to the meaning of the Sanskrit word *mandala*. Note that the Tibetan equivalent for *mandala* is *kyilkhor*, which in English is "center-circle." [EPK]

"Center" or *manda* means "essence" or *sara,* while *la* means "to take hold of" and therefore to capture the essence. Thus they explain the meaning of the word *mandala*. The "center" of the aggregates, elements, and sense-bases describes the "essence" *kunda*. This is the relative bodhichitta that forms the basis for great bliss. Taking hold of or capturing it by means of the (tummo practice of) blazing and dripping is explained as the hidden meaning of *mandala*.

Alternately, the essence of all the teachings describes the view of the Middle Way. This is the ultimate bodhichitta, free from constructs, which is the natural great bliss and compassion. Taking hold of or capturing it by practicing their unity is explained as the general meaning of *mandala*. Their merging, or the combination of word and meaning, expresses *mandala* itself.

Furthermore, "center" means that the natures of the aggregates, elements, sense-bases and objects, and disturbing emotions are the five families of male and female buddhas and the goddesses. "Circle" means cutting through the defilements.

In the context of the common development and completion, *mandala* means the support and the supported, while in the context of the completion stage, *mandala* means the union of emptiness and compassion. [JOKYAB]

56. The *Exposition Tantra of Guhyasamaja* is also called the *Vajra Garland*. [JOKYAB]

To explain this quotation: "E and VAM are the union of bliss and emptiness, emptiness and compassion, and of means and knowledge.

Since the coemergent wisdom of the omniscience of all the buddhas abides in the magical display of the union of these two syllables of means and knowledge, the E syllable of great emptiness and VAM syllable of great bliss, the syllables E and VAM are fully explained during the opening chapter at the beginning of teaching the profound and extensive aspects of the sacred Dharma. [JOKYAB] [DKR]

57. The 84,000 Dharma sections are remedies for the 84,000 disturbing emotions of those to be tamed. [JOKYAB]

This refers to the Dharma seal of the four seals of Mother Tantra. [JOKYAB]

The four seals are the Dharma seal, samaya seal, great seal, and action seal. [CNR]

58. "Sutras and tantras" refer to the common and the special teachings. According to the sutra system, EVAM MAYA [SHRUTAM EKASMIN SA-MAYE] means "Once upon a time I heard this spoken." "This" is the perfect place, "spoken" is the perfect teaching, "I" is the perfect teacher, "heard" is the perfect retinue, and "once upon a time" is the perfect time.

According to the system of tantra, the syllable E symbolizes knowledge, *prajna.* It is the nature of the space of the five consorts and is the perfect place, the dharmadhatu palace of Akanishtha. The syllable VAM symbolizes means, *upaya,* and is thus the perfect teacher, the buddha of the sixth family (Vajradhara). The bindu of the VAM syllable symbolizes union and is thus the perfect Dharma or teaching, the natural secret essence that is the continuity, tantra, of the indivisibly interconnected and uninterrupted ground, path, and fruition in which means and knowledge are a unity. The syllable MA stands for *mana,* cognizance, and is thus the sugata King of Consciousness. In a general way, MA is said to be the syllable that symbolizes mindfulness and is therefore *smriti.* Thus it is the perfect retinue because of retaining, with total recall, the meaning of tantra through the function of mindfulness. The syllable YA stands for the word *yada* meaning "upon a time" and therefore is the perfect time, because it is the particle showing the time at which this text was expounded. [JOKYAB]

E and VAM symbolize means and knowledge. There is no path within sutra and tantra that is not included within means and knowledge. When you gain full comprehension of E and VAM you also understand the full meaning of the tantras. [TUR]

59. The system of Phakshab is the tradition of Nagarjuna and his spiritual sons Aryadeva and Chandrakirti. The Father Tantras have the Five Stages, the Mother Tantras have the four seals, and the Nondual Tantras have the six unions. While the two latter will be explained below (in the following volumes), the Five Stages are as follows: the three solitudes of body, speech, and mind; illusory body; and unity. In another way, counting the solitude of body separately as the development stage, the Five Stages are: (1) the vajra recitation of the solitude of speech; (2) the meditation state of the solitude of mind, which is to meditate on the bindu in the heart center and then fix the mind upon it; (3) the illusory body, which is to visualize all appearances as the illusory deity and celestial palace; (4) the luminosity, which is to meditate on the luminosities of the three experiences and of the great emptiness after having gradually applied oneself to the former stages; and (5) the unity, which is to manifest again therefrom in the form of the deity, the nonduality of appearance and emptiness. [JOKYAB]

60. The "liberation of the upper gate" refers to one's own body as the upaya. [JOKYAB]

   The "secret lower gate" means the great bliss of the lower gate and refers to the union with another's body. [JOKYAB]

   "In this text" means in the later part of the Tibetan text, which is not included in volume 1. [EPK]

61. "Wisdom" is the Cutting Through of primordial purity, and "essence" is the Direct Crossing of spontaneous presence. [JOKYAB]

62. The basic dharmakaya refers to the pure all-ground and is the indivisibility of space and awareness. [JOKYAB]

63. To explain this quote: "Utterly free from the two obscurations and all kinds of confused concepts or, in other words, untainted by defilements, the ultimate and great coemergent wisdom dwells in everyone who has the vajra body endowed with the six elements and, moreover, it encompasses all things, outer and inner, animate and inanimate." [JOKYAB]

   Sambhuti (Skt. *Samputa*) is the name for the *Exposition Tantra of the Two Segments*. *Sambhuti* means "union" or "perfectly united." [JOKYAB]

64. The *Tantra That Prophesies Realization* is another name for the *Exposition Tantra of the Father Tantra Guhyasamaja*. [JOKYAB]

   This is *Sandhi Vyakarana* in Sanskrit, text no. 444 in the Derge *Kangyur*. [EPK]

65. The *Radiant Lamp* is Chandrakirti's commentary on *Guhyasamaja*. [JO-KYAB]

66. In the context of the ground that is to be realized or understood, it is called sugata essence, dharmakaya essence, buddha essence, and also essence of the victorious ones. [JOKYAB]

67. According to the common Mantrayana, space is the empty aspect, wisdom is the manifest aspect, and the ultimate nature is their inseparability, which encompasses all the phenomena of samsara and nirvana. [JOKYAB]

    According to Mahayoga of the uncommon Mantrayana, *Wisdom Essence* means the superior great dharmakaya of the purity and equality of the indivisible two truths. [JOKYAB]

    According to Anu Yoga, *Wisdom Essence* means the three mandalas of father, mother, and son—in other words, space, awareness, and their nonduality. [JOKYAB] [DKR]

68. According to Ati Yoga, the threefold wisdom refers to the dharmakaya wisdom of the primordially pure essence, the sambhogakaya wisdom of the spontaneously present nature, and the nirmanakaya wisdom of the unobstructed capacity. [JOKYAB]

69. The *Six Spheres* is one of the seventeen Dzogchen Tantras. [JOKYAB]

    According to Khenpo Ngak-chung, the *Tantra of the Six Spheres of Samantabhadra* teaches how to prevent rebirth in and purify the six realms and manifest the pure realms of self-display. [EPK]

70. In the context of the path, "essence" is that which brings about realization or understanding and is indicated by the Sanskrit word *sara,* which means ocean. Just like the ocean is the basis from which other precious jewels and manifold things appear or originate, "essence" indicates the means, upaya, which is the accumulation of merit. [JO-KYAB]

71. Means and knowledge should not be separated. [JOKYAB]

72. The natural is dharmakaya, the perfect enjoyment is sambhogakaya, and the body of emanation is nirmanakaya. The dharmakaya is the basis for the other two, both of which are called form bodies, rupakaya. The sambhogakaya has a form of rainbow light, while the nirmanakaya's form, in the case of an incarnation, is of flesh and blood. [TUR]

    The *Ornament of the Sutras* is one of the Five Teachings of Lord

Maitreya. Thrangu Rinpoche explains: "The *Ornament of Realization (Abhisamayalamkara)* clarifies the Second Turning of the Wheel of Dharma. The next three teachings are general works given to clarify all of Buddha Shakyamuni's teachings. These are called the *Ornament of the Sutras (Sutralamkara), Discerning the Middle and the Extremes,* and *Discerning Dharmas and Dharmata.* The fifth work taught by Lord Maitreya truly establishes the Third Turning of the Wheel of Dharma. It is called the *Uttaratantra.*" [EPK]

73. The two kayas are dharmakaya and rupakaya. The welfare of oneself, in this context, is not to be understood as meaning selfish, but in the sense that unless you realize dharmakaya you are utterly incapable of accomplishing the benefit of other beings by means of the two types of rupakaya, because the rupakaya cannot possibly manifest without dharmakaya. Once you realize dharmakaya, the rupakayas appear spontaneously. The dharmakaya is the splendor of oneself while the rupakaya is the splendor for others. [TUR]

74. In the context of fruition, the arrival at the final stage of realization and understanding, the qualities of freedom are the thirty-two dharmakaya qualities of freedom. The qualities of maturation are the thirty-two rupakaya qualities of maturation. Together these comprise the sixty-four qualities of freedom and maturation. [JOKYAB]

    These qualities are described in detail in the commentaries on the *Uttaratantra.* [EPK]

75. The everlasting and all-pervasive activities that are spontaneously present. [JOKYAB]

76. The expression of awareness manifests as knowledge when the nature of mind has been recognized, as opposed to manifesting as normal delusion. This is what removes the obscurations and lets the enlightened qualities appear. [TUR]

77. "The kayas as the support and the wisdoms as the supported are neither separate nor different. The ultimate nature is always beyond transformation or change." The rest of the quote is easy to understand. [JOKYAB]

    The *Tantra of Self-Arising Awareness* is one of the seventeen Dzogchen Tantras. [JOKYAB]

    The *Tantra of Self-Arising Awareness* teaches how to resolve the view, meditation, and action. [EPK]

78. About support and the supported, you can usually understand a temple and the images contained within it. For instance, the kaya is our physi-

cal body, and what it supports is our mind, the wisdom. In a further sense it is taught that everything is empty of all other things, but not of kayas and wisdoms; that is the intent of the buddhas. In brief, *kaya* means the two rupakayas, while *yeshe* is the mind within them. Moreover, dharmakaya is devoid of constructs, a body of space. The sambhogakaya is described as the "wisdom wheel of personal perception" with a form of light, like a rainbow. The nirmanakaya is usually defined as the vajra body endowed with the six elements. Thus the latter two are called rupakayas, form bodies, since even a rainbow has form, while the nirmanakaya is made of flesh and blood; one is subtle, the other is coarse. In the age of the five degenerations, a buddha must appear in the coarse body of a nirmanakaya in order to be perceived by other beings. That was about the kayas.

Next, about wisdom: the dharmakaya wisdom is unchanging, the sambhogakaya wisdom is all-pervasive, and the nirmanakaya is distinct, individual perception. Among the five wisdoms, the dharmadhatu wisdom refers to the state of dharmakaya; it is adorned with its four aspects, the other four wisdoms, which belong to the sambhogakaya state: the mirrorlike wisdom, wisdom of equality, discriminating wisdom, and all-accomplishing wisdom. The nirmanakaya wisdoms are the wisdom that knows the nature as it is and the wisdom that perceives all that exists. [TUR]

79. Just like a huge rope lying soaked in a lake can slowly be pulled up once you get hold of one end, the enlightenment of all the buddhas is placed in the palm of the hand of the practitioner when receiving the pointing-out instruction from a qualified master and can then slowly be "pulled in" through diligent training. [TUR]

80. The following is a quote from the end of the root text *Lamrim Yeshe Nyingpo*. The person speaking is Yeshe Tsogyal, in the company of King Trisong Deutsen and other close disciples of Padmasambhava. [TUR]

81. According to Jamdrak Rinpoche, Jamyang Khyentse Wangpo has said that this line refers to the general instructions and, in particular, that they should be understood to be the one hundred million heart practices of Guru Rinpoche. [JOKYAB]

The words that express are extensive, and the meaning that is expressed is profound. [JOKYAB]

The Wisdom Essence teaches the paths of the causal vehicles of phi-

losophy and the Three Outer Tantras of Mantrayana only in brief and
the paths of the Three Inner Tantras in detail. In short, it teaches in
completeness the stages of the path of Buddhadharma comprised of
Sutra and Mantra, unmistakenly and in its entirety.

Sutra means taking the cause as path. *Mantra* means taking the result
as path. [JOKYAB]

82. "Stages of the path," lamrim, means emphasis on the path among the
three aspects of ground, path, and fruition. However, the ground and
fruition are both implied. [JOKYAB]

Within the tradition of the glorious Atisha are his own *Stages of the
Path for the Three Kinds of Individuals* and Tsongkhapa's greater and
lesser *Stages of the Path for the Three Kinds of Individuals,* which are all
according to the Sutra system. [JOKYAB]

The *Stages of the Path of Enlightenment* is the lord Atisha's scripture
explaining the stages of the path for the three kinds of individuals.
Perfect faith is the path of the lesser individual, perfect renunciation is
the path of the mediocre individual, and perfect altruism is the path of
the superior individual. [JOKYAB]

As for the stages of the path according to Mantrayana, Aro's *Yogas
of the Greater Vehicle* is Kama, while *Padmey Lamrim* is a terma of Nyang
Ral Nyima Öser. [JOKYAB]

The *Padmey Lamrim, Padmakara's Stages of the Path,* is probably iden-
tical with *Sang-ngak Lamrim Radiant Jewel Lamp* found in vol. I of the
Rinchen Terdzö, a text combining the essence of the Three Inner Tan-
tras, which was passed down through the Oral Transmission Lineage,
Kama, as well as revealed in matching termas by Sangye Lama, Nyang
Ral Nyima Öser, Guru Chöwang, and Dorje Lingpa. [EPK]

The name Aro refers to Aro Yeshe Jungney, who also figures prom-
inently in the transmission of the Mind Section of the Great Perfection. [EPK]

Nyang Ral Nyima Öser (1124–1192) was the first of five Tertön
Kings and a reincarnation of King Trisong Deutsen. Several of his
revealed treasures are included in the *Rinchen Terdzö,* among which
the most well known is the *Assemblage of Sugatas,* known as *Kabgye
Deshek Düpa,* a cycle of teachings focusing on the Eight Sadhana
Teachings. Details of his life is found in Dudjom Rinpoche's *The
Nyingma School of Tibetan Buddhism.* His revelations translated into English include the biography of Padmasambhava called *The Lotus-Born*
and Padmasambhava's oral instructions entitled *Dakini Teachings,* both
published by Shambhala Publications. [EPK]

83. This means that *Lamrim Yeshe Nyingpo* is in fact no different from the *Two Segments,* the king of the tantras of the New Schools, nor from *Guhyagarbha,* the king of the tantras of the Nyingma School. Hevajra is also called [in Tibetan] *kye'i rdo rje, dgyes pa rdo rje, rol pa'i rdo rje,* and *dges pa rdo rje. Guhyagarbha* is [in Tibetan] called *Sangwey Nyingpo,* the *Essence of Secrets.* [JOKYAB]

84. Teachings named through analogy are, for instance, *White Lotus Sutra,* the *Precious Tala Sutra,* and the *Salu Sprout Sutra;* those named in terms of meaning are, for instance, *Transcendent Knowledge (Prajnaparamita), Middle Way (Madhyamaka),* or *Assemblage of Secrets (Guhyasamaja);* those named in terms of place are, for instance, the *Gayagori Sutra* or the *Sutra of the Descent to Lanka, Lankavatara Sutra,* and so forth; those named after their circumstance are, for instance, the *Sutra of Entering the City of Vaishali,* the *Sutra of the Meeting of Father and Son,* and so forth. Moreover, titles can be given after the one who requested the teaching, as for instance the *Sutra Requested by Tagmo* or the *Sutra Requested by Maitreya.* There are titles referring to the number of verses such as the *Hundred Thousand* or the *Twenty Thousand,* and others named after the teacher, such as the *Buddha Avatamsaka,* or after their function, such as the *Refutation of Criticism (Vigraha Vyavartani).* [JO-KYAB]

85. The Indian pandita Dignaga is among the Six Ornaments Which Beautify the Jambu Continent and the recipient of the transmission of *pramana,* valid cognition, to bring an end to confusion about meaning. [JOKYAB]

    The six ornaments are Nagarjuna, Aryadeva, Asanga, Dignaga, Vasubandhu, and Dharmakirti. [EPK]

    To explain this quote: "The knowledge *(prajna)* of emptiness transcends *(paramita)* samsara and is wisdom devoid of the duality of perceiver and perceived. The name *Prajnaparamita* demonstrates the scripture itself, the path to be traversed, and the fruition to be attained, because it contains the ultimate of what all the tathagatas of the three times accomplish." [JOKYAB]

86. To explain this quote: "Mamos and dakinis use symbols to make the meaning understood. When presented with symbolic gestures or symbolic sounds, they are skilled in responding unmistakenly by making symbolic replies. Since they understand exactly what exists in all the Sarma and Nyingma tantras, they link the ultimate essence back and

forth to symbolism, attaching symbols to what should be taught. Therefore, all the dakinis are the life-force of the samaya symbols." [JOKYAB]

87. To explain this quote: "Treasure letters possessing physical form are the body of magical creation, nirmanakaya. They are also speech for hearing and understanding sounds and words. When their meaning is expressed, one understands it. Thus, indirectly, they are also mind. [JOKYAB]

88. The seven symbolic letters demonstrate the seven collections of consciousnesses at the time of the ground, the seven bodhi-factors at the time of the path, and the seven cycles of the ultimate at the time of fruition. These aspects will be explained later. [JOKYAB]

   The symbolic letters are also said to be a magical city, because the tertön sees a city comprised of numerous words and meanings of treasure teachings within each single symbolic character. [DKR] [JOKYAB]

89. The symbolic script is Guru Rinpoche's seal of command. It is his emblem, the Dharma seal of his word. [JOKYAB]

   The terma sign instills doubtless trust in the fact that the treasure revealer himself is superior to other ordinary people. [JOKYAB]

   About the terma sign, according to the vision of Taksham Nüden Dorje, it is said that the two circles symbolize means and knowledge and the crescent moon their indivisible unity. This is, however, not totally fixed since the woodblocks at Mindröl Ling have only two circles without a crescent moon. [JOKYAB]

   Mindröl Ling is a major Nyingma monastery in central Tibet founded by Terdak Lingpa in 1670. [EPK]

   The indicating symbols are unaltered, the expressing words are unmistaken, and the expressed meaning is free from confusion. [JOKYAB]

90. Guru Rinpoche himself emanates the mandala deities of the sadhanas, and he also teaches the sadhana scriptures, the tantric expositions along with oral instructions. [JOKYAB]

   The Great Secret is a synonym for Vajrayana. [TUR]

91. To teach means to explain it to other fortunate people. To study means to receive teachings oneself from a qualified master. To meditate means to contemplate the meaning and meditate upon it correctly. To practice means to apply oneself to the practices of the stages of development, recitation, and completion. [JOKYAB]

92. The expedient meaning is the conventional homage of the gesture. The definitive meaning is the ultimate homage of recognition [of the natural face of awareness]. [JOKYAB]

    The ultimate homage of recognition means to sustain the view of Dzogchen, Mahamudra, or the Middle Way. [TUR]

93. The gurus are the root of blessings. The yidams are the root of accomplishments. The dakinis and wisdom protectors are the root of activities. [TUR]

94. Passionate means semiwrathful, just like a deity for the increasing or magnetizing activities. [JOKYAB]

    The sambhogakaya and nirmanakaya buddhas are of the nature of yidams. [JOKYAB]

    The tantras of Mantrayana are the extraordinary scriptures exalted above the sutras. [JOKYAB]

    The manifest aspect is the yidam, the empty aspect is the dakini, and their indivisibility is the guru, the Lord of the Circle, who is the chief figure of the mandala. [JOKYAB]

95. The *Body Tantra of the Assemblage of Realization* is probably a tantra belonging to the *Lama Gongdü* cycle revealed by Sangye Lingpa (1340–1396). [EPK]

96. The threefold wisdom—essence as the primordially pure wisdom of emptiness, nature as the spontaneously present wisdom of cognizance, and capacity as the all-pervasive wisdom of indivisibility—is in fact the very identity of the Three Roots, the Three Jewels, and the three kayas. [JOKYAB] [DKR]

97. The Three Precious Ones are the same as the Three Jewels: the Precious Buddha, the Precious Dharma, and the Precious Sangha. [CNR]

98. This is a quote from the *Vajra Mirror Tantra,* which belongs to the seventeen Dzogchen Tantras. "The guru as Vajrasattva is the chief figure of all the mandalas and the lord who encompasses all the families. In his realization, the guru and vajra-holder equals all the buddhas of the three times, while in relation to our own hopes and aims, his kindness is to be regarded as superior to all the buddhas." [JOKYAB]

    The *Vajra Mirror Tantra* may very well be the *Tantra of the Mind Mirror of Vajrasattva,* which teaches how the lamps are the self-display of awareness. By means of twenty-one pointing-out instructions, the different types of people recognize wisdom. It further teaches the four key points and how to practice. [EPK]

99. The following explanation describes each of the words in Padmasambhava's secret name, Powerful Vajra Wrath, Dorje Drakpo Tsal. First Vajra is explained, next Wrath, and finally Powerful. [EPK]

    The *Samayoga Tantra* is one of the Eighteen Tantras of Mahayoga. [JOKYAB]

    The full title of the *Samayoga Tantra* is *Sarvabuddha Samayoga,* the *Tantra of Equalizing All Buddhas.* A terma version of the sadhana of this tantra was revealed by Chokgyur Lingpa. [EPK]

100. To explain this quote: "I proclaim that the word *vajra* is used for the nature of emptiness itself, which is undifferentiated as to perceiver and perceived." [JOKYAB]

    The *Mirror of Magical Display* is one of the Eight Maya Sections, the eight divisions of Mayajala Tantras. [JOKYAB]

101. The natural state of the ground and the dharmakaya of all the victorious ones cannot be differentiated into a defiled samsara and an undefiled nirvana. In other words, the dharmakaya essence of samsara, the path, and nirvana are like the analogy of the space within pots of clay, copper, and gold. [JOKYAB]

    There is the ultimate vajra of emptiness, the conventional vajra of material substance with attributes, and the apparent symbolic or labeled vajra of the name. [JOKYAB]

102. As emptiness is externally (1) solid, firm, and unbreakable; internally (2) substantial; and (3) without hollowness, (4) impossible to cut into pieces, (5) impossible to split asunder or to destroy, (6) impossible to burn, and (7) finally imperishable, it is therefore described as the vajra of emptiness. These are the seven vajra qualities, such as being uncuttable, indestructible, and so forth, according to Jamdrak Rinpoche. [JOKYAB]

    The seven vajra qualities are the following: In the context of the ground, (1) emptiness is uncuttable by the obscuration of disturbing emotions and (2) indestructible by the cognitive obscuration. In the context of the path, (3) its essence is true, (4) its nature is solid, and (5) its function is stable. In the context of the fruition, (6) it is unfettered by the obscuration of disturbing emotions and (7) undefeatable by being unobstructed by the cognitive obscuration. [JOKYAB]

    The *Peak Scripture* is one of the three Yoga tantras known as *Splendor, Peak,* and *Space.* [JOKYAB]

103. The *Assemblage of Realization* can refer to either the chief scripture of Anu Yoga or to *Lama Gongdü,* the major collection of termas revealed by Sangye Lingpa. [EPK]

104. To explain this quote:

> Acts of gentleness will neither tame nor be of benefit to the hosts of rudras whose minds are extremely incorrigible and savage, to the type of beings to be tamed also called *karma krodha.* The natural wrath of the tamer, the wisdom krodha, which is the knowledge of emptiness (prajna), the dharmakaya state of equality, spontaneously defeats the two obscurations. Without moving from that state, the means (upaya) of great compassion shows its natural expression in the form of wrathful rupakayas. Thus, through the union of these two, means and knowledge, those to be tamed experience that the tathagatas manifest in wrathful forms. [JOKYAB]

In yet another way of explaining the above, the tamers, the wisdom krodhas, are the five heruka families according to the Tantra Section, and Eight Sadhana Teachings or Nine Glorious Ones according to the Sadhana Section. The ones to be tamed are the karma krodhas, the hosts of rudras or the loka krodhas, the eight major and minor classes of haughty spirits. [JOKYAB]

The Nine Glorious Ones are the chief herukas in the Eight Sadhana Teachings in addition to the *Guru Vidyadhara.* Sometimes the *Assemblage of Sugatas* is counted as the ninth. [EPK]

The Tantra Section and Sadhana Section are the two major divisions of Mahayoga, the first of the Three Inner Tantras. Mahayoga as scripture is divided into two parts: Tantra Section and Sadhana Section. The Tantra Section consists of the Eighteen Tantras of Mahayoga, while the Sadhana Section is comprised of the Eight Sadhana Teachings. Jamgön Kongtrül says in his *All-Encompassing Knowledge:* "Mahayoga emphasizes means (upaya), the development stage, and the view that liberation is attained through growing accustomed to the insight into the nature of the indivisibility of the superior two truths." The superior two truths in Mahayoga are purity and equality: The pure natures of the aggregates, elements, and sense factors are the male and female buddhas and bodhisattvas. At the same time, everything that appears and exists is of the equal nature of emptiness. [EPK]

105. Indra's vajra is made from the diamond bone of the rishi Curd Drinker and is endowed with a fourfold assurance. The analogy is that a dia-

mond is unmatched by any other precious stone, while the meaning is that Dorje Drakpo Tsal is totally unrivaled by anyone because he embodies the power and strength of all the wrathful ones. [JOKYAB]

What are the four assurances? It is thrown at whomever is hostile. It hits wherever it is thrown. Whoever is hit dies. Whoever dies is guided [to a higher rebirth]. [JOKYAB]

Krodha means wrathful beings. For the details of these wisdom krodhas, karma krodhas, and loka krodhas, see the above note. [EPK]

106. The explanation of the actual body of the text includes these five points: (1) the setting for the talk; what caused the instructions to be given in the context of tantras, statements, and instructions, (2) beginning the teaching; the conditions for this among all the causes and conditions, (3) the result; the meaning of the oral instructions to be fully understood among the three of causes, conditions, and result, (4) the reason for and the relationship to these oral instructions, meaning the four topics such as the reason and so forth, and (5) finally, giving directions to the retinue, the assembly of destined people, and entrusting them with the teachings. [JOKYAB]

The fourth and fifth of these five points appear at the end of Jamgön Kongtrül's commentary and will be part of the final volume. [EPK]

107. The threefold equality means being equal to all the buddhas in having perfected the accumulations, in being enlightened, and in accomplishing the welfare of beings. [JOKYAB]

The Matchless King of the Shakyas is another name for Buddha Shakyamuni. He is called matchless because his aspiration was superior to that of others. [JOKYAB]

Padmakara is called King of Victorious Ones because he conquered the enemy, the four maras. Padmakara means "lotus-born." [JOKYAB]

108. At this point, read Jokyab Rinpoche's further details in Appendix 5: Padmakara and the Four Vidyadhara Levels. [EPK]

The eight great vidyadhara receivers of the transmissions are listed as follows: (1) The receiver of the transmission of Manjushri (Yamantaka) was Manjushrimitra, the vidyadhara of Body. (2) The receiver of the transmission of Mighty Padma (Hayagriva) was Nagarjuna, the vidyadhara of Speech. (3) The receiver of the transmission of Vishuddha was Hungchen-kara, the vidyadhara of Mind. (4) The receiver of the transmission of Amrita Medicine was Vimalamitra, the vidyadhara of Qualities. (5) The receiver of the transmission of Kilaya was Prabhahasti, the vidyadhara of Activities. (6) The receiver of the transmission of Liberating Sorcery, Bötong, was Danasamskrita, the vidyadhara of Mamo. (7) The receiver of the transmission of Maledictory Fierce Mantra, Möpa, was Shantigarbha, the vidyadhara of Fierce Mantra. (8) The receiver of the transmission of Loka was Guhyachandra, the vidyadhara of Mundane Worship. [JOKYAB] [DKR]

In addition, the precious master of Uddiyana followed four masters for receiving the Four Rivers of Empowerment: Garab Dorje, who received the river of empowerment of yidam; King Ja, who received the river of empowerment of tantric scriptures; Buddhaguhya or Vimalamitra, who received the river of empowerment of spiritual teacher; and Shri Singha, who received the river of empowerment of the expression of awareness. [JOKYAB] [DKR]

The word *vidyadhara,* "knowledge-holder," means holding *(dhara)* or upholding the wisdom of knowledge *(vidya)* mantra. [JOKYAB]

109. *Dharmadhatu* means the "realm of phenomena," the suchness in which emptiness and dependent origination are inseparable—the nature of mind and phenomena, which lies beyond arising, dwelling, and ceasing. In his *Buddha Nature,* Thrangu Rinpoche said:

> In this context, the word for space is *ying* in Tibetan, *dhatu* in Sanskrit. It is the same word used in dharmadhatu, the realm or "space" of things. The word *space* is used because the dharmadhatu is like the body or realm of empty space where different things, like clouds, birds, and airplanes can fly around without obstruction. This is because the nature of space is empty and nonexistent. Due to this quality of openness, things can occur. Likewise, dharmadhatu is the essence of things—empty and inconcrete—where all phenomena such as trees, houses, mountains, oneself, other beings, emotions, wisdom, and all experiences can occur openly.

In this book, "dharmadhatu space" is often used as a synonym for buddha nature. [EPK] —

110. Concerning the naturally pure aggregates, elements, and sense-bases, the five aggregates are the five buddha families. The five elements are their five consorts (the five female buddhas). The twelve sense-bases are the male and female bodhisattvas. The purity of the body faculty and so forth are the male wrathful gatekeepers. The object and so forth are the female wrathful gatekeepers. [JOKYAB]

The five elements are earth, water, fire, wind, and space.

The twelve sense-bases are the twelve media for sense perception to occur: the faculties of eye, ear, nose, tongue, body, and mind and their corresponding sense objects—sight, sound, smell, taste, texture, and mental objects. [CNR]

The term "centers and surroundings" is the literal meaning of *mandala*, which in Jamgön Kongtrül's commentary is spelled out word by word. [EPK]

The forty-two peaceful deities and the wrathful deities such as Chemchok and so forth. [JOKYAB]

Forty-two peaceful deities: Samantabhadra and Samantabhadri, the five male and female buddhas, the eight male and female bodhisattvas, the six munis, and the four male and female gatekeepers. Fifty-eight herukas: The five herukas and consorts, eight yoginis, eight tramen goddesses, four female gatekeepers, and twenty-eight ishvaris. [TUR]

111. The channels, winds, and essences mean channels, energies, and essences. The channels are the 72,000 channels and the 40 million minor channels abiding in the body. The winds are the 21,600 winds circulating within the channels. Connected to the winds and permeating [the channels] are the essences, which are the white and red essences. [JO-KYAB]

The sacred places and countries refer to the twenty-four major places, the thirty-two major countries, and the eight charnel grounds. When added together, there are the sixty-four sacred places and countries. In the sixty-four places and countries are the dakas, such as Skull Pieces, and the dakinis, such as Ferocious Lady. [JOKYAB]

The wisdom protectors are the protectors of body, speech, mind, qualities, and activities. The Dharma protectors and guardians comprised of the three classes are: the male class, such as Legden; the female class, such as Mukhale; and the nondual class, such as Ma-ning, the "Neuter." [JOKYAB]

The seventy-two Palgöns, such as the eight classes of Mahadevas. The ten guardians of the directions, such as King Vajra Bearer. [JO-KYAB]

Appearance and existence (snang srid): appearance is the vessel-like world, and existence is the contents-like sentient beings. Also, it can mean "all that appears and exists" (snang tshad srid tshad). [JOKYAB] [DKR]

112. His one name, such as Mahaguru Padmakara, pervades the realms of the ten directions. The [supplication to Guru Rinpoche known as *Barchey Lamsel, Clearing the Obstacles of the Path*,] mentions:

One was Padmakara, *[Barchey Künsel]*
One was Padmasambhava, *[Yishin Norbu]*
And one was Lake-born Vajra. *[Tsokye Nyingtig]*
The secret name was Dorje Drakpo Tsal. *[Dorje Draktsal]* [JOKYAB]

These four names of teachings refer to the *Four Cycles of Guru Sadhana*. [TUR]

Also, within a single realm the number of his various names, such as the eight manifestations, are countless. [JOKYAB]

113. Within just this Saha buddha realm, he is known as the Lord Who Pervades an Ocean of Mandalas. In the pervaded, the infinite ocean of mandalas, the pervader is Guru Padmasambhava, the embodiment of all the families. The analogy is the sun in the sky, [the reflection of] which can be present in countless lakes. [JOKYAB]

114. These eight names are renowned as the eight manifestations of Guru Rinpoche: Padmasambhava, Loden Choksey, Padma Gyalpo, Nyima Öser, Senge Dradrok, Shakya Senge, Dorje Drolö, and Vajradhara of Uddiyana. [TUR]

115. The lotus family of supreme speech is one of the five buddha families. [JOKYAB]

116. In the dharmakaya realm of the Luminous Vajra Essence, the realm of the great, all-pervasive dharmadhatu, he is the original protector Changeless Light, the teacher of complete mastery in that realm. [JOKYAB]

Changeless Light is another name for the dharmakaya buddha Samantabhadra. [TUR]

117. The sambhogakaya realm shines with the natural light of the five wisdom families. The teachers are the five families of the buddha Immense Ocean. [JOKYAB]

The five certainties are: (1) The certain place is the Densely Arrayed Akanishtha. (2) The certain teacher is Vairochana Immense Ocean. (3) The certain retinue are bodhisattvas of the ten bhumis. (4) The certain teaching is the greater vehicle, Mahayana. (5) The certain time is the "continuous wheel of eternity." [JOKYAB]

The five certainties are the same as the five perfections. [CNR]

118. About semiapparent nirmanakaya: due to the power of compassion, the expression of the inner wisdom manifests outwardly in the realms of those to be tamed. Thus, all of the outwardly manifest and semiap-

parent realms, teachers, retinues, and so forth are the manifest aspect of both the buddhas and bodhisattvas. [DKR]

The realm of Great Purity refers to the first of the two types of nirmanakaya, the natural nirmanakayas and the nirmanakayas who tame beings. The realms of the five families of Great Purity are Sukhavati and so forth, with the five teachers being the five buddha families of Amitabha, and so on. [JOKYAB]

119. The nirmanakayas who tame beings are: in the realms of the ten directions of the six worlds, the teachers are the six munis and the gurus of the six classes. [JOKYAB]

120. Saha (Tib. *mi mjed*) means "undivided" because the karmas and kleshas, causes and effects, are not separately divided or differentiated. [JOKYAB]

The one hundred teachers of Sutra and Mantra are as described in the *Padma Kathang,* the *Chronicles of Padma.* [JOKYAB]

One version listing these teachers is the *Crystal Cave Chronicles* by Orgyen Lingpa, also known as *Kathang Sheldragma.* The other is the *Golden Garland Chronicles* by Sangye Lingpa (1340–1396), also known as *Kathang Sertreng.* [EPK]

121. In the teachings of Taksham [Nüden Dorje], Guru Rinpoche has five aspects of Immense Ocean. Each again has its own realms to be tamed and the teachers who tame. [JOKYAB]

122. The Jambu Continent is so-called because it is adorned with the Jambuvriksha tree. [JOKYAB]

The New Treasures refer to the termas revealed by Chokgyur Lingpa (1829–1870) and passed on to his chief recipients, including Jamyang Khyentse Wangpo (1820–1892), Jamgön Kongtrül Lodrö Thaye (1813–1899), the 14th Karmapa Tekchok Dorje (1798–1868), and 15th Karmapa Khakhyab Dorje (1871–1922). A translation of the *Wish-Fulfilling Tree* is found in the *Legend of the Great Stupa.* [EPK]

123. Dhanakosha is the name of a lake in the country of Uddiyana and literally means "Treasury of Wealth." [JOKYAB]

Dhanakosha is the lake or ocean where Padmasambhava miraculously took birth and was discovered by King Indrabodhi. [TUR]

124. *Uddiyana* is Sanskrit for the Tibetan word *Orgyen,* a corruption of the Indian word. The literal meaning is "vehicle of flying" or "going above," "going far." [JOKYAB]

Guru Rinpoche's miraculous birth is accepted by the termas as well as Dakpo Tashi Namgyal. His womb birth is accepted in the *Oral History of Kilaya* and by Taranatha. [JOKYAB]

125. The words "immature being" mean someone who has not yet reached the path of seeing, the first bhumi of the Joyous. [CNR]

126. At this point the lineage of the rulers of Tibet should be explained as descending from Licchavi, who was predicted by the Victorious King of the Munis. Beginning with King Nyatri Tsenpo, they were the Seven Namla Tri, the Six Sala Lek, the Eight Lokla Dey, the Five Tsigla Tsen, the Twelve and a Half Happy Generations, and so forth. In particular, the histories of the Three Ancestral Dharma Kings as well as of the lotsawa Tumi Sambhota should be briefly explained. [JOKYAB]

127. Trisong Deutsen was the son of King Namri Songtsen and a Dharma ruler from among the two types of king: Dharma ruler and secular ruler. [JOKYAB]

Shantarakshita means "Peace Sustainer." He was an incarnation of the bodhisattva Vajrapani, who dwells on the bhumis, and is also known as Bhikshu Bodhisattva Shantarakshita. [JOKYAB]

Also included among the 108 Indian panditas and siddhas were Buddhaguhya and Kamalashila. *Pandita* means "learned one." [JOKYAB] [DKR]

There were 108 translators headed by Vairochana and the others of the Seven Chosen Ones, and Namkhai Nyingpo and the others of the Five Bhikshus. The Sanskrit word for translator, used in Tibetan as *lotsawa,* means "the eye of the world." [JOKYAB]

The Seven Chosen Ones were, according to *Meaningful to Behold,* a biography of Padmasambhava: Shri Ratna of Bal, Shakyaprabha of Chim, Lekdrub of Tsang, Vairochana, the son of Nyasang of Shang, Palgyi Senge of Shubu, and Salnang of Ba, who received the ordination name Yeshe Wangpo. [EPK]

The outer temple is a palace, and the inner temple is the excellent teachings. [JOKYAB]

The two congregations of the Sangha: those with shaved heads and bare feet are the Vinaya followers, and those with braided hair and white robes are the Mantrayana followers. [JOKYAB]

He established the formerly nonexistent tradition of translating the Indian teachings into Tibetan as well as the traditions of expounding and practicing. He established teaching centers for the Tripitaka and sadhana centers for practice. [JOKYAB]

128. The Great Compassionate One is another name for Avalokiteshvara. [CNR]

129. "Matchless" is meant in the sense that Buddha Shakyamuni's resolve and aspiration were superior to those of other [bodhisattvas]. [JOKYAB] About this entrustment to Avalokiteshvara, [the Buddha] said:

> To the north of Vajrasana in the east,
> Lies Purgyal, the land of Tibet.
> It has lofty mountains like pillars of sky,
> Blue lakes like circles of turquoise,
> White glaciers like crystal stupas,
> And yellow meadows like mountains of gold.
> It has sweet scents of forests of medicinal plants,
> Summers adorned with turquoise meadows,
> And its lakes are beautified by golden flowers.
> Listen, Lord of the Snow Mountains, Avalokiteshvara,
> In that land is your pure realm.
> In that realm are your disciples. [JOKYAB]

130. The Tibetan equivalent for Mount Potala is *Riwo Dru-dzin,* "Boat Mountain." [JOKYAB] [EPK]

Potala is the pure realm of Avalokiteshvara, the bodhisattva of compassion. [TUR]

131. The four liberations are through seeing, hearing, remembering, and touching. The material things are the earth, stones, mountains, rocks, and so on. [JOKYAB]

If the teacher knows the narration of the Monkey Meditator, it should be told briefly at this point. [JOKYAB]

Before each name should be added "bodhisattva" such as "bodhisattva kings" and so forth. [JOKYAB]

Being barely able to talk, they would effortlessly, through the blessings of the Noble One, utter OM MANI PADME HUNG. [JOKYAB]

Another name for the snowy land of Tibet is *Silden,* literally meaning the "Cool Land." [JOKYAB]

132. As for "Statements and Realization," the Dharma of Statements is the Three Collections, the Tripitaka, while the Dharma of Realization is the Three Trainings. [JOKYAB]

At this point, read Jokyab Rinpoche's details in Appendix 6, "Shakyamuni's Prophecy about Buddhism in Tibet." [EPK]

The Twin Buddhas, means the representatives of the Buddha—the two Jowo Shakyamuni statues in Lhasa. [JOKYAB]

These two statues were said to have been enshrined in the upper stories of the stupa in Bodhgaya. Later they were brought to Tibet by the two brides to be married to King Songtsen Gampo. Today, one is situated in the Jokhang Temple and the other in the Ramochey Temple in Lhasa. [CNR]

133. The details of the magical display of the fourfold conversion possessed by a nirmanakaya are as follows: conversion through the perfect deeds of his body endowed with great merit, such as the Twelve Deeds and so forth; conversion through the direct perception of the great superknowledges of his mind, which are the six superknowledges; conversion through the great miraculous power of his inconceivable qualities and activities, which are the various magical displays of the deeds of his three secrets; conversion through the knowledge of teaching the five vehicles of his speech or conversion through the Mahayana teaching of his speech. The five vehicles are for gods, humans, shravakas and pratyekabuddhas, bodhisattvas, and the Secret Mantra. [JOKYAB]

These five never-ending adornment wheels refer to the twenty-five qualities of fruition—five each of body, speech, mind, qualities, and activities—that are never-ending, unceasing adornments of dharmadhatu. [TUR]

According to the commentary on the *Lotus Essence Tantra* by Pema Chögyal of Me-nyag, entitled *Radiant Lamp of Jewels,* these twenty-five qualities are described as follows:

The five kayas (bodies) are: (1) The tranquil dharmakaya, the perfection of the benefit for oneself. (2) The unified sambhogakaya, the spontaneously present benefit for others. (3) The manifold nirmanakaya, skilled in the means of taming whomever needs to be tamed. (4) The abhisambodhikaya, the distinct and unmixed apparent aspect of the three kayas. (5) The vajrakaya, their empty aspect and the fact that the three kayas are of one taste in being dharmadhatu.

The five types of speech are: (1) The ultimate speech of dharmakaya, purity beyond expression. (2) The symbolic speech of sambhogakaya, illustrated by bodily forms. (3) The verbal speech of nirmanakaya, possessing the melodiousness of Brahma. (4) The knowledge speech of abhisambodhikaya, appearing as the individual voices of those to be tamed. (5) The wisdom speech of vajrakaya, the nonduality of resounding and being empty.

The five types of mind are: (1) The dharmakaya mind of the wisdom of dharmadhatu. (2) The sambhogakaya mind of discriminating wisdom. (3) The nirmanakaya mind of all-accomplishing wisdom. (4) The abhisambodhikaya mind of mirrorlike wisdom. (5) The wisdom-vajra mind of the wisdom of equality.

The five types of qualities are the perfect qualities of the realm, celestial palace, rays of light, throne, and ornaments.

The five activities are the pacifying, increasing, magnetizing, subjugating, and spontaneous accomplishment of the four activities.

These never-ending adornment wheels of body, speech, mind, qualities, and activities remain unceasing for as long as the space pervades, appearing spontaneously and effortlessly for the welfare of all sentient beings, as many as fill the space. [EPK]

These qualities are the domain of only the tathagatas, the buddhas who have gone (gata) to the state of innate suchness (tatha). It is needless to mention ordinary beings, shravakas, and pratyekabuddhas, since they are not even within the domain of the bodhisattvas of the ten bhumis. [JOKYAB]

134. For details of the places Ngari and Dokham: Mount Tisey surrounded by snow mountains, Gugey surrounded by slate mountains, and Purang surrounded by water are the Three Districts of Ngari in Upper Tibet, which were formed in the manner of a pond. Lharu and Geru in Tsang and Yeru and Yönru in Central Tibet are the four districts of Ü and Tsang in the middle, which were formed in the manner of an irrigation channel. The Six Ridges are Zalmo Ridge, Tsawa Ridge, Markham Ridge, Menyag-rab Ridge, Pobor Ridge, and Mardza Ridge. The Four Rivers are Machu, Dzachu, Drichu, and Ngulchu. These are the Six Ridges and Four Rivers of Lower Dokham, which were formed in the manner of a plough furrow. Thus it has been told.

It is also said that the Three Districts of Ngari in Upper Tibet were formed in the manner of a warrior's battle axe, the Four Districts of Ü and Tsang in the middle were formed in the manner of a precious gold belt, and the Six Ridges and Four Rivers of Lower Dokham were formed in the manner of a beautiful lining of plush silk. [JOKYAB]

135. *Vikramashila* means "Subjugating Disposition." [JOKYAB]

Since the king was the ruler of Tibet, the lower story was made in

Tibetan style with deities of clay [mixed with bark paper]. Since China was the "uncle," the middle story was made in Chinese style with deities of leather. Since India was the source of the Dharma, the upper story was made in Indian style with deities of plaited cloth [glued together]. [JOKYAB] [TUR]

According to the Abhidharma cosmology, the four continents surrounding Mount Sumeru are called Superior Body, Jambu Continent, Cow Utilizing, and Unpleasant Sound. [EPK]

The inner representations were representations of body, such as Mahabodhi; representations of speech, such as chiefly the Indian copies of the sutras and tantras; representations of mind, such as the four kinds of stupas, and so forth. [JOKYAB]

136. Guru Rinpoche predicted the translators Vairochana, Kawa Paltsek, and Chok-ro Lui Gyaltsen. The training they were given was chiefly in the science of languages. The lotsawas and panditas were placed together in pairs. [JOKYAB]

137. The ripening empowerments and liberating instructions are those of Vajrayana. [JOKYAB]

There are the tantras of tantra, the statements of tantra, and the instructions of tantra, [and so forth]. This is to be combined also with the statements and instructions, making nine aspects in all. [JOKYAB]

Tantras, statements, and instructions are usually equated with the Three Inner Tantras of Maha, Anu, and Ati, but it is also taught that each of the Three Inner Tantras has the three aspects of tantra, statement, and instruction. [JOKYAB]

138. Often the phrase "king, subject, and companion" means King Trisong Deutsen, the translator Vairochana, and the dakini Yeshe Tsogyal. [TUR]

139. The four grand snow mountains of Tibet are the Yarlha Shampo snow mountain, Nöjin Gangsang, Jomo Gangkar, Tidro Gang; these are in the four intermediate directions. [JOKYAB]

The eight great caves are Yangdzong Phuk, Chimphu Phuk, Kharchu Phuk, Sheldrak Phuk, Senge Dzongphuk, Yerpa Phuk, Yama Lungphuk, and Namkha Dingphuk at Chuwori. [JOKYAB]

The four renowned lakes are Yamdrok Yutso, Trishö Gyalmo, which is the same as Lingtso Ngönmo, Tso Mapham, and Namtso to the north. [JOKYAB]

The five lands are, according to the *Chronicles [of Padma]:*

In the center is the Sabbu land of Shang.
In the Kongpo district to the east is the Jönpa land.
To the south is the Sibtsen land of Mön.
To the west is the Phagri land of Go.
To the north is the Droma land of Kyi. [JOKYAB]

The three valleys are, again, according to the *Chronicles of Padma:*

To the southwest is the secret land of the Dremo Valley [Sikkim].
To the northwest is the secret land of the Khenpa Valley.
To the northeast is the secret land of the Lungsum Valley.
[JOKYAB]

About the secret countries and great districts, the *Chronicles of Padma* further says:

To the southeast is the secret country of Padma Ling.

This and the others are the great districts. The other districts I have not been able to identify from any reliable source, so please include them here when they have been established. [JOKYAB]

140. The primordially established major sacred places, such as Potala and Uddiyana. [JOKYAB]

141. Destined disciples have liberation occurring simultaneously with realization, as in the case of King Indrabhuti. [JOKYAB]

The disciples of lesser fortune were implanted with the seed of emancipation from samsara. [JOKYAB]

142. Image treasures are statue representations. Dharma treasures are Guru Sadhana, Great Perfection, and sadhanas of the Great Compassionate One. Wealth treasures are things of great value. Substance treasures are samaya substance, attributes, and so forth. [JOKYAB]

143. From the Fourth Guide [Buddha Shakyamuni] until the Fifth Guide [Maitreya], treasure revealers and treasure teachings will appear and continually accomplish the welfare of beings. [JOKYAB]

The difference between central and surrounding lands is whether a place is endowed with Dharma teachings or is a barbaric borderland. [JOKYAB]

This is the direct valid perception of all intelligent and wise people of the present times. [JOKYAB]

144. It is generally accepted that Padmasambhava spent fifty-five years and six months in Tibet and Kham. Scholars disagree as to the exact dates. See Tulku Thondup's *Hidden Teachings of Tibet.* [EPK]

145. In this chapter, Jamgön Kongtrül quotes only the beginning and end of these two sections from the root text. The main body of this chapter, including the root text interspersed with "filling-in commentary" by Jokyab Rinpoche, is found in Appendix 8, "Establishing the Basis for Beginning the Teaching," and Appendix 9, "The Actual Beginning of the Teaching." [EPK]

146. Designations are [usually] of three types: cognitive, expressive, and engaged [describing the domains of thought, word, and deed]—mental designations of cognition, verbal designations of expression, and physical designations of engagement. [JOKYAB]

   Nonconcurrent formations are defined as any formation that is neither endowed with matter nor [concurrent with a cognitive state of] mind. In this case matter is composed of material particles, and mind is what is conscious and cognizant. [JOKYAB]

   The Dharma seal is one of the four seals also called four *mudras*. [JOKYAB]

   Deities: to develop the deity from a seed syllable or accomplishing the deity by a mantra and so forth is defined as "deity." [JOKYAB]

   Buddhas are defined as buddhas among the Precious Ones. [JOKYAB]

   Appearance is from among appearance and emptiness. [JOKYAB]

   Indivisible: since buddhas and the syllables are indivisible, they are defined as one. [JOKYAB]

   There are six considerations due to the differences in people's conceptions and due to the different types of context. [JOKYAB]

147. The luminous nature of mind is itself spontaneously manifest as syllables, and besides that there does not exist any concrete thing whatsoever to be called "syllables." [JOKYAB]

148. To explain this quote further: In a sutra [the Buddha] says, "Subhuti, syllables transcend superficial convention and are in the ultimate sense the unborn natural state, the nonarising essence of A endowed with the three emancipations. The empty essence of this A is itself the luminous nature of mind; it utterly transcends all confines of mental constructs, such as the permanence of being concrete or the nothingness of being inconcrete." [JOKYAB]

149. Longchen Rabjam, the great Omniscient Lord of Dharma, taught these [four types] as: (1) the syllables E and VAM, which are the ultimate natural state, (2) the vowels and consonants, which are the nadi sylla-

bles abiding in the body, (3) the [Buddha's] Words and the Treatises, which are the audible syllables of utterance, and (4) the final syllables of fruition, which are exclusively sublime teaching. [JOKYAB]

Syllables also have the three levels of being impure, half pure, and utterly pure, as well as the aspects of ground, path, and fruition. [JO-KYAB]

150. Jokyab Rinpoche's teachings on the sixty aspects of melodious speech are explained in Appendix 10, in accord with both Sutra and Tantra. [EPK]

151. The wind of luminosity is the wind that manifests from the extremely subtle wisdom wind. From this wind of luminosity appears the slightly more coarse wind of the manifest aspects of "appearance, increase, and attainment." From that again appear the coarse ten winds, such as the life-upholding wind. [JOKYAB]

152. The vajra body and so forth appearing from the fivefold great emptiness means the five syllables of great emptiness, as follows. In the center is the short A in the form of a curved knife, which symbolizes all-pervading space. To the east is the syllable E in the shape of a staff, which symbolizes the vajra wisdom of wind. To the south is the syllable RI in the shape of a circle, the anusvara, which symbolizes the vajra speech of fire. To the east is the syllable LI in the shape of a plowshare, which symbolizes the vajra body of earth. To the north is the syllable U in the shape of a visarga, which symbolizes the vajra mind of water. For the details about them, see the drawings accompanied by annotations. [JOKYAB]

These drawings are missing from our original manuscript. [EPK]

The anusvara, the two circles of the vowelless MA, is the vajra body. The two A syllables are the vajra mind. The two visarga circles are the vajra speech. The two indestructible HA syllables are the vajra wisdom.

One must examine how they are combined with the four vajras: the [two] anusvaras are the vajra body, the [two] A syllables are the vajra speech, the circles are the vajra mind, and the [two syllables] HA are the vajra wisdom. [JOKYAB]

The circles in this context are the two small circles after the syllable AH or HOH. [EPK]

At this point a short sound-practice is required, so it is excellent if one knows how, otherwise it is also permissible to omit. [JOKYAB]

153. *Ali Kali* means the A-string and the KA-string. [JOKYAB]

The sixteen vowels and thirty-four consonants of the Sanskrit sylla-

bary are: A Ā I Ī U Ū Ṛ Ṝ Ḷ Ḹ E AI O AU AM AḤ and KA KHA
GA GHA NA CA CHA JA JHA ÑA ṬA ṬHA ḌA ḌHA ṆA TA
THA DA DHA NA PA PHA BA BHA MA YA RA LA VA ŚA ṢA
SA HA KṢAḤ. [EPK]

The secret mantras, the knowledge mantras, and the dharani mantras have many different connotations, such as secret mantras being
Father Tantra, knowledge mantras being Mother Tantra, and dharani
mantras being Nondual Tantra. Here all the root mantras, essence
mantras, and quintessence mantras taught in the Father, Mother, and
Nondual Tantras are secret mantras. The Six-Syllable Mantra, the
GATE mantra (OM GATE GATE PARAGATE PARASAMGATE BODHI SVAHA)
are knowledge mantras. The Vajra Vidarana mantra and so forth are
dharani mantras. [JOKYAB]

154. In his notes, Jokyab Rinpoche quotes this line as "The sacred syllable
of the great meaning." [EPK]

155. These lines are explained as: "Arising from within sound, it is by nature without arising. Beyond expression as words such as A, it is the
supreme cause of all expressions." [JOKYAB]

156. *Nada* means "tone of sound." [JOKYAB]

A is name-and-form, U is the sense-bases, MA is contact, A is sensation, AH is craving, the two visarga circles are grasping, H is becoming,
U is birth, MA is old age and death, HA is ignorance, U is formation, HA
is consciousness, or the visargas are consciousness. [JOKYAB]

Here the vowelless HU symbolizes ignorance. The reason why HU is
defined as ignorance is mentioned in the *Kalachakra:* "Ignorance is
defined as the transference of the elements, and here the root of existence is symbolized by the syllable HU, the nature of the transferring
elements of the union of male and female." [JOKYAB]

The four vajras are the unchanging vajra body, the unceasing vajra
speech, the undeluded vajra mind, and indivisible vajra wisdom. [TUR]

The fact that each of the four vajras has the nature of the three kayas
means that there are twelve when combining each of the four vajras
with the three kayas, such as the dharmakaya of the vajra body, the
sambhogakaya of the vajra body, the nirmanakaya of the vajra body,
and so forth. [JOKYAB]

157. The manifestation of these syllables appearing as body, speech, and
mind means that the syllables at the time of the ground are body,
speech, and mind. At the time of the path they are the vajra recitation

of the three syllables. At the time of fruition they are the three vajras. [JOKYAB]

158. "Hooded" means the hood of a snake and therefore [the realm of] the nagas. [JOKYAB]

159. The three doors are the body, the voice, and the mind. [TUR]

160. This line refers to the syllable HOH. [JOKYAB]

161. The engaging consciousnesses are the five sense-consciousnesses. [JO-KYAB]

To explain briefly the four vajra syllables mentioned, Jamyang Khyentse Wangpo has taught that at the beginning of the *Hevajra Tantra,* the quintessence of the Mother Tantras, is written EVAM MAYA SHRUTAM EKASMIN SAMAYE. The tantra, which was translated into Tibetan, [continues with:] "The essence of the body, speech, and mind of all the blessed tathagatas abides in the bhaga of the Vajra Queen." This sentence summarizes the entire meaning of the *Hevajra Tantra* from beginning to end. Similarly, in this context, the four vajra syllables summarize the entire meaning of *Lamrim Yeshe Nyingpo* from beginning to end. [JOKYAB]

162. The state of passion is the conceptual notion of passion belonging under the mind consciousness or mental cognition. [JOKYAB]

The obscuration of transference refers to the obscuration of the transference of the white and red elements. [JOKYAB]

163. The four empowerments: The vase empowerment has the four aspects of approach and accomplishment. The secret empowerment has the four aspects of channels, winds, essences, and mind. The knowledge empowerment has the four aspects of the wisdoms of the four joys. As for the word empowerment, Trekchö has the four aspects of cognizance, emptiness suffused with awareness, and indivisibility. Tögal has the four visions. [JOKYAB]

The four visions are four stages in the practice of the Great Perfection: manifest dharmata, increased experience, awareness reaching fullness, and exhaustion of concepts and phenomena. [TUR]

The four yogas are the shape yoga of the development stage, the profound yoga of mantra, the ultimate yoga of Dharma, and the yoga of total purity. [JOKYAB]

Relative self-consecration means the upper gate of one's own body. [JOKYAB]

The mandala circle means the lower gate of another's body, the phonya path of great bliss. [JOKYAB]

164. The wisdom of emptiness is the dharmadhatu wisdom, here symbolized by the syllable HOH. [JOKYAB]

165. The three kayas are the dharmakaya, sambhogakaya, and nirmanakaya. The three kayas as ground are essence, nature, and capacity; as path they are bliss, clarity, and nonthought; and as fruition they are the three kayas of buddhahood. The three kayas of buddhahood are the dharmakaya, which is free from elaborate constructs and endowed with the twenty-one sets of enlightened qualities; the sambhogakaya, which is of the nature of light and endowed with the perfect major and minor marks perceptible only to bodhisattvas; and the nirmanakaya, which manifests in forms perceptible to both pure and impure beings. [TUR]

166. There are three types of "tantra of words": tantra manifest as sound is mind transmission or both the transmission of mind and symbol; tantra uttered as sound is the oral transmission of great masters; and tantra turned into symbols is the letter characters of the scriptures. For example, the terma teachings belong to the category of the three types of tantra of words: the mind transmission is to keep in mind what Padmasambhava initially heard, the oral transmission is what he uttered to the king and the subjects as the natural sound of dharmata, and the Word Transmission of Yellow Parchment is the teaching written down on the yellow parchment [and concealed as a terma for later discovery and propagation]. [JOKYAB]
The "tantra of meaning" is ground, path, and fruition. [JOKYAB]

167. Both the *Tantra of the Union of Sun and Moon* and the *Talgyur Root Tantra* are counted among the Seventeen Dzogchen Tantras. [JOKYAB]
According to Khenpo Ngak-chung, the *Tantra of the Union of Sun and Moon* shows the experiences a person undergoes in the intermediate state, the bardo, after passing away. It teaches how to resolve one's master's oral instructions during the bardo of this life, how to stabilize awareness during the bardo of dying, how to attain enlightenment through recognizing awareness during the bardo of dharmata, and, if necessary, how to be assured of a rebirth in a natural nirmanakaya realm during the bardo of becoming and there attain buddhahood without further rebirths. The *Talgyur Root Tantra,* the chief tantra of the Instruction Section of Dzogchen, explains how to attain the level

of nirmanakaya and how to accomplish the welfare of others through practices related to sound. [EPK]

168. The ordinary setting is covered in Chapter 4. [EPK]

169. The five aspects of the basis are the five perfections. The realms of the three kayas are regarded as three kinds. [JOKYAB]

170. HE is the cause or ground, dharmakaya, the future, and the emancipation of nonformation. RU is the place, disintegration, the path, and thus it is the past, the emancipation of marklessness. KA is the particular, the fruition, and thus it is the present, nirmanakaya, and the emancipation of wishlessness.

In another way, *hela* means "drinking" or "enjoying," *rudhira* means "blood," and *kapala* means "bliss sustainer" or "skull cup." Translated into Tibetan *heruka* means "drinking the blood of the skull." That is to say, having drunk the blood of the ego-clinging and disturbing emotions in one's own stream of being, the heruka drinks the blood of the ego-clinging and disturbing emotions in the stream of being of other disciples. In short, *heruka* means "blood drinker." [JOKYAB]

171. The realm of the Great Sphere: Among the six types of Akanishtha mentioned by Buddhaguhya, this is the real or ultimate Akanishtha, which is called Palace of Dharmadhatu. According to the Great Perfection, the dharmakaya realm is called the Luminous Vajra Essence. This was stated by Manjugosha [Jamyang Khyentse Wangpo]. [JOKYAB]

Concerning pure realms, Sukhavati, the Blissful Realm, and so on are celestial; the Glorious [Copper-Colored] Mountain, Potala, and so on are terrestrial. The impure realms are the abodes of the six classes of beings. [JOKYAB]

Sukhavati is the pure realm of Buddha Amitabha. [EPK]

172. The supramundane beings are the triple Sangha of shravakas, pratyeka-buddhas, and bodhisattvas, as well as the vidyadhara Sangha, such as the Five Eminent Ones. The mundane beings are the six classes of sentient beings. [JOKYAB]

The Five Eminent Ones were five vidyadharas who received the first Anu Yoga teachings in this world: a god, a naga, a yaksha, a rakshasa, and the human vidyadhara Vimalakirti. [TUR]

173. The dharmakaya teaching is the Great Perfection Ati Yoga. The sambhogakaya teachings are the Three Outer Tantras of Secret Mantra as

well as the two inner of Maha and Anu. The nirmanakaya teachings are the three causal vehicles of the shravakas, pratyekabuddhas, and bodhisattvas. [JOKYAB]

174. The fourth time of equality of dharmakaya should be identified as meaning the equality of the four times: the conditioned three transient times and the unconditioned, single, unchanging time. [JOKYAB]

The threefold ripening of disciples is the ripening of nature, faculty, and thought. The nature is ripened through having trained in the Dharma and the path during many former lives. By the power of that, the faculties are ripened, since the five ruling faculties of perfection have become extremely sharp. By the power of that, discriminating knowledge has ripened from the present intelligence obtained at birth.

It is also held that the threefold ripening of disciples is of nature, interest, and thought. But the meaning is identical, since interest is the five ruling faculties of faith and so forth. [JOKYAB]

175. The three types of pleasing actions are to please by means of material things, service, and practice. The last is the most eminent of the three. The first two perfect the accumulation of merit and the latter the accumulation of wisdom. [JOKYAB]

176. Ajita [Maitreya], the Undefeatable, said: "Having first of all adorned his mind stream with the immense light of discriminating knowledge, which establishes knowable objects resulting from learning the philosophical root texts and so forth from a spiritual guide, the wise bodhisattvas will quickly engage in all the ultimate experiences of the buddhas." [JOKYAB]

177. Separating or joining is synonymous with growing distant or close. [JOKYAB]

178. The word "space" (Tib. ying, Skt. dhatu) here refers to the dharmadhatu nature that is synonymous with the sugata essence. It is called "space" because of being uncompounded, beyond mental constructs, and beyond arising, dwelling, and ceasing. The use of the word "space" in this context should not be mistaken for physical space, which totally lacks a cognizant quality. The dharmadhatu space of one's buddha nature is always indivisible from wakefulness. [TUR]

179. The victorious Maitreya taught in the *Uttaratantra:*

> Like earth on water and water on wind,
> Wind fully dwells on space.

But space does not dwell on anything.
Similarly, the aggregates, elements, and sense-bases
All dwell on the karmic actions and disturbing emotions,
And the karmas and disturbing emotions dwell on incorrect
   thinking.
Incorrect thinking dwells fully on the purity of mind
But the natural qualities of mind
Do not dwell on any of them.

Explaining the last four lines of this quotation, "The individual karmas and disturbing emotions dwell on incorrect thinking while the incorrect thinking, which clings by mistaking nonexistence for existence, the obscuration of mental fabrications, dwells on the purity of the mind, the sugata essence. But the naturally pure qualities of the mind-essence do not dwell on any of the karmas or disturbing emotions." [JOKYAB] [DKR]

180. Explaining this quotation from the *Uttaratantra*, "Just as the example of the sky is all-pervading and present throughout all of the other four elements, having the nature of being without the concept of good or evil, likewise, the meaning of this is that the immaculate dharmadhatu space of the mind's nature similarly pervades and is present everywhere throughout samsara, nirvana, and the path." [JOKYAB]

The *Uttaratantra*, literally "Unexcelled Continuity," is one of the Five Doctrines of Maitreya, written down by the great Indian master Asanga. A translation of the *Uttaratantra, The Changeless Nature* by Katia and Ken Holmes, is available from Samye Ling in Scotland. For a discussion of its general meaning, see Khenchen Thrangu Rinpoche's *Buddha Nature* (Rangjung Yeshe Publications, 1993) and *The Uttara Tantra: A Treatise on Buddha Nature* (Sri Satguru Publications, 1994). [EPK]

181. The word "potential" (rigs) is sometimes also translated as "family" or "nature." It is synonymous with sugata essence, tathagata-garbha, and buddha nature. [EPK]

182. For Jokyab Rinpoche's details about the different Buddhist philosophical schools' view about this nature, see Appendix 4, "The Sugata Essence." [EPK]

183. To explain the quotation from the *Sutra of the King of Samadhi*: "Pure by being free from the two temporary obscurations and crystal clear because dharmakaya does not dwell on anything whatsoever, the nature of mind is primordially luminous because of not being tainted by

obscuration. It is unstirred or undisturbed by the primary and subsidiary disturbing emotions, as well as being uncompounded by causes
and conditions. This, the all-pervading sugata essence, is the original
nature that is primordially present." This explanation was according
to Jamdrak Rinpoche. [JOKYAB] [DKR]

184. Concerning what has been taught in all the profound tantras of Secret
Mantra: the Three Outer Tantras of Mantrayana define the sugata essence as "profound and luminous nondual wisdom." The Inner Mantrayana defines the ground in any of the different classifications of
ground, path, and fruition as "nature" or "basic condition." In regard
to having purified the temporary defilements and having actualized
the ground by the power of dispelling them, it is defined as "fruition."
[JOKYAB]

   E and VAM are what was described in the quotations [in Chapter 2].
Vajra being is the unity of emptiness and compassion and the inseparability of emptiness and bliss. Tantra (continuity) is the ground tantra of
the indivisible two truths. The great unchanging sphere means the
primordial ground of the single sphere of dharmakaya that is free from
angles or corners. Luminosity is the uncompounded nature, present
throughout all of samsara and nirvana. In particular, the New Schools
of Secret Mantra use the phrase "ultimate coemergent wisdom," while
the Nyingma School uses "self-existing wakefulness." This will be
further explained below in the context of identifying the deity to be
accomplished. [JOKYAB] (To appear in *The Light of Wisdom*, vol. 2.)
[EPK]

185. To explain this quote from the *Hevajra Tantra:* "The precepts and samayas of all the perfect buddhas without exception fully abide as the
letters E and VAM, the empty bliss that is the unity of emptiness and
compassion and the unity of development and completion." [JOKYAB]

186. To explain the whole quotation: "That which is called 'potential' (rigs)
is explained with the term 'continuity of ground.' This ground continuity is taught to be the pure essence of dharmata, which is present
since primordial time. Indestructible in the end, beyond dwelling in
the between, and without arising in the beginning, this is proclaimed
to be the primordial ground of the all-pervading and original sovereign lord." [JOKYAB]

   Why is it called "continuity of ground" or "continuity of cause"?
It is the ground or cause from which both samsara and nirvana arise,

since samsara and nirvana are produced depending upon whether or not it has been embraced by some means. And since its nature remains unchanged and continual from sentient being to buddhahood, it is called "continuity." [JOKYAB]

187. The two types of potential are the naturally present potential and the developed potential. [EPK]

At the time of the ground, the naturally present potential is emptiness, and the developed potential is cognizance. At the time of awakening the naturally present potential, one feels immeasurable interest, devotion, and joy when hearing about the nature of emptiness, and at the time of awakening the developed potential, one sheds tears out of compassion for sentient beings. An analogy for these two potentials is that the naturally present potential is present as the essence of emptiness, like a jewel mine, and the developed potential is present as the developed qualities of the path, like cultivating a wish-fulfilling tree.

At the time of the path, the two types of potential are, respectively, the five paths that are caused by the forming cause of emptiness and conditioned by the coproducing condition of compassion, as well as the ten bhumis that are caused by the forming cause of compassion and conditioned by the coproducing condition of emptiness.

At the time of fruition, the naturally present potential is dharmakaya, and the developed potential is sambhogakaya. Hence they are of the nature of the sixty-four qualities of freedom and maturation. [JOKYAB]

188. To explain this quote from the *Uttaratantra:* "If you and all sentient beings had not the potential for awakening, you would not feel weary of samsaric pain. You would not feel enthusiastic desire for the pure qualities of nirvana, nor would you even pursue the relinquishment of suffering and the attainment of happiness, or aspire for it with the desire to attain the fruition." [JOKYAB]

This phrase is also found in the *Sutra of the Lion's Roar of Queen Shrimala,* included in *A Treasury of Mahayana Sutras* (Pennsylvania State University Press, 1983). [EPK]

189. To explain this quote from *Uttaratantra:* "Perceiving the different faults of suffering and the virtues of happiness of samsara and nirvana, the three levels of impure existence and the three types of pure nirvana result from having the potential of buddha nature. Why is that? It is because sentient beings without the potential for the two bodies of

buddhahood to arise would have no such perception or understanding of the fault of suffering and the virtue of happiness." [JOKYAB]

190. The *Vajra Dome,* which is the *Instruction Tantra of the Two Segments* says: "In the element of space, whatever exists—which means all that is pervaded by space—in the thousands of world systems—which means in the mental continuum of the sentient beings in the countless worlds of the three realms—the mind of the Awakened One, Mahamudra, which is the union of emptiness endowed with the supreme of all aspects and the perfect and most eminent unchanging great bliss, always remains present, like the sky, which is beyond analogy." This was said by Jamdrak Rinpoche. [JOKYAB]

191. For an explanation of this quote see the reference under "look truly into the true" in the index. [EPK]

192. The six classes of beings are gods, demigods, humans, animals, hungry ghosts, and hell beings. [TUR]

193. "Confusion arising from the presence of a basis" means being deluded while possessing the sugata essence, which is the ground of both samsara and nirvana. An example for this is coemergent ignorance, like a person with blurred eyesight meeting together with conceptual ignorance, like the time of dusk, engaging in the cognition that apprehends, due to the cause and condition of these two kinds of ignorance, the five sense objects of visual form, sound, and so forth, for instance, a mottled rope being seen to be a snake, because of the existence of snakes in a certain area. [JOKYAB]

Confusion arising from no presence, the temporary confusion, is like an eye with the blurred vision of coemergent ignorance seeing an apparition of hair in the sky, the conceptual ignorance. [JOKYAB]

Confusion arising from indivisibility of the two [above] is like the essence of camphor having two abilities—just as confusion and liberation both take place from the ground—because it can be a medicine for the disease of heat and a poison for the disease of wind, and thus both samsara and nirvana appear. [JOKYAB]

194. The single-nature ignorance is the presence of the mere quality of not recognizing the pure nature of the sugata essence, the subtle cause for the cognitive obscuration in not recognizing one's nature at the time of the space of the all-ground, which is undecided as to being pure or impure and which has not split up into the division of confusion and liberation. [JOKYAB]

The cause that is concurrent with the preceding and the proceeding is the ignorance that is accompanying or coemergent with the pure dharmata. This is the cognizant and nonconceptual all-ground consciousness, which is the actual cognitive obscuration and is present as the potential for the confusion of the seven collections to arise when meeting with an object condition. [JOKYAB]

The mutually cooperating cause is the conceptual mind consciousness, the conceptual ignorance that is the cognizant quality of this all-ground which, without any other assistance than itself, apprehends as a self-entity itself as being the inner subject, the empty aspect, and which labels as good or bad the external objects, the manifest aspect, as the five sense objects. [JOKYAB]

The perpetuating cause, from the obscuration of disturbing emotions that have appeared, to virtue and nonvirtue that will appear due to the seven collections and their subsidiary aspects, is what has the power of definitely yielding its individual result of virtue or nonvirtue through accumulating the karmic tendencies of the seven collections. It is present in [or as] the all-ground consciousness. [JOKYAB]

195. The mind consciousness, which is subtle thought occurrence, can be divided into two aspects: disturbed-mind consciousness and subsequent cognition. (1) The disturbed-mind consciousness is gross feelings of like and dislike that fixate on a self-entity with regard to the all-ground by thinking "I am" and makes the consciousnesses [cognitions] disturbed with desire, anger, and delusion or causes weariness. (2) The subsequent mind is so-called because it is the extremely subtle thought occurrence, which forms the cause for a sequence of cognition. It is the six collections—consisting of the five sense consciousnesses, such as visual cognition, in addition to the mental cognition of subtle thought occurrence—that create the uninterrupted flow of a sequence of sense objects, such as visual form arising and ceasing, and place the seeds of karmic powers for accumulating disturbing emotions in the all-ground. [JOKYAB]

All-ground consciousness, alaya-vijnana: The basis for these two aspects of subsequent cognition and disturbed-mind consciousness and the retainer of all the manifold tendencies and seeds of virtue and nonvirtue is known as the "labeling basis for confusion," and thus it is in all the scriptural traditions defined as the all-ground consciousness. In particular, the following are its synonyms for an identical nature: all-ground for true application, all-ground for manifold tendencies, perpetuating consciousness, mistaken cognition, single-nature ignorance or coemergent ignorance, tendencies for the three experiences of transference, and cognitive obscuration.

The all-ground consciousness and the disturbed-mind conscious-ness are directed inward. The six collections are directed outward. In particular, the mental cognition assists in both outward and inward direction. [JOKYAB]

196. Nontransferring karmic action is to take rebirth in the Realm of Form, because of having cultivated the four dhyanas, or in the Four Spheres, because of having cultivated the four formless states. [JOKYAB]

197. The all-ground consciousness is not recognizing one's natural face as the cognizant quality. In the first moment of the subtle mind con-sciousness, the disturbed-mind consciousness of formation stirred and labeled the outer objects, the manifest aspect, and the inner, the empty aspect, as being a separate self and other. [JOKYAB]

From that came the five sense consciousnesses perceiving visual form, sound, and so on; sensation, which is the mind consciousness; and conception, which is the disturbed-mind consciousness. [JOKYAB]

At this point, read Appendix 7, "The Five Aggregates." [EPK]

198. The related causes of outer dependent origination are root, trunk, branch, leaf, flower, and fruit. The related conditions are stabilizing earth, adhering water, maturing fire, expanding wind, accommodating space, and gradually changing time.

The twelve related causes of inner dependent origination are de-scribed in a sutra: "Because of ignorance, formation arises; likewise, successively, consciousness, name and form, the six sense-bases, con-tact, sensation, craving, grasping, and becoming. Because of birth arises old age and death, sorrow, lamentation, misery, unhappiness, and distress. Thus this great mass of total suffering arises."

The six related conditions are as mentioned above. For further de-tails look in the *Salu Sprout Sutra.* [JOKYAB]

199. There is nothing that is not embraced by this unfabricated continuous instant, the sugata essence of dharmakaya. There is also nothing that is not produced by the obscuring continuous instant of deluded think-ing, the temporary confusion. [JOKYAB]

In his *Repeating the Words of the Buddha,* Tulku Urgyen Rinpoche says: "That which connects one's mind with all the negative karma or imprints from the past is conceptual thinking. The moment conceptual thinking is absent there is nothing to tie samsara together; it is cut, just like a rope that has been cut cannot bind. Look into what samsara is based on, and see it is the moment-to-moment delusion. This string of deluded moments is called the "continuous instant of delusion," and is the basis of samsara. Among the five aggregates, it is called formation."

200. The eight gates manifesting as outward luminosity are described as follows. The eight gates of spontaneous presence, which are the self-display of awareness rising from the ground, manifested from the stirring of the wisdom wind, breaking the seal of the youthful vase body, the original ground space of primordial purity. At that moment the dharmakaya manifestation of primordial purity appeared above, like a cloudless sky, and the luminous sambhogakaya realms filled the expanse of sky straight ahead. From the expression of that, the great ground-manifestation appeared below, and from its expression below appeared the sambhogakaya manifestations, the manifestation of nirmanakaya realms in the cardinal and intermediate directions. Further below, from the gate of samsara, appeared the infinite self-manifest realms of the six classes of beings. All of this appeared naturally from the manifestation of the eight gates of spontaneous presence, and thus the great display of samsara and nirvana manifested simultaneously. Thus it has been taught. [JOKYAB]

When the inner luminosity appeared as outward luminosity, the manifestation of essence was unobstructedly self-luminous, the manifestation of nature was primordially radiant as five lights, and the manifestation of compassion was self-manifest from the quality of openness, like a cloudless sky. [JOKYAB]

The eight gates of the manifestation modes are described in the *Tantra of the Great Graceful Auspiciousness:* "Unobstructed space manifests as compassion, unobstructed appearance manifests as five lights, unobstructed enjoyment manifests as wisdom, unobstructed essence manifests as kayas, unobstructed view manifests as nonduality, unobstructed means manifests as liberation from extremes, the perfected entrance gate of pure wisdom, and unobstructed impure capacity like a precious wish-fulfilling jewel." The eminent Jamdrak Rinpoche described them as being identical with the eight collections of consciousness. [JOKYAB]

201. The *Lelag* is propably the *Leulag Magical Net,* one of the eight sections of scriptures on *Magical Net (Mayajala).* [EPK]

202. The *Abhidharma Sutra* explains that samsara has neither beginning nor end when considering sentient beings in general. When considering a particular person, although samsara is without beginning and end, the individual possesses the cause for bringing an end to samsaric existence when awakening his potential and attaining liberation. [JOKYAB]

203. The unwholesome habits of the habitual tendencies of one's mind are like the rigidity of a piece of wood or the unyielding quality of an uncultivated field. A "hard virgin field" means wild lands or wild meadows, which are hard and difficult to cultivate. [JOKYAB]

    Grain free from the defects of blight, frost, or rot. [JOKYAB]

204. "Wrongdoing" literally means "unmentionable," in the sense that, needless to say, it is something which one should not commit, but also which one should not dare speak about, or which is not appropriate to mention. [JOKYAB]

    In short, his conduct of body and speech is pure by possessing the disciplines. He accepts disciples by possessing the superior intention. He is learned in what should be known by possessing discriminating knowledge. According to Mantrayana, he should, in addition, possess experience and a lineage. Among all these qualities, the most important is to have superior intention, which means an altruistic attitude and compassion. [JOKYAB]

205. The *Sutra of the Descent to Lanka* says:

    > As long as there are different conceptions,
    > There will be no end to the number of vehicles.

    Thus the master should have distinguished the nature of all the teachings by means of studying, reflecting upon, and practicing the innumerable stages of the paths corresponding to the innumerable vehicles. [JOKYAB]

    See also Appendix 1, "The Six Limits and Four Modes." [EPK]

    To be endowed with the signs of progress is as follows. The lesser signs of progress are to equalize the eight worldly concerns and to have sense pleasure arise as helpers for the practice. The medium signs of progress are the qualities of elimination, acceptance, and the gazes. Beyond that are the greater signs of progress. The signs of progress should be combined with the path of accumulation, joining, and the rest of the five paths. [JOKYAB]

    The eight worldly concerns are: attachment to gain, pleasure, praise, and fame, and aversion to loss, pain, blame, and bad reputation. [CNR]

206. The details of the three qualities of knowledge, compassion, and ability can be found in the authoritative scriptures. [JOKYAB]

For instance, see Thrangu Rinpoche's *Buddha Nature,* Chapter 1. [EPK]

207. The three ways of pleasing the master are to offer whatever one has; to render respectful service, such as attending, arranging his seat, and so forth; and to serve by the practice of sadhana. [JOKYAB]

These are the three notions: to regard the master as the wish-fulfilling jewel, which dispels poverty; to regard him as the nectar of immortality, which can resurrect the dead; and to regard him as one's heart, which is the abode of the life-force. [JOKYAB]

208. "Careful" means to be cautious in thought and deed. [JOKYAB]

The three secrets are the life examples of his body, speech, and mind. [JOKYAB]

209. To explain this quote: "Fortunate son of a noble family, how do all the tathagatas, the buddhas, and their heart sons, all the bodhisattvas, regard the object of respect, the vajra master? They regard him as being exactly the indestructible vajra mind of enlightenment, the manifest essence of compassion." This was according to Jamdrak Rinpoche. [JOKYAB]

210. *Approaching the Ultimate* (Skt. *Paramartha Seva*) was written by Pundarika, the second Kulika (Tib. Rigden) King of Shambhala. It is text no. 1348 in the Derge *Tangyur.* [EPK]

211. A worthy recipient is someone who respects his master with great faith, takes delight in Dharma practice with great diligence, has sharp mental faculties with great intelligence, and is able to keep the secrecy of the samayas. The teachings should be given to a person whose temper is steady, like the flow of a river, whose character is precise like spiritual practice, whose intentions are excellent like gold, whose mind is stable like a mountain, and who is able to surrender his body and possessions to the Dharma and his master. [JOKYAB]

212. Padmasambhava, the precious master of Uddiyana, has taught in detail on the necessity of having faith, diligence, and discriminating knowledge, and how one is not a suitable recipient for the Secret Mantra when lacking faith. See also the *Notes on the Seven Chapters* by Karma Chagmey. [JOKYAB]

The *Notes on the Seven Chapters* have been translated into English by H. E. Kalu Rinpoche's translator, Lama Ngawang. [EPK]

213. Action Tantra means Kriya Tantra. Unexcelled Yoga means Anuttara Yoga. [EPK]

214. The topics included in the main part, comprised of teachings on the preliminary practices and the development stage, are planned to appear in *The Light of Wisdom,* volume 2. [EPK]

215. Sudden jump here means to jump to a higher level while skipping the grades or steps in between. [JOKYAB]

216. Distraction here means associating with many people and your mind becoming distracted due to being agitated by a lot of talk and activities. [JOKYAB]

217. The *Sutra That Admonishes One to Superior Intention* says:

> Maitreya, there are twenty defects of distraction. What are these twenty? Maitreya, they are not to have controlled your body, not to have controlled your speech, not to have controlled your mind, to have great desire, to have great hatred, to have great dullness, to be tainted by mundane conversation, to have completely strayed away from supramundane conversation, to associate with people who do not respect the Dharma, to have fully cast away the Dharma, to consequently be harmed by the maras, to associate with people who are careless, to be careless oneself, to be dominated by conception and discernment, to completely stray away from great learning, to fail to achieve shamatha and vipashyana, to fail to quickly maintain pure conduct, to completely stray away from rejoicing in the Buddha, to completely stray away from rejoicing in the Dharma, and to completely stray away from rejoicing in the Sangha. Maitreya, understand that these twenty are the defects of taking delight in distraction. A bodhisattva after having applied examination will take delight in solitude and never become completely disheartened. [JOKYAB]

The quotation in the *Sutra of the King of Samadhi* is:

> Compared to someone who makes offerings to many millions of buddhas
> Throughout many millions of aeons,
> To take seven steps toward a solitary place
> Is of a much superior merit. [JOKYAB]

218. The Secret Mantra is the path of blessing. Blessing is the path of devotion. Devotion is the path of supplication. [JOKYAB]

219. The "freedoms and riches" is the usual synonym for the precious human body. [EPK]

220. There are, however, also the eight unfree states due to an unfortunate frame of mind and the eight unfree states due to temporary conditions. What are they? The *Wish-Fulfilling Treasury* explains:

> Being bound by fetters and having extremely unwholesome conduct,
> Not feeling weary about samsara and not possessing the slightest faith,
> Engaging in unvirtuous misdeeds and separating mind and Dharma,
> And corrupting one's precepts and samayas—
> These are called the eight unfree states due to an unfortunate frame of mind.

Moreover, the same text says:

> Being disturbed by the five poisons, deluded, and possessed by the maras,
> Being lazy and letting the sea of evil karma overflow,
> Being controlled by others, seeking shelter from fear, and pretending to be dharmic—
> These are the eight unfree states due to temporary conditions.
> [JOKYAB]

221. The word *udumbara* literally means "especially eminent" or "supremely exalted." [JOKYAB]

222. Chandragomin's name means "Moon of the Gomin Clan." [JOKYAB]

223. The *Jewel Mound Sutra,* also known as *Ratnakuta,* is a collection of forty-nine different sutras, half of which are found in English in *A Treasury of Mahayana Sutras.* [EPK]

224. The *Udana Varga* is text no. 326 in the Derge *Kangyur.* Another version, compiled by Dharmatrata, is found as no. 4100 in the *Tangyur.* [EPK]

225. Emancipation means liberation from the three realms of samsara, as for instance the attainment of an arhat. In the context of Vajrayana, emancipation can also mean rebirth within a natural nirmanakaya realm. [TUR]

226. The *Jewel Garland* by Nagarjuna is sometimes counted among his *Six Scriptures on Reasoning.* [EPK]

227. The physical misdeeds are to kill, to take what is not given, and to engage in sexual misconduct. The verbal misdeeds are to lie, utter divisive talk, harsh words, and gossip. The mental misdeeds are to harbor covetousness, ill-will, and wrong views. These actions have the four factors of object, intent, engagement, and completion. In the instance of killing, the object is to be unmistaken that someone is, for example, a human being. The intent is the desire to kill. The engagement is, for example, to take a weapon. The completion is that the life-faculty is interrupted. The other misdeeds are shown through this example. [JOKYAB]

The sub-aspects of killing are to hit, beat, or oppress others and so on. The sub-aspects of stealing from others are to profiteer in business, to solicit and be pretentious, and so on. The sub-aspects of sexual misconduct are to engage in wanton talk and so on. The other sub-aspects are shown through these examples. [JOKYAB]

228. The ten virtuous actions are the opposites of the above ten unvirtuous actions. [JOKYAB]

The three types of emancipation are those of the shravaka, pratyekabuddha, and bodhisattva. [JOKYAB]

229. The result of white virtuous actions is pleasure. The result of black evil deeds is pain. Neutral actions bear no result. [JOKYAB]

230. The ripened result (Tib. rnam smin gyi 'bras bu) of these unvirtuous actions is the three lower realms. The result resembling the cause is of two types:

1. The result of experience resembling the cause, for each of the ten nonvirtues, respectively, is to have a short life span, lack necessities, have much strife in family life, meet with a lot of slander, have no friends, hear unpleasant words, hear pointless talk, have no result from one's hopes, always have fear, and meet with wrong views.

2. The result of action resembling the cause is naturally to take delight in the particular aspects of the ten nonvirtues that one has been accustomed to in former lifetimes.

The dominant result is that the environment has little splendor, much hail and frost, abundant dust, deep undulations, briny soil, disordered seasons, little crops, deep abysses, and lack of water.

The result of the acting person is that the cause, though small, can be increased into many results. [JOKYAB]

The four types of impelling and completing, performed and accumulated, have four aspects: A white impelling karma while the completing is black; a black impelling karma while the completing is white; both being white; both being black. Similarly, the performed and accumulated have four aspects: a black karma with a white ripening; a white karma with a black ripening, and so forth. [JOKYAB]

231. *The Clouds of Precious Jewels* is the *Arya Ratnamegha Sutra.* [EPK]

232. The five perpetuating aggregates are the aggregates of forms, sensations, conceptions, formations, and consciousnesses. [JOKYAB] See Appendix 7, "The Five Aggregates."

The eight sufferings of human beings are the four major sufferings and the four subsidiary sufferings. [JOKYAB]

These eight are: to take birth, to grow old, to fall sick, and to die; and in addition to be separated from what is beloved, to meet with what is unwanted, to fail to obtain what is desired although one strives for it, and the all-pervasive suffering of formation. [EPK]

233. To clarify the last clause: "Because they have perceived with knowledge what is suffering, the effect of the states of gods and men, what is the cause of this suffering, the karmas and the disturbing emotions of the origin, and what is the cessation of both the cause and effect of suffering by means of stopping the karmas and disturbing emotions." [JOKYAB]

234. In the context of the shravakas of the lesser vehicles, the Buddha is nirmanakaya Shakyamuni, the Dharma is the four truths, and the Sangha is four: the stream-enterers, once-returners, nonreturners, and arhats. [JOKYAB]

According to the Mahayana, the Buddha is the four kayas and five wisdoms endowed with the twofold purity—the primordial purity of essence and the perfect purity of nature. The four kayas are dharmakaya, sambhogakaya, nirmanakaya, and svabhavikakaya, while the five wisdoms are the wisdom of dharmadhatu and so forth. The Buddha possesses the twofold welfare: the benefit of self, which is the qualities of purity, peace, and realization; and the benefit of others, which is the qualities of knowledge, compassion, and ability. [JOKYAB]

The Dharma has two aspects: the truth of cessation, which is the three qualities of inconceivability, nonduality, and nonthought; and the truth of the path, which is the three qualities of purification, clarity, and remedial power. [JOKYAB]

The Sangha has two aspects; the three qualities of knowledge, which are the wisdom of the nature as it is, the wisdom of all that exists, and the inner wisdom; and the three qualities of freedom—from attachment, impediment, and inferior obscuration. [JOKYAB]

235. To take refuge in the Three Jewels is the causal refuge, and to recognize that essence, nature, and capacity are the mandala of the Three Jewels and the Three Roots is the refuge of fruition. [JOKYAB]

236. Having taken refuge in the Buddha, one should not bow down to non-Buddhist mundane gods. Having taken refuge in the Dharma, one should not cause harm to sentient beings. Having taken refuge in the Sangha, one should not keep the company of non-Buddhist friends. One should keep faith in, respect, and admiration for the sacred images, even down to a piece of a tsa-tsa; for the scriptures, even down to a single letter; and for the sacred robes, even down to a piece of saffron-colored cloth. [JOKYAB]

One should follow sublime spiritual teachers; study, reflect upon, and practice the sacred Dharma; and having entered the gateway of the teachings of the Victorious One, one should not let the senses run rampant toward sense objects, but cherish the trainings. [JOKYAB]

In addition, according to Ngari Panchen: (1) One should not abandon the Three Jewels for gifts, or even at the cost of one's life. (2) One should not seek other means even in dire need. (3) One should not omit the time for worship, (4) but establish self and others in the refuge. (5) One should pay homage to the buddha of the direction to which one is going. These five were accepted by Atisha as being general trainings. [JOKYAB]

237. To explain the quote from this sutra: "Because of protecting the inferior type of person from all material and immaterial harms and from the three lower realms, such as the hells and so forth; because of protecting the intermediate type of person from those who are not skilled in the means for attaining liberation from samsara and from the twenty peaks of the view of the transitory collection present in the mind of an immature ordinary person; as well as protecting the superior type of person from the lower vehicles of both shravakas and pratyekabuddhas, they are taught to be the supreme refuge." This was according to Jamdrak Rinpoche. Thus it is the refuge that is in conformity with the paths of the three types of individuals. [JOKYAB]

238. The four samadhis are to focus one-pointedly on the four immeasurables, such as the samadhi of love and so forth. [JOKYAB]

239. Concerning the strength of the cause, helper, and so forth, the *Ornament of the Sutras* says:

> The strength of the cause is the awakening of the naturally present potential.
> The strength of the helper is the strength of the spiritual friend.
> The strength of the root is the strength of having gathered roots of virtue.
> The strength of learning results from cultivating the virtues of learning, reflection, and meditation.
> Through this one does not adhere to the strength of the helper, but the strengths of the cause, root, and learning become more stable.
> This is explained as the generating of bodhichitta taught by others. [JOKYAB]

240. (1) The bodhichitta of devoted engagement for ordinary people on the paths of accumulation and joining. (2) The bodhichitta of pure superior intention on the seven impure bhumis. (3) The bodhichitta of maturation on the three pure bhumis. (4) The bodhichitta of abandoning all obscuration on the level of buddhahood. [JOKYAB]

The twenty-two analogies given in the *Ornament (Abhisamayalamkara)* are:

> These are like the earth, gold, the moon, and fire,
> Like a treasure, a jewel mine, and the ocean,
> Like a diamond, a mountain, medicine, and a teacher,
> Like a wish-fulfilling jewel, the sun, and a song,
> Like a king, a treasury, and a highway,
> Like a carriage and a fountain,
> Like a lute, a river, and a cloud—
> Thus there are twenty-two kinds.

These twenty-two are examples for pursuing the aim and so forth up through dharmakaya. When combining them with the five paths: pursuance, intention, and superior intention are the path of accumulation; application is the path of joining; the paramita of generosity is the path of seeing; discipline, patience, diligence, concentration, discriminating knowledge, means, strength, aspiration, and wisdom are the nine stages of the path of cultivation; superknowledges, [the accumulations of] merit and wisdom, the thirty-seven factors conducive to enlightenment, shamatha and vipashyana, recall and courageous eloquence—five altogether—comprise the special path of three pure bhumis together; and the banquet of Dharma, the singular journeyed path, and the possession of dharmakaya comprise the three aspects of preparation, main part, and conclusion of the stage of buddhahood. You should know that all of them can be combined with three aspects: analogy, helper, and quality; for instance, the helper is the subject, the bodhichitta concurrent with pursuing the aim of enlightenment. The analogy is that it is like the earth, because it serves as the basis for all virtuous qualities. [JOKYAB]

These are the two types defined according to their characteristics, aspiration, and application: the bodhichitta of aspiration is the four immeasurables, and the bodhichitta of application is the six paramitas. According to the system of Nagarjuna, the bodhichitta of aspiration is to pledge the effect, and the bodhichitta of application is to pledge the cause. According to the system of Asanga, the intention is the bodhichitta of aspiration, and the engagement is the bodhichitta of application. The bodhichitta of aspiration is the wish to attain buddhahood, like intending to travel. The bodhichitta of application is to train in bodhichitta, the means for attaining buddhahood, like traveling. [JOKYAB]

241. The important Mahayana scriptures *Bhumi Sections* by Asanga consist of five sections, including the *Bodhisattva Bhumi,* and are found in the Derge edition of the *Tangyur,* no. 4035 and following. [EPK]

Dharmata is the innate nature of phenomena and mind. [EPK]

242. The way of generating bodhichitta according to Mantrayana, such as in the context of the Lamdrey of the glorious Sakya School, is to chant the "I take refuge in the Three Jewels" and so forth immediately after the seven branches. This style of generating bodhichitta is similar to the Middle Way. [JOKYAB]

These seven branches are: prostrating to the Three Jewels, confessing negative actions, making offerings, rejoicing in the virtue of others, requesting to turn the wheel of Dharma, beseeching to not pass into nirvana, and dedicating the merit to the enlightenment of all sentient beings. [CNR]

243. The four black deeds are:

To deceive a venerable person, to cause someone to regret what is not regrettable,
To disparage a sublime person, and to deceive sentient beings.

The four white deeds are the opposites of these. [JOKYAB]

244. The four impure aspects are: (1) impure intention or motivation is self-interest and ill-will toward others, (2) impure materials are poisons, weapons, and so forth, (3) impure recipients are the non-Buddhist Jain ascetics and so forth, (4) impure method is what is temporarily or ultimately harmful. [JOKYAB]

The four pure aspects are: (1) pure intention is the motivation of bodhichitta; (2) pure materials are, unlike poison, weapons, and the like, things to be given away, such as food, medicine, clothing, and so forth; (3) pure recipients of gifts are, upward, the Precious Ones and, downward, beggars and so forth; (4) pure methods are what is ingenious and conducive to the welfare of other beings to be tamed. [JOKYAB]

The four objects are: (1) one's parents, who are the benevolent objects, (2) one's preceptors and teachers, who are the respectable objects, (3) the buddhas and bodhisattvas, who are the qualified objects, (4) the poor and destitute, who are the unprotected objects.

Alternately: (1) the master and the Precious Ones are the object of qualities, (2) one's parents are the objects that brought benefit, (3) sick people and so forth are the objects that suffer, (4) enemies and evil spirits are the sublime objects that bring harm.

In another way: (1) the buddhas and bodhisattvas are the objects of qualities, (2) parents are the objects that benefit, (3) one's master is both of those, (4) unprotected sentient beings are the objects of suffering. [JOKYAB]

245. Possessing this threefold purity means to control one's body, speech, and mind against wrongdoing and to engage in what is virtuous. [JOKYAB]

246. These four qualities are: to take the bodhichitta vows, to observe these vows, to maintain the purity of the vows, and, if violated, to restore them or make confessions. Thus they are called the four aspects of taking, observing, purity, and restoring. [JOKYAB]

247. The seven types of Individual Liberation are male and female lay persons, male and female novices, monks and nuns, and candidate nuns. [JOKYAB]

The Traditions of the Two Chariots are the systems of Nagarjuna and Asanga.

According to the system of Nagarjuna, the Chariot of the Profound

View, [the precepts are to refrain from the following:] to steal the
funds of the Three Jewels; to commit the act of forsaking the Dharma;
to punish or cause to lose the precepts and so forth, people who possess
or have lapsed from the trainings; to commit the five acts with immediate result; to violate the five definite precepts for a king, such as
keeping wrong views and so forth; to violate the five definitive precepts for a minister, such as destroying a village, valley, city, district, or
country; to give premature teachings on emptiness to people who
have not trained in the Mahayana; to aspire toward the shravakas of
the Hinayana after having reached the Mahayana; to train in the Mahayana after forsaking the Individual Liberation; to disparage the Hinayana; to praise oneself and disparage others; to be highly hypocritical
for the sake of honor and gain; to let a monk receive punishment and
be humiliated; to harm others by bribing a king or a minister in order
to punish them; to give the food of a renunciant meditator to a reciter
of scriptures and thus causing obstacles for the cultivation of shamatha.
The eighty subsidiary infractions are to forsake the happiness of another being and so forth.

According to the system of Asanga, the Chariot of the Vast Conduct, the precepts for the bodhichitta of aspiration are as follows: to
never forsake sentient beings, to remember the benefits of bodhichitta,
to gather the accumulations, to exert oneself in training in bodhichitta,
as well as to adopt and avoid the eight black and white deeds as mentioned above.

The four precepts for the bodhichitta of application are [to avoid
the following]: (1) out of desire, to have exceeding attachment to
honor and gain and to praise oneself and disparage others, (2) out of
stinginess, to refrain from giving material things, Dharma teachings,
and wealth to others, (3) out of anger, to harm others and be unforgiv-
ing when offered an apology, (4) out of stupidity, to pretend that indo-
lence is Dharma and to teach that to others. The forty-six minor
infractions are to refrain from making offerings to the Three Jewels
and so forth. [JOKYAB]

248. The twelve ways of benefiting others, as mentioned in the *Bodhisattva
Bhumi,* are:

> To keep company with those who perform meaningful actions.
> To dispel the misery of suffering sentient beings.
> To teach discriminating knowledge to those who have no
> methods.

To reward and acknowledge actions, benefiting people in return.
To protect from all fears.
To clear away the sorrow of all types of misery.
To make those who have no possessions obtain their necessities.
To gather assemblies by means of the Dharma.
To engage in what is in harmony with people's inclinations.
To delight others with true virtues.
To fully guide [others away from errant paths].
To instill fear and determination by means of miraculous powers.
[JOKYAB]

249. The five notions are according to the *Bodhisattva Bhumi:* "It is taught that one should generate and meditate upon these five notions: cultivate the notion that harmdoers are your beloved ones, the notion of simply following the Dharma, the notion of impermanence, the notion of suffering, and the notion of completely cherishing [other beings]." [JOKYAB]

The nine considerations are according to the view of the master Shantideva: "To consider that others who harm oneself have no self-control, to consider the shortcomings of one's own actions, to consider the shortcomings of the physical body, to consider the shortcomings of the mind, to consider harmdoers without making a difference, to consider those who benefit, to consider those who are most kind, to consider how to please the buddhas, and to consider what has great benefit and to be patient." [JOKYAB]

250. These two are the absence of the individual self and of the self-entity of phenomena. [JOKYAB]

251. The eight types of application that discard the five shortcomings are according to *Discerning of the Middle and the Extremes:*

> The eight types of attention that discard the five shortcomings
> Result from the cause of application.
> [1] Laziness and [2] forgetfulness of instructions,
> [3] Dullness and agitation,
> [4] Lack of application and [5] overapplication;
> These are regarded as the five shortcomings.
> To not forget the object of reference,
> To discern both dullness and agitation,
> To fully apply what discards them,
> And, when they have subsided, to enter the innate.

These five are: (1) laziness and (2) forgetfulness that obscure the preparatory stage of dhyana; (3) dullness inwardly and agitation outwardly, which obscure the main part [of dhyana]; (4) lack of application of the remedies against dullness and agitation; and (5) overapplication of the remedies after dullness and agitation have subsided. [JOKYAB]

The eight types of application that discard these five shortcomings are: faith, determination, effort, pliancy, mindfulness, conscientiousness, attention, and equanimity. The first four discard laziness. That is to say, for the attainment of samadhi, through determination with faith and through striving one attains pliancy by generating effort and thus discards laziness. Mindfulness means not to forget the instruction. Conscientiousness means to discern the occurrence of dullness and agitation. If they do occur, attention is the application of the remedies to discard them. Equanimity means to rest with no application of conceptual thinking when they have subsided. These are progressively the remedies against forgetfulness of the instruction and so forth. [JOKYAB]

252. The nine means of mental stillness are:

Resting, continual resting, and repeated resting,
Fully resting, taming, and pacifying,
Fully pacifying, one-pointedness, and settling in equanimity.

Resting is to direct the mind toward the object. Continual resting is to maintain the continuity of that. Repeated resting is to discard forgetfulness and distraction and then return to the object. Fully resting is to progress further and further by resting in that way. Taming is to contemplate the virtues of samadhi and take delight in them. Pacifying is to regard distraction as a flaw and to make dislike for samadhi subside. Fully pacifying is to pacify the causes for distraction, such as the subsidiary disturbing emotions, as well as all the mental eruptions of covetousness, sluggishness, sleep, mental pain, and so forth. Together with the actualization of that, one-pointedness is to attain stillness. Following that, settling in equanimity is to attain the natural stillness in regard to the object of focus, without having to apply effort. [JOKYAB]

253. For more details, including the seven types of attention, see Appendix 3, "The Four Dhyanas and Formless States." [EPK]

The ten totalities are the totality of earth, water, fire, wind, blue, yellow, red, white, space, and consciousness. They are ten qualities, such as not sinking into water and so forth, abilities perfected by gaining control over the inner elements and sense-bases. [JOKYAB]

The eight masteries are: (1–2) The two masteries over all external sentient and insentient forms by means of the conception that they are inner forms. (3–4) The two masteries over all external sentient and insentient forms by means of the conception that they are inner formlessness. (5–8) The four masteries of emitting rays of light to gain mastery over the external colors of blue, yellow, red, and white by willing them to be absorbed within. [JOKYAB]

The eight emancipations are the emancipation of regarding what has form to be form, the emancipation of regarding the formless as having form, the emancipation of the repulsive and clearing away hindrances, the four emancipations of the four formless states, and the emancipation of cessation. [JOKYAB]

"And so forth" indicates the nine serene states of successive abiding, which are the four dhyanas, the four formless states, and the serenity of cessation. [JOKYAB]

There are countless billions of samadhi doors, such as the vajralike samadhi and so forth. [JOKYAB]

254. The eleven ways of benefiting others are as explained [six notes] above. [JOKYAB]

255. The three spheres are subject, object, and action, or in the instance of giving, the thing given, the act of giving, and the recipient of the gift. [JOKYAB]

256. Language, logic, craftsmanship, healing, and so forth, can be included within three topics: elimination, safekeeping, and all-knowing. The knowledge of language eliminates the delusion about words, and the knowledge of logic eliminates the delusion about meaning. The knowledge of craftsmanship is beneficial for external physical enjoyments, and the knowledge of healing is beneficial for inner physical disorders. The Three Collections (Tripitaka) are for the purpose of achieving personal all-knowing, and thus one should train in the inner topics of knowledge, such as the Vinaya, Abhidharma, Middle Way, Prajnaparamita, and so forth. As is said, "Even noble and eminent beings do not achieve omniscience unless they become learned in the five sciences. Therefore, exert yourself in them in order to eliminate [ignorance], to safeguard other beings, and to gain personal all-knowing." [JOKYAB]

The five minor sciences are merely subsidiary aspects. That is to say, they are five ways of not being ignorant. When knowing calculation you are not ignorant about numbers; when knowing poetics you are not ignorant about literary embellishments; when knowing composition you are not ignorant about verse meters; when knowing synonyms you are not ignorant about words; and when knowing dramatics you are not ignorant about types of language. When added together, these are known as the ten topics of knowledge. [JOKYAB]

The well-spoken Words of the Buddha are of three types: words spoken personally, words spoken through blessing, and words spoken with permission. [JOKYAB]

The treatises that explain their meaning include explanations by bodhisattvas, such as the *Trilogy of Commentaries by Bodhisattvas,* explanations by shravakas, such as the *Great Treasury of Exposition,* explanations by ordinary beings, learned masters who have entered the path, such as the treatises renowned in India and Tibet. [JOKYAB]

There are also treatises that summarize the extensive, treatises that elucidate the profound, treatises that revive the declined, treatises that gather the scattered, and treatises that arrange the disordered into sequence. [JOKYAB]

257. The four special qualities are to be free from fixation and clinging because of not conceptualizing the three spheres, to have no expectation of a reward, to increase [the virtue] by dedicating at the end, and to possess the methods of the union of emptiness and compassion. These are clarified in the text itself. [JOKYAB]

The three levels of enlightenment are the enlightenment of the shravaka, the enlightenment of the pratyekabuddha, and the great enlightenment, which is the state of buddhahood. [JOKYAB]

The knowledge that does not conceptualize the three spheres is prajna, the direct insight into emptiness that does not form notions of a subject, an object, or an action related to them as having any concrete, true, independent existence. [CNR]

258. When mentioning that each of the six paramitas can be divided further into six, in the instance of generosity, generosity is the material being given, discipline is the purity, patience is to avoid being angry even when someone begs repeatedly, diligence is to give quickly, concentration is to focus one's attention one-pointedly upon that, and knowledge is to refrain from conceptualizing the three spheres. [JOKYAB]

259. The extensive classifications mentioned in the *Sutra of the Good Aeon* are 121 types, beginning with the statement, "There are the six paramitas of the perfect training of the King of Supreme Joy" and concluding with, "The six paramitas of fully distinguishing sacred remains." [JOKYAB]

260. The four attributes of a virtuous practitioner are not to respond with anger toward anger, not to respond with insult when insulted, not to respond with accusations when accused, and not to respond with beating when beaten. [JOKYAB]

261. To explain this quotation:

> The generosity of not having expectation for a reward in the future; the discipline of not desiring the fruition of a rebirth among gods or human beings; the patience toward everything with or without form, having abandoned aggression toward all beings; the diligence of quickly cultivating all white virtuous qualities, in general, and all the virtues of freedom and maturation, in particular; the concentration that is not a mundane state of dhyana because of transcending the realms of form and the formless states; and the knowledge of emptiness endowed with skillful means of compassion—thus those who adhere to these six paramitas of generosity and so forth should practice them perfectly. [JOKYAB]

262. The *Ornament of the Sutras* says: "The first means by being in harmony with generosity; the second means teaching that to disciples by using words spoken pleasantly; the third is to act meaningfully by personally applying what should be adopted or avoided; and the fourth means to be consistent with the meaning of liberation by following it oneself. This is regarded as the sequence." [JOKYAB] [DKR]

263. To explain this quotation: "Because giving is the means for bringing temporal and lasting benefit, because pleasing words are what accepts disciples, because meaningful action is what makes them enter the path, and likewise because consistency causes them to follow the conduct of the sons of the victorious ones, they are called the four means of attraction." [JOKYAB]

264. Emancipation means liberation from the three realms of samsara, such as rebirth in a pure buddhafield. Omniscience (Tib. rnam mkhyen, thams cad mkhyen pa) is the same as complete enlightenment or buddhahood. [TUR]

265. The *Seven Points of Mind Training* are: stating the preliminaries, the supporting teachings; training in the main part, the awakened mind; turning negative circumstances into the path of enlightenment; stating concisely the practice for the entire life; the commitment of mind training; the precepts of mind-training; and evaluation of mind training. [JOKYAB]

266. The word "self-nature" here means an inherently existent identity and independent substance of the individual self or of phenomena. [CNR]

267. Tirthikas are usually the name for non-Buddhist teachers of philosophy adhering to the extreme views of eternalism or nihilism. However, His Holiness Dilgo Khyentse Rinpoche once told me that the tirthikas are within ourselves as different forms for incorrect understanding, as are the shravaka and pratyekabuddha views in the form of partial understanding. [CNR]

268. To explain this quote by Nagarjuna, alias Phakshab: "If the existence of a certain impermanent thing is established in dependency upon something permanent, that impermanence is itself also dependent upon permanence. And if the existence of the dependent permanent object is to be established based on the given label 'impermanence,' well then, tell me how you can establish the true existence of something that is only the word 'permanence' dependent upon the word 'impermanence' "? [JOKYAB] [DKR]

269. To explain this quote: "All outer and inner composite things are devoid of a permanent essence which, according to the tirthikas, has an indestructible nature and a substance that remains into the following instant. The proof of this is, respectively, because their nature does not remain but changes into some other situation and because their continuity appears to cease. According to the Middle Way, things are devoid of an essence. Why? Because all things are asserted to be emptiness devoid of a 'me' and 'mine,' there also exists no true attribute such as 'impermanence' based thereon." [JOKYAB] [DKR]

270. The three realms are the samsaric realms of Desire, Form, and Formlessness. The Realm of Desire is comprised of the abodes of hell beings, hungry ghosts, animals, humans, asuras, and the gods of the six abodes of Desire gods. It is called "Realm of Desire" because of the tormented mental pain caused by gross desire and attachment. The Realm of Form is comprised of seventeen samsaric heavenly abodes, consisting of the threefold Four Dhyana Realms and the Five Pure

Abodes. The beings there have bodies of light, long lives, and no painful sensations. The Realm of Formlessness consists of the most subtle states of samsaric existence, the abodes of unenlightened beings who have practiced the four formless states. These beings dwell in unchanging equanimity for long durations of time, after which they again return to lower states within samsara. [EPK]

271. To explain this quote:

> Moreover, when all these phenomena comprised of cause and effect are by the very identity of their nature devoid of coming forth and devoid of going away, and likewise abide neither in the middle nor in extremes, then how can karmic deeds, as the causes, and the ripening of karmic deeds, as the results, have any reasonable true existence? They don't! Being nonexistent also in the ultimate sense that transcends the relative, they have no coming or going whatsoever, neither in space nor in time. In terms of the conventional truth, however, there are the teachings of entering the path of accepting and rejecting causes, as well as of the white and black ripening of the results of karmic deeds. [JOKYAB] [DKR]

272. Details of the Vaibhashikas are included in Appendix 11, "The Four Schools of Buddhist Philosophy." [EPK]

273. The *Commentary on the Vajra Heart* mentions that there are four Buddhist philosophical schools:

> The Buddhists have four schools;
> A fifth is not the intent of Shakyamuni.

> Although the Hinayana has the two divisions of shravakas and pratyekabuddhas, the view of the pratyekabuddhas is equivalent to the Sautrantika, while their resolve and conduct resembles the general system of the shravakas. These points are therefore not mentioned separately. [JOKYAB]

274. To explain this quote:

> Two types of truth, conventional and ultimate, have been taught. What are their definitions? When something, as a jug, for instance, can be destroyed into pieces, it is no longer perceived by the mind and so has conventional existence, as in the example of the jug that no longer yields the concept "vase" once it has been smashed into pieces. Or, when something can be eliminated by

the intellect, it will not be perceived by the mind and therefore also has conventional existence, as in the example of water that no longer yields the concept "water" once the mind eliminates its attributes, such as physical form. Since they are nothing but their imputed names, a thing, just like a jug or water, does exist conventionally because it is not an untruth. But ultimate existence is different from that. [JOKYAB]

275. To explain this quote: "Since the center particle is touched at six points in different directions, the most subtle particle has six directional parts and thus the claim of partlessness is defeated. If the six directional particles were a single spot, even a heap the size of Mount Sumeru would be only the size of one partless particle and would therefore be like empty space." [JOKYAB]

276. For Jokyab Rinpoche's further details, see Appendix 11, "The Four Schools of Buddhist Philosophy." [EPK]

277. To explain this quote, "Like a star, an apparition, or a flame," among these nine analogies to illustrate conditioned phenomena, a star is visible at night but not in the daytime. Its shimmering movement, which does not remain from one moment to the next demonstrates the arising and ceasing of conditioned things. An apparition is like the person suffering from an eye disease, making him see double floating strands of hair. The flame from a butter or oil lamp burns and perishes every instant from the moment it was lit until the continuity of burning is suddenly destroyed by a wind, for instance. The rest is easy to understand. [JOKYAB]

278. To explain the quote: "If the self were the aggregates, then this self would be subject to arising and perishing. But if the self is different from the aggregates, the self would have none of the aggregates' characteristics, such as arising, remaining, or perishing." [JOKYAB]

279. To explain this quote: "The self does therefore not exist as something other than the aggregates, because there is no existent basis for holding the self as any other thing besides the aggregates." [JOKYAB]

280. The Buddha moreover said: "One is one's own protector. One is also one's own enemy. When doing good or evil, one is one's own witness." And, "When thoroughly having tamed himself, the wise achieves the higher realms." [JOKYAB]

281. To explain this quote, "Just as with the end of an instant of completed action or of the finality of time, you should also examine whether at first it has a beginning and next a middle. Similarly, because you must examine these three aspects of an instant, a world possessing continuity does in fact not abide for even one moment." [JOKYAB]

The *Precious Garland, Ratnavali,* was authored by Nagarjuna and is translated under the same name by Jeffrey Hopkins. [EPK]

282. To explain this quote: "The claim that things do exist is the belief in permanence, while the claim that things do not exist is the belief in nihilism. For this reason all learned people abide neither in existence nor in nonexistence." [JOKYAB]

283. About nonarising: in the aspect of ultimate truth, all phenomena are devoid of an independent, concrete identity and have therefore no basis for such attributes as arising, dwelling, or ceasing, i.e., coming into being, remaining in time and place, and ceasing to exist. [EPK]

284. "Moons of Speech" is synonymous with buddhas. [TUR]

The constructs of the eight limits are the mental formulations of mind or phenomena having such attributes as arising and ceasing, being singular or plural, coming and going, and being the same or being different. [CNR]

285. To explain this quote:

> From this sugata essence there is nothing whatsoever of the faults of the two obscurations to remove, since it is primordially untainted by defects, nor is there, moreover, even the slightest new thing to add or new achievement to gain because of being primordially endowed with the basis for freedom through being devoid of extraneous, momentary elements, as well as with the qualities of freedom and maturation. Look correctly and truly into the true and unmistaken view, the basis that is not empty of the elements of unexcelled qualities and which is free from something to accept or reject, remove or add. And thus, to see the true fruition is the total and unexcelled freedom from the two obscurations. [JOKYAB]

286. To explain this quote: "I, a bodhisattva, have no such pretense as holding the individual notions of settling in the meditation state of emptiness, which is like space, or emerging from it during the postmeditation, which is like a magical illusion. And why is this? It is

because of fully realizing that emptiness is forever the nature of all knowable phenomena." [JOKYAB]

287. Jamgön Kongtrül here plays on the literal meaning of shamatha and vipashyana: "calming down and remaining" and "seeing clearly." [EPK]

288. All the extremely profound sutras state that the complete realization of the twofold egolessness, which is not seeing any fixation on concreteness, free from extremes, and utterly unbiased—that is the true seeing of the suchness of the buddhas. [JOKYAB]

289. The two obscurations are the obscuration of disturbing emotions and the cognitive obscuration. [JOKYAB]

The five eyes are the physical eye, the divine eye, the eye of knowledge, the Dharma eye, and the buddha eye. [JOKYAB]

The six superknowledges are the superknowledge of miraculous power, divine hearing, divine sight, perceiving the minds of others, recollecting former lives, and of the exhaustion of defilements. [JOKYAB]

Unforgetting recall, dharani, is the [four of] words, meaning, courage, and forbearance. The *Sutra Requested by the King of Dharanis* mentions eight: The dharani of perfect melodiousness, the dharani of the inexhaustible casket, the dharani of unending retention, the dharani of the ocean seal, the dharani of the lotus array, the dharani of the unattached union, the dharani of constant definitiveness, and the dharani that is blessed by the awakened ones. [JOKYAB]

What are the eight great treasure mines of courageous eloquence? The *Lalitavistara* mentions:

> The treasure mine of remembrance because of never forgetting, the treasure mine of intelligence because of having fully developed the intellect, the treasure mine of comprehension because of having understood the various meanings of all the sutras, the treasure mine of recall because of having fully retained everything heard, the treasure mine of courageous eloquence because of having satisfied all beings with eloquent expositions, the treasure mine of the Dharma because of having protected all the teachings, the treasure mine of enlightenment because of not having interrupted the bloodline of the Three Jewels, and the treasure mine of accomplishment because of having achieved the acceptance of the nature of nonarising. Thus you will achieve these eight great treasure mines. [JOKYAB]

The miraculous power of mastery over wind and mind is the ability to display uninhibited miraculous powers, such as emitting flames from one's torso, water from the lower part of the body, or raise above seven banana plantain trees or above the summit of existence. [JOKYAB]

The samadhi of the stream of Dharma; there is a countless number of such samadhis, including the samadhi known as not conceiving the identities of all phenomena and the samadhi known as renunciation resulting from knowing the identity of all phenomena. [JOKYAB]

The five paths are the path of accumulation, the path of joining, the path of seeing, the path of cultivation, and the path beyond training. [JOKYAB]

The ten bhumis of bodhisattvas are: The first bhumi of the Joyous, the second bhumi of the Stainless, the third bhumi of the Radiant, the fourth bhumi of the Brilliant, the fifth bhumi of the Hard to Conquer, the sixth bhumi of the Realized, the seventh bhumi of the Reaching Far, the eighth bhumi of the Unshakable, the ninth bhumi of the Good Intelligence, and the tenth bhumi of the Cloud of Dharma. [JOKYAB]

For more details by Jokyab Rinpoche, see Appendix 12, "The Bodhisattva Bhumis." [EPK]

290. The sixteen moments of cognition, ensuing cognition, acceptance, and ensuing acceptance of the Dharma for each of the four truths, at the end of the stage of supreme mundane attribute, are first the four concerning suffering: the acceptance of cognizing the attributes of suffering, the cognition of these attributes, the acceptance of ensuing cognition, and this ensuing cognition; thus there are four aspects of wisdom. When combining the other three—origin, cessation, and path—in the same fashion, there are in all sixteen wisdoms.

There exist numerous different ways in which the Hinayana schools define the sixteen moments mentioned above; the Mahayana schools as well have several positions.

There are said to be sixteen since the objects discerned, the four truths, each have four aspects, which are understood gradually and not all at once. Hereby one acquires the capability to be unafraid of the nonarising nature of things. [JOKYAB]

291. There are 112 discards through the path of seeing, arrived at by multiplying the four truths and the three realms with: desire, anger, arro-

gance, ignorance, doubt, belief in the transitory collection, belief in adhering to extremes, perverted belief, holding a belief to be paramount, holding a discipline or ritual to be paramount. [JOKYAB]

The seven bodhi-factors are: concentration, full discernment of phenomena, mindfulness, diligence, rejoicing, pliancy, and impartiality. [EPK]

292. The 414 discards through the path of cultivation are arrived at by subdividing desire, anger, arrogance, ignorance, doubt, the belief in the transitory collection, and the belief in adhering to extremes, each with the levels and the major and middling degrees. [JOKYAB]

293. These thirty-seven factors conducive to enlightenment are summarized in the following way:

> The four applications of mindfulness
> Are of body, sensation, mind, and phenomena.
> The four right endeavors are said to be
> Not to give rise to nonvirtue, to abandon the ones that have arisen,
> To give rise to virtuous qualities, and to not degenerate the ones that have arisen.
> The four legs of miraculous action are
> Determination, diligence, attention, and discernment.
> The five ruling faculties are
> Faith, diligence, mindfulness, concentration, and discrimination.
> These five strengthened are the five powers.
> The seven bodhi-factors are
> Mindfulness and full discernment of phenomena,
> Diligence, joy, and pliancy,
> Concentration and impartiality.
> The eightfold path of noble beings is
> Right view and right thought,
> Right speech, action, and livelihood,
> Right effort, mindfulness, and concentration.

The ten qualities of the stage beyond training are the right view of the stage beyond training up to and including the right concentration of the stage beyond training—thus the eightfold noble path—and in addition the right liberation of the stage beyond training and the right understanding of the stage beyond training.

These ten are also included within the five undefiled aggregates: right speech, livelihood, and action are the aggregate of discipline;

right mindfulness and concentration are the aggregate of samadhi; right view, thought, and effort are the aggregate of discriminating knowledge; plus the aggregate of liberation and the aggregate of the wisdom that sees liberation. [JOKYAB]

294. Appendix 12, "The Bodhisattva Bhumis," contains a detailed definition of bhumi. [JOKYAB]

The five kinds of fear are as stated in a sutra: "As soon as you attain the first bhumi of the Joyous you are totally free from these five kinds of fear—the fear of lacking the means of livelihood [having nothing to eat], the fear of no verse [of praise from others], the fear of death, the fear of the lower realms, and the fear of being intimidated amidst an [even oceanlike] gathering [when expounding the Dharma]." [JO-KYAB]

The twelve times one hundred qualities are described like this: on the first bhumi you realize twelve times one hundred qualities, including meeting one hundred buddhas simultaneously. [JOKYAB]

Jokyab Rinpoche's further details of these qualities are mentioned in Appendix 12, "The Bodhisattva Bhumis." [EPK]

295. The ten masteries on the eighth bhumi are described like this:

> Through mastery over wealth, rebirth, and life,
> Wisdom, interest, mind, and action,
> Miracles, aspiration, and all teachings,
> He is the mighty king of the three realms.

The four right discriminations on the ninth bhumi are the right discrimination of definitive words, meaning, phenomena, and courageous eloquence. Their respective causes are language, the Collections, scientific calculus, and reasoning. [JOKYAB]

296. To explain this quote: "Having fully turned the three successive Dharma Wheels of the causal teachings of the philosophical vehicles, which apply the causes for a buddhahood that is not a fruition in the present situation, [the Buddha prophesied] that the short path of the resultant Vajra Vehicle, which applies the fruition of buddhahood in the present situation, 'will appear twenty-eight years after I have passed into nirvana.'" [JOKYAB]

297. Generally speaking, the causal vehicles are so-called because of being led along or journeying "by means of this," while the resultant vehicles are so-called because of being led or journeying "right here."

Thus Mantrayana is superior because of embodying both cause and result. [JOKYAB]

298. The eight collections of consciousnesses are the all-ground, the defiled mental consciousness, the mental cognition, and the cognitions of eye, ear, nose, tongue, and body. [JOKYAB]

299. The paths of ripening and liberation are two vital parts of Vajrayana practice: the empowerments that ripen one's being with the capacity to realize the four kayas and the liberating oral instructions enabling one actually to apply the insight that was introduced through the empowerments. [CNR]

300. Development and completion are the two main aspects—the "means and knowledge"—of Vajrayana practice. Briefly stated, development stage means positive mental fabrication, including visualization and mantra recitation, while completion stage means resting in the unfabricated nature of mind. [EPK]

301. In this Mantrayana statement about the special qualities of objects, time, situation, and mental faculties, "objects" means to enjoy the five sense pleasures, "time" means to swiftly achieve the fruition, "situation" means to experience everything as purity, and "mental faculties" means the methods that correspond to the person of the highest and other types of capacity. [JOKYAB]

302. Dombi Heruka accepts five special qualities of Mantrayana:

> Here there is the special quality of the recipient,
> The special quality of the teaching given,
> The special quality of the scriptures, and of the path;
> Thus through the special quality of fruition,
> The vehicle of Mantra is especially exalted.

According to Indrabhuti, Mantrayana is superior due to these seven: the special quality of the master, recipient, ritual, activities, commitment, view of training, and conduct.

Moreover, according to the master Jnana Shri, Mantrayana is superior because of these eleven qualities: the skillful means of focusing on the unexcelled aim, of unexcelled practice, of unexcelled wisdom, of unexcelled exertion, of the capacity to accept all disciples without exception, of consecration of the disturbing emotions, of swift blessings, of quick results, of the abandonment of disturbing emotions, of unexcelled attitude, and finally, the skillful means of unexcelled conduct. [JOKYAB]

303. The Tripitaka—the Three Collections—and the 84,000 entrances to the Dharma are described in the following way.

> The 21,000 pitakas of the Vinaya were taught
> As the remedy to tame the disturbing emotion of desire.
> The 21,000 pitakas of the Sutra were taught
> As the remedy to tame the disturbing emotion of anger.
> The 21,000 pitakas of the Abhidharma were taught
> As the remedy to tame the disturbing emotion of delusion.
> The 21,000 pitakas of the Secret Mantra were taught
> As the remedy to tame the combination of the three poisons.
> [JOKYAB]

The twelve aspects of excellent speech are: General Discourses; Proclamations in Song; Prophecies; Poetic Pronouncements; Special Aphorisms; Declarations; Narratives; Parables; Succession of Former Lives; Extensive Sayings; Marvels; and Established Doctrines. [JO-KYAB]

These are the twelve main divisions of the Buddhist canon. According to the Mahayana perspective of Asanga, the first five are considered to be the Shravaka Collection, the next four are Vinaya, the following two are the Bodhisattva Collection, and the last is the Abhidharma. [EPK]

The nine gradual vehicles are the three of the shravakas, pratyeka-buddhas, and bodhisattvas, and the three of the Kriya Tantra, Charya Tantra, and Yoga Tantra. According to the New Schools, the additional three are those of the Father Tantra, Mother Tantra, and the Nondual Tantra. According to the Nyingma School, they are Maha, Anu, and Ati. [JOKYAB]

304. The level of Great Regent refers to the tenth bhumi of the Cloud of Dharma, the level at which the regents of Buddha Shakyamuni abide, as for instance Avalokiteshvara, Manjushri, Vajrapani, and the other of the Eight Close Sons. [TUR]

The defilement of the tendencies of the three experiences of transference refers to the actual obscuration of the transference of the elements during union, but to define it as just that is too small a scope. It also covers the channels, winds, and essences; body, speech, and mind; the three realms; and the outer, inner, and secret.

The phrase "three experiences of transference" means the three aspects of appearance, increase, and attainment. The initial transference from the nadi abodes during union and the final emission of transference from the body are both coarse. The coarse as well as the subtle and intermediate all manifest as the obscuration that prevents the meditation state from being unceasing. The three experiences occur no matter what arises, be it virtuous, evil, or neutral. This is the subtle cognitive obscuration mentioned in the teachings of Mantrayana.

The coarse version is the [process of] dying or union. The intermediate is when fainting or falling asleep. The subtle is during a sneeze or a hiccup. The extremely subtle happens unceasingly during any thought occurrence. However, the degree of subtlety between sleep and union can be reversed.

It is generally taught that this subtle defilement of the three aspects of appearance, increase, and attainment is more subtle during union than when falling asleep. The reason for this is that slight breathing still takes place during deep sleep, while it is said that the movement of breath ceases for a moment when the bodhichitta of the union transfers.

The obscuration of transference of the kunda-like bodhichitta of union is the manifest obscuration. The obscuration of the tendencies is unmanifest and subtle. The obscuration of union taught in the context of the *Uttaratantra* refers to dullness, lethargy, and drowsiness, and to agitation, excitement, and thought occurrence, which obscure the unified state of dhyana. [JOKYAB]

305. The path connected to the fourth empowerment is the Great Perfection, including the practices of Trekchö and Tögal. [TUR]

306. Mother Tsogyal is the dakini Yeshe Tsogyal. [TUR]

307. Prince Damdzin was the second son of King Trisong Deutsen. [TUR]

308. Do-ngak Lingpa is the tertön name of Jamyang Khyentse Wangpo. Trisong Deutsen is called "gentle" because he was an emanation of Manjushri, whose name literally means "Gentle Splendor." [EPK]

309. Chimey Tennyi Yungdrung Lingpa is the tertön name of Jamgön Kongtrül, who himself was the reincarnation of the Tibetan translator Vairochana. [TUR]

310. The *Heruka Galpo Tantra* is one of the Eighteen Mahayoga Tantras, focused on Vishuddha Mind, the heruka of the tathagata family among the five families. It is found in Vol. RA of the *Nyingma Gyübum,* the collection of the Three Inner Tantras. [EPK]

311. This is a reference to a past life of Buddha Shakyamuni in which he killed a man named Spear-Wielding Criminal (Minag Dungtung Chen) in order to save the life of 500 others, and another story of having sex with a chieftain's daughter in order to save her from committing suicide. Both instances are often used as examples of how a bodhisattva in rare cases will commit seeming misdeeds of body or speech in order to accomplish the welfare of other beings. The three misdeeds of mind—craving, ill will, and holding wrong views—are never condoned. [CNR]

312. The Three Turnings of the Wheel of Dharma are described like this: the first set of teachings on the Dharma Wheel of the four noble truths, the second set of teachings on the Dharma Wheel of the absence of attributes, and the last set of teachings on the Dharma Wheel of the complete uncovering. The First Turning of the Wheel of Dharma was primarily on the sixteen aspects of the four truths, taught by the Buddha at the Deer Park in Sarnath. The Second Turning of the Wheel of Dharma was primarily on emptiness and transcendent knowledge, taught by the Buddha at Vulture Peak Mountain. The Third Turning of the Wheel of Dharma was primarily on the sugata essence, as well as on the three natures—the imagined, the dependent, and the absolute. [CNR]

313. This well-known phrase is often explained: "Mind itself is devoid of conceptual thinking because the nature of mind is luminous cognizance." [TUR]

314. The two denominations are samsara and nirvana. [EPK]

315. This quote plays on the literal meaning of Vajrasattva, "courageous vajra mind." [EPK]

316. The eight charnel grounds mentioned above are: (1) Cool Grove (Sitavana), in the east, (2) Perfected in Body, to the south, (3) Lotus Mound, to the west, (4) Lanka Mound, to the north, (5) Spontaneously Accomplished Mound, to the southeast, (6) Display of Great Secret, to the southwest, (7) Pervasive Great Joy, to the northwest, and (8) World Mound, to the northeast. There are, however, numerous other lists of charnel grounds. [JOKYAB]

317. Lords of the Three Families are the three bodhisattvas Avalokiteshvara, Manjushri, and Vajrapani. [TUR]

318. The following two appendices are composed in the traditional style called "filling-in commentary," a way in which the structure of the

original text is interspersed with additional words to clarify the meaning of the text. In Jokyab Rinpoche's manuscript, the extra words are marked with a tiny circle underneath. But here, the reader can compare the original text included in the root text in the beginning of the book. Due to the nature of this type of literature, the sentences can sometimes seem slightly wordy and lengthy. [EPK]

319. Abbot, the Master, and the Dharma King are Shantarakshita, Padmasambhava, and Trisong Deutsen. Shantarakshita is often called Khenpo Bodhisattva. [TUR]

320. "Abandonment and realization" is a synonym for buddhahood or enlightenment; all obscurations are abandoned and all enlightened qualities are realized. [CNR]

321. The nine regions of Tibet and Kham: The Regions of Jewel Light are the three upper districts between the slate and snow mountains, which are governed by elephants and deer. The Regions of Four Sogdian Areas are the three middle districts between rock and meadow mountains, which are governed by rock demons and monkeys. The Regions of Peacocks Below are the three lower districts between the jungles and forests, which are governed by birds and rakshasas. At this time there were no human beings. But here, "the center of the nine regions" is defined as being Samye in the center surrounded by the four cardinal and four intermediate directions of Tibet and Kham, altogether nine. This is the view of Jamyang Khyentse as has been told by Jamdrak. [JOKYAB]

322. The secular as well as the religious systems. [JOKYAB]

323. The five ruling faculties are: faith, diligence, mindfulness, concentration, and discrimination. [CNR]

324. "Eye of the World" is the translation of *loka-chakshu,* the Sanskrit word from which the Tibetan *lotsawa,* meaning "translator," is derived. [EPK]

325. The word for lotus here is "born from a lake" as in the analogy of a lotus flower being untainted by the mud of the swamp in which it grows. [EPK]

326. The two accumulations of merit with concepts and wisdom beyond concepts. [CNR]

327. The five degenerations are: (1) the degeneration of views due to the decline in the virtue of renunciants, meaning wrong views; (2) the

degeneration of disturbing emotions due to the decline in the virtue of householders, meaning coarse-natured minds in which coarseness refers to strong and long-lasting disturbing emotions; (3) the degeneration of times due to the decline in enjoyments, meaning the decreasing Aeon of Strife; (4) the degeneration of life span due to the decline of the sustaining life-force, meaning a decreasing life span, finally reaching the length of ten years; and (5) the degeneration of sentient beings, meaning the decline of body due to inferior shape and lesser size, the decline of merit due to lesser power and splendor, the decline of mind due to lesser sharpness of intellect, power of recollection, and diligence. Thus, the degeneration of sentient beings in whom the three types of decline have come together, meaning that their minds are difficult to tame. [JOKYAB]

328. The two orders refer to the ordained monks and nuns, and ngakpas, the tantric practitioners. [EPK]

329. There are various descriptions of the eight classes of gods and demons, but in the sutras the most general is: devas, nagas, yakshas, gandharvas, asuras, garudas, kinkaras, and mahoragas. All of them were able to receive and practice the teachings of the Buddha. These eight classes can also refer to various types of mundane spirits who can cause either help or harm, but remain invisible to normal human beings: ging, mara, tsen, yaksha, rakshasa, mamo, rahula, and naga. On a subtle level, they are regarded as the impure manifestation of the eight types of consciousness. [EPK]

330. In this regard, it is accepted that the "single recollection" of the Sarma Schools and the "single mudra" of the Nyingma School are identical. [JOKYAB]

331. My copy differs from the text used by Jokyab Rinpoche, so an alternate translation may be: "with his vajra voice of dharmata, his audible and yet empty vajra speech, this, the ultimate stages of the path. . . ." [EPK]

332. The *Great Treasury of Detailed Exposition* is a major collection of Abhidharma teachings, compiled after the passing of Lord Buddha by 500 arhat monks in agreement. It was translated into Tibetan from the Chinese version. [EPK]

333. The *Seven Sections of Abhidharma* are seven treatises composed by seven arhats and form the basis for the Sarvastavadin school of Buddhism. [EPK]

334. Jamgön Kongtrül in his *All-Encompassing Knowledge* defines the imagined [phenomena] lacking attributes as "that which is labeled by thought even though it in fact does not exist, as for instance the idea of a self or substantial existence." [EPK]

335. Dharani, in addition to mantra and incantation, also means the ability to remember a vast amount of the Buddha's teachings and therefore extraordinary memory and comprehension. [EPK]

336. The three great tertöns and vidyadharas were Jamgön Kongtrül, Jamyang Khyentse Wangpo, and Chokgyur Lingpa. The pair of Jamgöns may be Khyentse and Kongtrül, or Khyentse and Mipham Rinpoche. [TUR]

337. The Vajra Essence is a synonym for the innermost teachings of the Great Perfection. [TUR]

The Mind Seat of Chokgyur Lingpa was named Mindröl Norbu Ling and is situated at Neten. About this place, Orgyen Tobgyal Rinpoche says, "At Yegyal Namkhadzö near Riwoche, Chokgyur Lingpa established the monastery of Neten called Tenchok Gyurmey Ling, Sanctuary of the Changeless Supreme Teaching, which became his spiritual residence. While human beings were building by day, gods and demons were seen building by night. Here he started a monastic residence and his own quarters, named Sang-ngak Phodrang, the Mansion of Secret Mantra." His Body Seat and Speech Seat were respectively at Karma Gön and at Kela Monastery near Riwoche, between Central Tibet and Kham. For more information on Chokgyur Lingpa, see *The Life and Teachings of Chokgyur Lingpa* (Rangjung Yeshe Publications, 1988). [EPK]

Index

Index

Index

Dhyana Realms (bsam gtan gyi gnas ris): 173, 272

Dignaga, 226; details of, 226; quote by, 35

Dilgo, clan, xxxvi

Dilgo Khyentse Rinpoche, xvi, xvii, xxvi, xxvii, xxxi, xxxiii, 272; his lineage for *Lamrim Yeshe Nyingpo,* xxiv

diligence, 129, 130; three types, 125

Direct Crossing of spontaneous presence (lhun grub thod rgal). *See* Tögal

Discerning Dharmas and Dharmata (chos dang chos nyid rnam 'byed), 223

Discerning the Middle and the Extremes (dbus mtha' rnam 'byed), 204, 223; quote from, 267

disciple (slob ma): characteristics of, 91; expl. of qualities, 257; six principal virtues of, 92

discipline (tshul khrims): expl., 123; four aspects of taking, observing, purity, and restoring, 265; four qualities, 265; three types of, 123

discriminating knowledge (shes rab), 97, 123, 142, 147, 150, 203, 248, 256, 257, 263, 266, 279

Display of Great Secret (gsang chen rol pa): charnel ground, 283

distraction ('du 'dzi), 96, 258

disturbed-mind consciousness (nyon yid), 61, 184, 253, 254; def., 183; expl., 79, 184, 253; of formation ('du byed kyi nyon yid), 254

Dodrub Chen Rinpoche, xxvi

Dokham (mdo khams), 50; details of places in, 239

Dombi Heruka, 218; quote by, 280

Döndrub Tulku, 209

Do-ngak Lingpa. *See* Jamyang Khyentse Wangpo

Dorje Drag (rdo rje brag), xxxvi

Dorje Drakpo Tsal (rdo rje drag po rtsal), xxi, 7, 8, 37, 63, 217, 231, 234; details of revelation, xxiii; Innermost Cycle, xix; innermost sadhana (yang gsang sgrub pa rdo rje drag rtsal), 215; Padmasambhava's manifestation, 193; Power-

ful Vajra Wrath, xxii, 40, 229; secret cycle, xxiii; ultimate meaning of, 64

Dorje Draktsal. *See* Dorje Drakpo Tsal

Dorje Drolö (rdo rje gro lod), xxii, 234; one of the eight manifestations, 45; thirteen Tiger's Nests, 209

Dorje Düdjom, 189

Dorje Lingpa, 208, 225

Dorje Lobpön, xxxix

Dorje Ziji Tsal. *See* Jamyang Khyentse Wangpo

Dremo Valley ('bras mo ljong), 241

Drichu, 239

Droma land of Kyi (skyid kyi gro ma lung), 241

Dru Jamyang Drakpa. *See* Jamyang Drakpa

Dudjom Rinpoche, 225

Dusum Sangye prayer, xxii

Dza Chukha, xxxvii

Dzachu, 239

Dzigar Kongtrül Rinpoche, xxv, xxvi

Dzogchen: *See* Great Perfection

Dzogchen Monastery, xxxvi

Dzongsar Jamyang Khyentse. *See* Khyentse Chökyi Lodrö

Dzongsar Monastery, xxi, xxxvii, 210

Dzongshö (rdzong shod), xxxvii

E and VAM, 29, 250; as synonym for sugata essence, 72; expl., 219, 220

Early Translation School (snga 'gyur). *See* Nyingma School

Earth Treasure (sa gter), 211

eight aspects of the main stage of the dhyanas, 173

eight aspects of the preparatory stage, 173

Eight Chariots of the Practice Lineage (sgrub brgyud shing rta brgyad), xix; listing, 210

eight charnel grounds (dur khrod brgyad), 179, 233; listing, 283

eight classes of gods and demons (lha srin sde brgyad), 285

eight classes of Mahadevas (lha chen brgyad), 233

Index

Index

Index

ence from Hinayana, 199; listing the sevenfold greatness, 212; the result, 148; two divisions of, 199

Mahayoga (chen po'i rnal 'byor), 212, 216, 222; approach and accomplishment, 210; details, 215; expl., 230; Father Tantra, 212; listing of Eight Sadhana Teachings, 208; lit. meaning, 213; meaning of Wisdom Essence, 31

Mahayoga (rnal 'byor chen po), 248

mahoraga, 285

Maitreya (byams pa), 52, 176, 258; quotes by, 28, 31, 69, 70, 74, 109, 248

Malaya, Peak of, 47

Maledictory Fierce Mantra (dmod pa drag sngags), 208; transmission of, 232

mamo, 193, 226, 285

Mamo Bötong, 232

mandala (dkyil 'khor), 44; expl., 233; lit. meaning of, 219; special meaning of, 219

mandala-circle (dkyil 'khor gyi 'khor lo), 60, 62; expl., 246

Mandarava, 179

Ma-ning (ma ning), 233

Manjugosha. *See* Jamyang Khyentse Wangpo

Manjushri ('jam dpal dbyangs), xxxvii, 3, 48, 187, 281, 282, 283

Manjushri Body ('jam dpal sku), 208

Manjushri Yamantaka ('jam dpal gshin rje), transmission of, 231

Manjushrimitra ('jam dpal bshes gnyen), 231

Mansion of Secret Mantra (gsang sngags pho brang), 286

Mantra. *See* Mantrayana; Sutra and Mantra

mantras (sngags): expl., 244; three types, 59, 190

Mantrayana (sngags kyi theg pa), 30, 38, 88, 93, 153, 163, 212, 236, 280; common (sngags thun mong), 222; comparison with the Sutra system, 153; eleven special qualities, 280; explanation of cognitive obscuration, 282; five special qualities of, 280; meaning of Wisdom

Essence, 28; outer and inner sections, 212; scriptures for the stages of the path, 225; seven special qualities of; listing, 280; special version of the Three Jewels, 112; superiority of, 280; tantras of (sngags rgyud), 228; tradition of bodhichitta vow, 119; uncommon (thun min sngags), 222

mantrika (sngags pa), 5, 189

mara, 285

Mara (bdud), 4, 5, 6, 96, 189, 192; of the Realm of Desire, 187

Maratika Cave, xiii, 179

Mardza Ridge, 239

Margyenma. *See* Queen Margyenma

Markham Ridge, 239

Marvels (rmad du byung ba), aspects of excellent speech, 281

master (slob dpon, bla ma): characteristics of, 87; expl. qualities, 256; how to follow, 90

Master of Uddiyana. *See* Padmasambhava

Master Padmakara. *See* Padmasambhava

Matchless King of the Shakyas. *See* Buddha Shakyamuni

material finality, 138

maturation, qualities of (rnam smin yon tan), 33

Maya (sgyu 'phrul). *See also* Magical Net

Maya Sections, Eight (sgyu 'phrul sde brgyad), 229

Maya Tantra (sgyu 'phrul), 56

Mayajala (sgyu 'phrul drva ba), 255

Mayajala Tantras (sgyu 'phrul gyi rgyud), 229

Meaningful to Behold (mthong ba don ldan), 236

means and knowledge (thabs dang shes rab), 32, 38, 222; as terma signs, 227; E and VAM, 219, 220; expl., 32; in Vajrayana, 280; union of, 40; unity of, 149, 153, 219, 220, 230; vowels and consonants, 57

means and liberation (thabs grol), of Mahayoga, 215

meditation state of the solitude of mind (yid dben mnyam bzhag), 221

Index

Medium Prajnaparamita (yum bar ma), 119
mental cognition (yid kyi rnam shes), 253.
See also mind consciousness
Menyag-rab Ridge, 239
Meyshö, 209
Middle Dharma Wheel. See Dharma
Wheels
Middle Way (dbu ma), 140, 175, 226, 269,
272; as the sugata essence, 76; expl.,
200; Great Middle, 146; Padmasambhava's definition, 15; view of, 219; viewpoint of the noble potential, 176
Mighty Padma (pad ma dbang), transmission of, 231
Miarepa, xxxvi
Milky Lake ('o ma can gyi rgya mtsho),
179
mind consciousness (yid kyi rnam shes),
61, 184, 245, 254; conceptual (yid shes
rtog bcas), 79, 253; def., 183; expl., 184;
two aspects, 79, 184
Mind Lineage of the Victorious Ones
(rgyal ba dgongs brgyud), 216
Mind Only School (sems tsam pa), 175;
def. of name, 199; expl., 199; view, 140;
viewpoint of the noble potential, 175
Mind Seat, of Chokgyur Lingpa, 207
Mind Section (sems sde), of Dzogchen,
225
mind training (blo sbyong): expl., 95;
tong-len practice, 132
Mind Treasure (dgongs gter): among the
seven transmissions, 211
Mindröl Ling, xxxvi, 227; expl., 227
Mindröl Ling Monastery, 215
Mindröl Norbu Ling, 207, 286
Mipham Rinpoche, xxxii
miraculous power of mastery over wind
and mind, 277
Mirror of Magical Display (sgyu 'phrul me
long), 229; quote from, 39
misdeeds (sdig pa), 260. See also karma
mistaken cognition ('khrul pa'i sems): as
syn. for the all-ground, 254
Mön, 4, 186, 241
Monkey Meditator (sprel sgom), 237

Moons of Speech. See Precious Buddha
Mother Scripture (Prajnaparamita) (yum), 89
Mother Tantra (ma rgyud), 218, 220, 221,
244, 245, 281; Anu Yoga, 212
Mount Potala. See Potala
Mount Sumeru, 50, 240, 274
Mount Tisey, 239
Mukhale, 233
mundane dhyanas ('jig rten pa'i bsam
gtan), 13, 126
mundane wisdom resulting from meditation (sgom byung 'jig rten pa'i ye shes),
150
Mundane Worship ('jig rten mchod bstod),
208, 232
Murub Tseypo, xvii; background information on past life of Chokgyur Lingpa
by H. H. Dilgo Khyentse Rinpoche,
xvi; Prince Damdzin, 282; Prince
Translator, xvii
Mutri Tseypo, xvi. See Murub Tseypo
mutually cooperating cause (lhan cig byed
pa'i rgyu), in terms of ignorance, 253

nada, 244
nadi (rtsa). See channels
nadi-element (rtsa khams), 61
nadi syllables (rtsa yig), 57, 243
nadi-wheels (rtsa 'khor), 30, 57
naga, 247, 285
Nagarjuna, 226, 259, 265; expl. of quote,
272; on bodhichitta training, 265;
quotes by, 30, 70, 74, 128, 137, 138,
140; system of bodhichitta, 264; system
of Phakshab, 221
Nagarjuna(garbha) (klu sgrub snying po),
231
Namkha Dingphuk (nam mkha' lding
phyug), 240
Namkhai Nyingpo, 189, 236
Namtso (byang gi gnam mtsho), 240
Nangchen (nang chen), province in East
Tibet, xxxviii
Nangchen Tsechu Monastery (nang chen
tshe chu dgon pa), xxxviii

Index

Index

313

Index

word empowerment (tshig dbang), 62; four aspects, 245

Word Transmission of Yellow Parchment (shog ser tshig brgyud), 246

Words and Treatises. See *Kangyur; Tengyur*

Words of the Outcaste Rishi (gdol pa'i drang srong gtam), 217

World Mound ('jig rten brtsegs), charnel ground, 283

world-system ('jig rten gyi khams), 46

worthy recipient (snod ldan), qualities, 257

wrathful (drag po), expl. of Powerful Vajra Wrath, 40

wrongdoing (kha na ma tho ba), 256

Yabje Rigdzin (Serpa Tersey) Gyurmey Tsewang Gyatso, xxv

yaksha (gnod sbyin), 247, 285

Yama Lungphuk (gya' ma lung phug), 240

Yamantaka (gshin rje), 231

Yamdrok Yutso (yar 'brog gyu mtsho), 240

Yangdzong Phuk (yang rdzong phug), 240

Yangleshö, xiii, 179

yangter (yang gter), rediscovered treasures, xli

Yarlha Shampo snow mountain (yar lha sham po gangs), 240

Yegyal Namkhadzö, 286

yellow parchment (shog gser), xxiii, xxv

Yenlak Meypey Dorje (yan lag med pa'i rdo rje), 218

Yerpa Phuk (yer pa phug), 240

Yeru, 239

yeshe (ye shes), 27

Yeshe Nyingpo. See Wisdom Essence

Yeshe Rölpa Tsal. *See* Murub Tseypo

Yeshe Tsogyal, 37, 159, 240, 282; as Vajra Yogini, 208; summary of her life by Jamgön Kongtrül, xv; vision of Padmasambhava's specific manifestations, 46

Yeshe Wangpo (ye shes dbang po), 236

yidam (yi dam), xxxvii; expl., 37, 228; Mahayoga, 208; passionate forms (chags), 228; peaceful and wrathful, 3, 190; practice, 211; river of empowerment, 232; six Tantra sections (rgyud sde drug gi yi dam), 216. *See also* Three Roots

ying (dbyings). *See* dharmadhatu

Yishin Norbu Sampa Lhündrub (yid bzhin nor bu bsam pa lhun grub), 234. See *Sampa Lhündrub*

Yoga of Nonaction, 94

Yoga Tantra (rnal 'byor rgyud), 94, 212, 229, 281

Yogas of the Greater Vehicle (theg chen rnal 'byor), 34, 225

yogini (rnal 'byor ma), 45; eight, 233

Yogini Chito, 218

Yönru, 239

Yönten Gyatso (yon tan rgya mtsho). *See* Jamgön Kongtrül

Zalmo Ridge, 239

Zurgyen (zur rgyan), xxxi